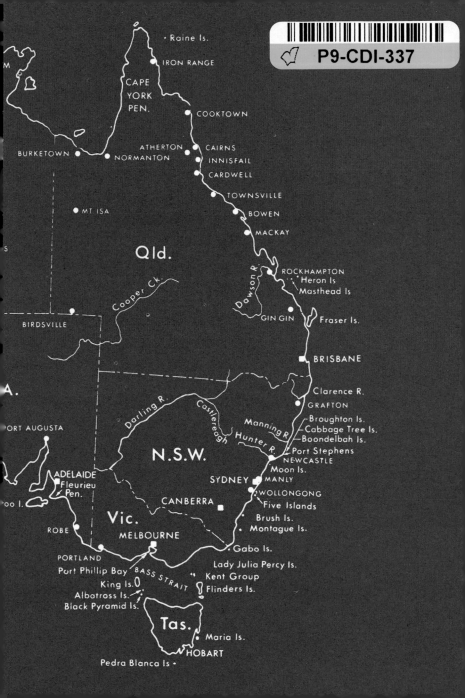

For George
Christmas 1981
with the hope
you'll get back
to the land of
"footie" again.

love,
Dot

# A FIELD GUIDE TO
# AUSTRALIAN BIRDS
## VOLUME TWO

*Also by Peter Slater*
A Field Guide to Australian Birds, Volume One (Non-passerines)

*With Pat Slater*
Wildlife in Colour
Australian Moths and Butterflies

A FIELD GUIDE TO

# AUSTRALIAN BIRDS

## VOLUME TWO

### PASSERINES

# PETER SLATER

**RIGBY**

National Library of Australia
Cataloguing-in-Publication entry

**Slater, Peter**
    A field guide to Australian birds: passerines/
    [by] Peter Slater.—Adelaide: Rigby, 1974.
    Index.
    A companion volume to A field guide to
    Australian birds: non-passerines.
    ISBN 0 85179 813 6.
    1. Passeriformes.   2. Birds—Australia.
    I.   Title.

    598.80994

RIGBY LIMITED • ADELAIDE • SYDNEY
MELBOURNE • BRISBANE • PERTH
First printed November 1974
Reprinted January 1975
Reprinted September 1975
Reprinted August 1976
Reprinted January 1978
Reprinted May 1979

# CONTENTS

# PLAN OF BOOK

This guide, like its predecessor which dealt with non-passerines, has only one aim—to facilitate the field identification of Australian birds.

Approximately 350 of the nearly 750 species of birds occurring in Australia belong to a single order of birds, *Passeriformes*. These form the subject of this volume. The remainder, comprising members of numerous and diverse orders such as emus, birds of prey, cuckoos, and seabirds, are treated in a companion volume, *A Field Guide to Australian Birds: Non-passerines*.

Passerines are often called songbirds, although many have songs less pleasing to human ears than those of some non-passerines; they are often referred to as perching birds, although many live on the ground and only rarely perch, and many non-passerines perch. The characters by which passerines are separated from other birds are mainly anatomical and not obvious to the eye, therefore the beginner has some difficulty in deciding which birds are passerines and which are not. When examined closely, the foot of the passerine will be found to have three toes directed forwards, free of any webbing or joining, and one toe directed backwards. The hind toe joins the leg at the same level as the front toes. In other orders of birds the toe arrangement is different. Many, such as cormorants, seabirds, and ducks, have the toes attached by webbing. Others have no hind toe. Others, such as cuckoos, have two toes directed forwards and two backwards. Frogmouths, kingfishers, and rollers have the front toes joined for part of their length, while wading birds, quail, and herons have the hind toe joining the leg higher up than do the front toes.

Most passerines are quite small, the exceptions being the lyrebirds and crows. None of them swim or make their living on salt or fresh water. As a generalisation they may be thought of as "small bush birds."

The best way for the beginner to learn to differentiate passerines from non-passerines is to compare the illustrations of the birds in the two volumes, or to study photographs in a pictorial encyclopaedia of birds.

The passerines occurring in Australia are classified, according to their relationships, into approximately thirty-five families. Some of these are endemic to Australia, e.g. *Menuridae* (lyrebirds), *Atrichornithidae* (scrub-birds), and *Ephthianuridae* (Australian chats); others are confined to the Australian region, e.g. *Meliphagidae* (honeyeaters), or are found in many parts of the world, e.g. *Sylviidae* (warblers) and

*Sturnidae* (starlings). Some are represented in Australia by only one species, e.g. *Nectariniidae* (sunbirds) and *Dicruridae* (drongos); others by many species, e.g. *Meliphagidae* (honeyeaters) and *Sylviidae* (warblers). A few families, e.g. *Ploceidae* (weaver-finches) and *Pycnonotidae* (bulbuls), are represented by introduced species.

A number of categories of birds may be recognised:

**1. Resident birds:** those species that reside and nest within a fairly limited locality, e.g. White-browed Scrub-wren.

**2. Nomadic birds:** those species that wander in response to meteorological conditions, having no regular paths of movements, e.g. Masked Wood-swallow, Crimson Chat.

**3. Breeding migratory birds:** those species that move from one place to another along regular flight paths, usually returning to much the same area. Some perform their migrations within Australia, e.g. Yellow-faced Honeyeater; others migrate beyond Australia, e.g. Spangled Drongo.

**4. Non-breeding migratory birds:** those species that regularly visit Australia but do not breed there, e.g. Barn Swallow.

**5. Casual visitors:** those species that occur spasmodically, usually as a result of extraordinary conditions, e.g. Yellow-headed Wagtail, Ceylon Crow.

**6. Introduced species:** those exotic species that have been introduced either deliberately or accidentally, e.g. House Sparrow, Starling.

At the moment there is no concensus of opinion among taxonomists on the number of species of Australian birds, particularly regarding passerines. This is due in part to different interpretations put on the definition of a species, which may be summarised as "a group of populations capable of interbreeding but reproductively isolated from other groups." When the group of populations is continuously distributed there is no real diversity of opinion, even if the birds at extremes of the total range are different in appearance, e.g. Banded Finch. But when distribution is discontinuous and there is detectable difference between isolated populations, then opinion is sharply divided. For example, the three separate populations of emu-wrens are considered by some to represent three races of one variable species; others suggest that they have evolved sufficiently to be regarded as separate species. There is also disagreement in some cases where related but distinctive forms meet and interbreed, so that there is an overlap. If the overlap covers a wide area and the intergradation between the two forms is gradual, it is widely held that only one species is involved. But if the intergradation takes place over only a small area then some taxonomists feel that two related species may be involved; others maintain that the interbreeding proves that the two forms belong to one species.

As this is a field guide, and the great majority of people using it are interested only in putting names to the birds they see, the general criterion used here is that distinctive forms are treated separately unless there is gradual intergradation between them. The critical reader will find inconsistencies for which I make no apologies—taxonomy is the only science in which opinion is as important as other criteria.

## ILLUSTRATIONS

In the introduction to the first volume, I wrote: "The illustrations are intended to be an aid to identification, not works of art." Several critics remarked that this was obvious! I repeat, the illustrations in this volume are not works of art; they are directed solely at making field identification as easy as possible. The colours of the original paintings are as close to life as possible; the method used is the Villalobos system, which consists of coloured squares of 100 graduated hues for each colour, over 7,000 in all. In the centre of each hue a hole has been punched, so that when it is held over the bird's feathers a direct comparison may be made. Paint is then mixed to match the colour closest to the original. Where possible a fresh museum specimen of a typical example of each species was used for colour-matching. The original paintings were subjected to a lengthy process of colour printing, and regardless of how carefully the printer worked some colour shift in some colours inevitably resulted. These are often less than those caused by chromatic aberrations in the average pair of binoculars.

## TREATMENT OF SPECIES

Each species is generally treated in the following order:

**Vernacular name:** The vernacular names are based on the CSIRO *Index of Australian Bird Names*, which is comprehensive and includes a list of alternative names. I strongly recommend that at least until the revised checklist of the Royal Australian Ornithologists' Union is issued the CSIRO *Index* should be added to your library. In some cases other names have been used; this is so that there is some uniformity with other books of a similar nature.

**Scientific name:** In most cases a binomial is used, but in some instances where a sub-species is easily recognisable in the field, a trinomial has been employed.

**Measurements:** Approximate total length, measured from bill-tip to tail-tip is given in centimetres. In most instances knowledge of the length of a bird is of little help in the field unless comparison with another species is possible.

**Description:** An introductory sentence emphasises the features most likely to register at a first glance, or by which distinction can be made from a similar species. This is followed by a general description of the bird, and of female and immature plumages where they differ from the male; the colours of bill, eyes, and legs; and any distinctive habits. Where confusion with another species is likely, a brief description of the differentiating features is given. See page 84 for the names used for parts of a bird.

**Voice:** The sounds made by birds are often important aids for identification, particularly in the case of similar birds such as the corvids, but in most cases a verbal description is unsatisfactory. For this reason a reference is given to a good recording that is available commercially, e.g.

> "VOICE: Rich vigorous 'ch-ch-ch-choo-wee-a' repeated often (Hutchinson 40)"

means that track 40 on John Hutchinson's *Index of Australian Bird Calls* gives a good recording of the bird involved. The record of fifty calls is available for $9 including postage, either as a disc or cassette, from John Hutchinson, Wildlife Sound Studios, Balingup, W.A. 6253.

**Habitat:** The key to the distribution of many Australian birds lies in their habitats: preferred areas where they are best able to live and reproduce. The major vegetation assemblages are shown on the accompanying maps. Within these assemblages there are minor divisions which more accurately limit the distribution of birds, e.g. within the spinifex assemblages, the Thick-billed Grass-wren prefers spinifex on flat country and the closely similar Thin-billed (Dusky) Grass-wren prefers spinifex-clad hills and rocky outcrops.

**Movements:** The precise study of passerine movements in Australia is in its infancy. Most of what is known is due to the efforts of bird-banders. A feature of the Australian avifauna is the number of nomadic species which move without any regular seasonal pattern, but rather in response to rainfall.

**Range:** It is not possible to place accurate limits on the distribution of any great number of Australian birds, because of the lack of observers in outback areas and the changes being made to the environment by cultivation. The ranges of some species with very specific habitat requirements, e.g. Noisy Scrub-bird, have shrunk quite rapidly; other birds, such as pipits, have increased enormously in numbers with man-made habitats. The maps must be regarded as approximate only; they are intended to be a further aid to identification. Obviously, if a bird is found to be a long way outside the range shown on the map, there is a possibility that a mistake has been made in identification. If a check reveals that the identification is not mistaken, then it is worth noting the details of the observation and submitting them to a suitable ornithological journal.

# ACKNOWLEDGMENTS

This volume would have taken considerably longer to produce without the assistance of Mr J. D. Macdonald, formerly keeper of birds at the British Museum and leader of the Harold Hall ornithological expeditions to Australia. Not only did he make available his notes and extensive field knowledge of Australian birds, but also, through his contact with many of the world's best painters of birds, he was able to suggest to me many subtleties of technique that vastly improved my ability to delineate them.

Mr D. Vernon, the curator of birds at the Brisbane Museum, was most helpful in selecting and discussing the skins in the collection.

In addition to those mentioned already in the first volume, I wish to acknowledge my indebtedness to Shane Parker, who was more than generous in his assistance; to Mrs Billie Gill, who was able to correct many of my misconceptions concerning birds of the rain forest and north Queensland; and to Mr J. S. Robertson, who made valuable suggestions.

Improvements suggested by critical comments on the first volume, especially those by R. K. Carruthers, S. G. Lane, Dr Raby, Fred T. H. Smith, and R. Stranger, were incorporated in this volume. Many people studied the maps and suggested amendments in the light of their knowledge, particularly G. Beruldsen, S. Breeden, D. D. Dow, I. Fien, R. Garstone, E. Lindgren, R. Lovell, J. D. Macdonald, B. Morgan, S. Parker, and M. Schrader.

# LIST OF PLATES

COLOUR PLATES

*PLATE 1* 5

# PITTAS, SCRUB-BIRDS, and BRISTLE-BIRDS

*PLATE 2*                     7

# LYREBIRDS

*PLATE 3* 9

# SWALLOWS and SWIFTS

Swifts *(Apodidae)* are not related to swallows *(Hirundinidae),* but because of the similarity in appearance between the two groups of birds they are illustrated here to aid in identification.

*Scale 1—1 : 4*                                                                 *Page*

1. Welcome Swallow: rusty forehead and throat.                           92
2. Barn Swallow: black border to rusty throat.                            92
3. White-backed Swallow: white head, throat, and back.                    91
4. Tree Martin: rusty forehead, whitish rump.                            93
5. Fairy Martin: rusty head and nape, white rump.                        93

*Scale 2—1 : 6*

6. Grey Swiftlet: white rump.
7. Glossy Swiftlet: white belly.
8. Uniform Swiftlet: dark rump, grey belly.
9. Fork-tailed Swift: white rump, forked tail.
10. Spine-tailed Swift: white undertail.

*PLATE 4*                11

## LARKS, PIPITS, and WAGTAILS

Ground birds of open country.                               *Page*

*PLATE 5*                                          13

## CUCKOO-SHRIKES

*PLATE 6*

15

# THRUSHES, BULBULS, and LOG-RUNNERS

*PLATE 7*                                    17

# QUAIL-THRUSHES

Quail-thrushes are ground-frequenting birds, usually found on stony ridges or hillsides; when alarmed they rise with a quail-like whirr.

*PLATE 8*    19

# BABBLERS, WHIPBIRDS, and MUDBUILDERS

All of these birds spend a lot of time on the ground, but nest in bushes or trees.

*Pronounced "chuff."

*PLATE 9*

21

# WRENS

*PLATE 10*    23

## WRENS

*PLATE 11* 25

# GRASS-WRENS

Grass-wrens are streaked with white; they have a preference for spinifex or cane grass, usually feeding on the ground. As a rule they are difficult to see because they keep under cover.

*PLATE 12* 27

# WARBLERS of REEDS and LONG GRASS

*PLATE 13*                                    29

## FAIRY WARBLERS

Warblers differ from thornbills (Plate 14) in behaviour, lack of freckled foreheads and ear coverts, and lack of streaking on the breast. Warblers never
feed on the ground, many thornbills do so.

A. Pale-breasted warblers with white in tail.                    *Page*

1.  White-tailed (Western) Warbler: pale grey-brown back,
    extensive white in tail; drier woodland.                      145
2.  Brown Warbler (race *richmondii*): brown back, grey breast,
    white spots in tail tip; eastern rain forest.                 144
3.  Brown Warbler (race *mouki*): grey-brown back, buff breast,
    white spots in tail tip; north-eastern rain forest.           144
4.  Mangrove Warbler *immature*: pale lemon underparts.           144
5.  Mangrove Warbler (race *cantator*): brown back, grey breast,
    white spots in tail tip.                                      144
6.  Mangrove Warbler (race *levigaster*): grey-brown back, buff
    breast, white spots in tail tip.                              144

B. Pale-breasted warblers without white in tail. (All in mangroves).

7.  Green-backed Warbler: grey-brown head without eyebrow,
    olive-green back, white below, with olive-yellow flanks.      142
8.  Dusky Warbler: pale buff forehead and eyebrow, white eye,
    rufous-brown back, pale buff underparts.                      143
9.  Large-billed Warbler: brownish-olive head without eyebrow,
    brownish-olive back, white below, with pale buff flanks.      143

C. Yellow-breasted warblers.

10. Fairy Warbler *female*: olive-green back, white throat.       141
11. Fairy Warbler *immature*: olive-green back, yellow throat.
    (Most commonly observed plumage.)                             141
12. Fairy Warbler *male*: olive-green back, black chin, white throat,
    white spots in tail tip.                                      141
13. White-throated Warbler *adult*: grey-brown back, white throat,
    white at base of tail and tail tip.                           140
14. White-throated Warbler *immature*: grey-brown back, yellow
    throat.                                                       140
15. Black-throated Warbler *immature*: olive-green back, yellow
    throat.                                                       141
16. Black-throated Warbler *female*: olive-green back, white throat. 141
17. Black-throated Warbler *male*: olive-green back, blackish or
    brownish throat, white moustache, no white in tail.          141

*PLATE 14* 31

## THORNBILLS and WEEBILLS

Thornbills are often difficult to identify on first acquaintance. Many of them are very similar in appearance, and are probably best distinguished by behaviour, habitat, and range. Weebills lack streaked ear coverts.

A. Warbler-like thornbills feed in treetops and outer foliage. *Page*

B. White-eyed thornbills often on ground; all have freckled foreheads.

C. Dark-eyed thornbills seldom if ever feed on the ground.

*This species is variable; it is probably best not to try to identify the race.

*PLATE 15*                                                33

# GROUND-FREQUENTING WARBLERS

Small birds that spend much of their time feeding on the ground (or, in one case, on sandstone); most of them may also be seen in bushes or trees but seldom far above the ground.

*Page*

*This is a very variable species: the illustrations show two of several forms. It is probably best to think of all as field-wrens rather than to try to pin race names on birds observed.

*PLATE 16*                                                     35

## SCRUB-WRENS

Scrub-wrens are small birds most often observed on or near the ground in dense undergrowth, or on the rain forest floor. Numbers 2–5 are often considered to belong to one species, but can in most cases be differentiated by their distribution and appearance.

PLATE 17                    37

# FLYCATCHERS and ROBINS

A. Small robin-like flycatchers with short legs and broad gapes; usually sit on an exposed perch and take insects in the air.

B. Females of the red-breasted robins: usually sit on exposed perches and take insects on the ground.

C. Males of the red-breasted robins: all have white foreheads except the Red-capped Robin; usually sit on exposed perches and take insects on the ground.

*PLATE 18* 39

# ROBINS

*PLATE 19*　　　　　　　　　　　41

## FANTAILS and MONARCH FLYCATCHERS

Fantails are very active, often fanning tails.　　　　　　　*Page*

1. Willie Wagtail: black throat, white eyebrow, wags tail sideways.　178
2. Grey Fantail: grey breast, white line behind eye, very active.　177
3. Northern Fantail: grey, breast streaked white, no white line behind eye, not active.　177
4. Rufous Fantail: rufous forehead and rump.　178

Monarch Flycatchers (genus *Myiagra*) have harsh, frog-like calls.

5. Restless Flycatcher: white throat, harsh "scissors-grinding" call.　182
6. Broad-billed Flycatcher: shiny blue-grey above, rusty throat and breast, white edge to tail; mangroves.　181
7. Shining Flycatcher *female*: black head, chestnut back.　181
8. Shining Flycatcher *male*: shining black.　181
9. Satin Flycatcher *male*: shining black with white abdomen.　180
10. Satin Flycatcher *female*: brownish blue-grey above, rusty throat.　180
11. Leaden Flycatcher *female*: brownish-grey above, rusty throat and breast.　179
12. Leaden Flycatcher *male*: leaden-grey above, throat dark grey, breast and abdomen white.　179

*PLATE 20* 43

## MONARCH FLYCATCHERS

The two species of frill-necked flycatchers are pied in colour and have erectile frills on the nape (not always fluffed out as shown). Also, the white lower back feathers often protrude through the wing, giving the impression of a white wing patch.

*PLATE 21* 45

# WHISTLERS

*PLATE 22*                                                    47

## SHRIKE-TITS and SHRIKE-THRUSHES

Shrike-tits are crested, yellow-breasted birds with powerful notched bills adapted for pulling bark from tree trunks and branches.

Shrike-thrushes are large-headed, stout-billed birds with mellow voices.

*PLATE 23* 49

# CHATS

*"Gibber" is pronounced with a hard "g."

*PLATE 24* 51

## SITTELLAS and TREE-CREEPERS

Sittellas are small, dumpy birds usually seen in small flocks hopping up or down tree branches. They are all very similar in behaviour and virtually replace each other geographically, so that only one form is found in any one area.

*Page*

Tree-creepers are usually seen spiralling up tree trunks, but often feed on the ground and among fallen timber. They have orange or buff patches in the wings, visible in flight.

A. Tree-creepers with prominent eyebrows.

B. Tree-creepers without prominent eyebrows.

*PLATE 25*                53

# FLOWER PECKERS (PARDALOTES and MISTLETOE-BIRD)

*PLATE 26*                                               55

## SUNBIRD, SILVEREYES, and SMALL HONEYEATERS

*The colour of this honeyeater is close to Ridgeway's orange-citrine, which is nearer to olive than to brown; perhaps it should be known as Brown's Honeyeater, after its discoverer, Robert Brown.

*PLATE 27*                                                57

# LONG-BILLED HONEYEATERS

*PLATE 28* 59

## TYPICAL HONEYEATERS

White-gaped honeyeaters: greenish or greyish-olive in basic colour, these species are best distinguished by their head colours. The top row depicts three confusing species that occur in the rain forests of north-eastern Queensland. They may be identified on bill length, eye colour, and call. The Lewin Honeyeater occurs only in upland rain forest in its northern Queensland range.

*Page*

1. Graceful Honeyeater: blue eyes, slender bill, small yellow ear patch closer to eye than in other two species; calls "plik."    226
2. Lesser Lewin Honeyeater: brown eye, long stout bill; the feathers touching the yellow ear patch are dark above the gape, pale below; calls "ee-yeu."    225
3. Lewin Honeyeater: blue eye, short stout bill; the feathers touching the yellow ear patch are silvery-grey; utters a loud musical staccato.    225
4. White-lined Honeyeater: greyish-brown with faintly streaked breast; Arnhem Land gorges.    227
5. White-gaped Honeyeater: plainly coloured, greyish-olive with white gape; tropical mangroves and river margins.    224
6. Bridled Honeyeater: bi-coloured bill with gape extended into a yellow "bridle;" upland rain forest in north-eastern Queensland.    227

Masked honeyeaters: greenish or yellowish-olive honeyeaters with distinctive head patterns.

7. Yellow-tufted Honeyeater: yellow forehead, throat, and ear tuft, little white in tail; south-east.    228
8. Helmeted Honeyeater: curled feathers on forehead; restricted to a few localities in southern Victoria.    229
9. Yellow-throated Honeyeater: yellow throat; Tasmania and Bass Strait islands.    228
10. White-eared Honeyeater: black throat, white ear patch.    227

Bare-eyed honeyeaters: mottled long-billed rain forest honeyeaters with bare yellow skin below the eye.

11. Tawny-breasted Honeyeater: faintly streaked tawny breast; Cape York.    236
12. Macleay's Honeyeater: boldly streaked above and below; north-eastern Queensland.    236

PLATE 29                                                 61

# TYPICAL HONEYEATERS and MASKED HONEYEATERS

Typical honeyeaters are rather similar in general appearance, being various shades of yellowish or greyish-olive. They are best identified by the head and breast patterns.

Masked honeyeaters all have a broad black band through the eye, below which is a yellow or yellow-and-white streak.

*PLATE 30*      63

# WHITE-NAPED HONEYEATERS and STRIPED HONEYEATER

*PLATE 31* 65

# YELLOW-WINGED HONEYEATERS and TAWNY-CROWNED HONEYEATER

*This species is often called either Yellow-winged or White-eyed Honeyeater.

*PLATE 32*                    67

# MINERS, FRIAR-BIRDS, and WATTLE-BIRDS

Friar-birds are large, noisy honeyeaters with naked skin on the head and a basic similarity of body shape and colour.

The next three species occur in the northern areas of the Northern Territory. They are best distinguished by the size of the knob on the forehead, colour of facial skin, call, size, condition of nape feathers, and habitat.

*PLATE 33* 69

# FINCHES

*PLATE 34* 71

## FINCHES and SPARROWS

*PLATE 35* 73

# STARLINGS, ORIOLES, FIGBIRD, and DRONGO

PLATE 36                                             75

# WOOD-SWALLOWS

*PLATE 37* 77

## BUTCHER-BIRDS and MAGPIES

PLATE 38                                              79

## BOWER-BIRDS and CATBIRDS

PLATE 39                                      81

# CROWS, CURRAWONGS, RIFLE-BIRDS, and MANUCODE

Australian crows and ravens are difficult to differentiate, all looking much the same (see p. 83 for identification hints). Indian (or Ceylon) Crows are sometimes seen near Australian ports after escaping from ships which have inadvertently carried them from Indian ports.

Currawongs are large crow-like birds with yellow eyes and white patches in the wings and under the tail; they fly with looping wingbeats and have loud calls.

Birds of Paradise are represented by four species with iridescent plumage. They are confined to rain forest.

# RAVENS

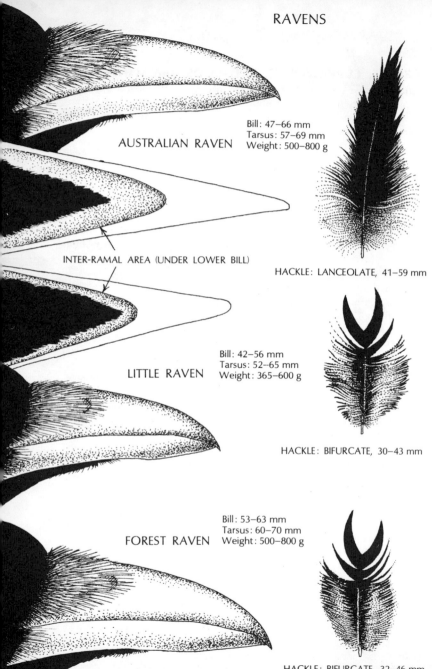

**AUSTRALIAN RAVEN**

Bill: 47–66 mm
Tarsus: 57–69 mm
Weight: 500–800 g

INTER-RAMAL AREA (UNDER LOWER BILL)

HACKLE: LANCEOLATE, 41–59 mm

**LITTLE RAVEN**

Bill: 42–56 mm
Tarsus: 52–65 mm
Weight: 365–600 g

HACKLE: BIFURCATE, 30–43 mm

**FOREST RAVEN**

Bill: 53–63 mm
Tarsus: 60–70 mm
Weight: 500–800 g

HACKLE: BIFURCATE, 32–46 mm

# CROWS

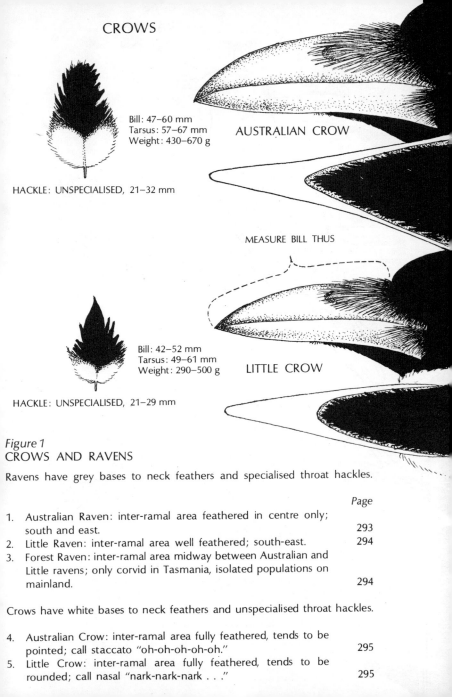

Bill: 47–60 mm
Tarsus: 57–67 mm
Weight: 430–670 g

HACKLE: UNSPECIALISED, 21–32 mm

AUSTRALIAN CROW

MEASURE BILL THUS

Bill: 42–52 mm
Tarsus: 49–61 mm
Weight: 290–500 g

LITTLE CROW

HACKLE: UNSPECIALISED, 21–29 mm

*Figure 1*
## CROWS AND RAVENS

Ravens have grey bases to neck feathers and specialised throat hackles.

Crows have white bases to neck feathers and unspecialised throat hackles.

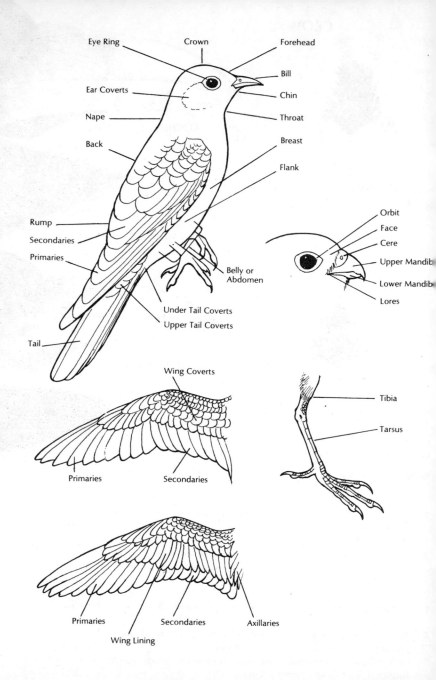

# PASSERIFORMES

## PITTAS—Pittidae

Pittas are short-tailed, long-legged, brightly coloured ground birds found in rain forest and mangroves. They seldom fly when disturbed, but when they do show white "bull's-eyes" in the wings. Their cries are loud, usually uttered from the ground, but they sometimes climb quite high into trees to call. Food, consisting of insects, snails, and other invertebrates, is taken on the ground. Often a stone or log is used as an anvil to break snail-shells.

Most species are migratory, but in Australia the Rainbow Pitta and, in some areas, the Noisy Pitta, are sedentary. The Blue-winged Pitta has been recorded on only a few occasions.

The nest is built near or on the ground and is round in shape, often with a platform leading to the side entrance. Three or four glossy eggs are laid.

### NOISY PITTA *Pitta versicolor* SEE p. 5

17·5 cm. A buff-breasted pitta. Above, brilliant green; shoulder and rump, blue; head, black, with brown crown; wing with white "window;" below, buff; centre of abdomen, black; undertail, red. Bill, black; eyes, brown; legs, pink.

VOICE: "Did you work."

HABITAT: Rain forest, feeding on the ground, though roosting in trees.

RANGE: Eastern Australia, from Cape York to northern New South Wales.

Noisy Pitta

Blue-winged Pitta

At least some migrate to New Guinea. Larger southern birds migrate north to northern Queensland; smaller northern birds apparently sedentary.

## BLUE-WINGED PITTA *Pitta moluccensis*                                  SEE p. 5

25 cm. A buff-breasted pitta with a white throat. Above, brilliant green; shoulder and rump, blue; head, black with brown crown; wing with white "window;" below, buff with white throat; undertail, red. Bill, black; eyes, brown; legs, pink.

A very rare migrant, distinguished from the Noisy Pitta by the white throat.

VOICE: Not recorded.

HABITAT: Rain forest and mangroves.

RANGE: Recorded in Australia on the north-west coast.

Migrates between South-east Asia and the islands to the north of Australia.

## RAINBOW PITTA *Pitta iris*                                             SEE p. 5

16 cm. A black-breasted pitta. Above, brilliant green; shoulder and rump, blue; wing with white "window;" head, black, with buff eyebrows; below, black; undertail, red. Bill, black; eyes, brown; feet, pink.

VOICE: Loud clear whistle, "want-a-whip."

HABITAT: Rain forest, mangroves, bamboo thickets, river margins, feeding on the ground, roosting in trees.

RANGE: Kimberley coast and rivers, Northern Territory coast and rivers, Melville Island, and Groote Eylandt.

Sedentary.

## BLUE-BREASTED PITTA *Pitta mackloti*                                   SEE p. 5

16 cm. A blue-breasted pitta. Above, brilliant green; shoulder and rump, blue; wing with white "window;" head, brown, with reddish nape; breast, blue, separated by a black line from red abdomen. Bill, black; eyes, brown; feet, grey.

Rainbow Pitta

Blue-breasted Pitta

VOICE: A rasping "karaa-karaa" (Rand & Gilliard).
HABITAT: Rain forest, feeding on the ground, roosting in trees.
RANGE: Cape York, northern Queensland.
Migrates to New Guinea.

## LYREBIRDS — Menuridae

Lyrebirds are found only in Australia. They are among the largest of all passerines, rivalled in body size only by the corvids, and must be numbered among the most remarkable of all birds. The polygamous male performs a dance on a mound or scrape on the forest floor, spreading the long tail over its back. It accompanies the display with rich and varied song, including mimicry of other species. The female prepares a nest either on the ground, on a rock ledge, or a tree stump. The nest is large, made of sticks and with a side entrance. Only one egg is laid.

All food is taken on the forest floor, scratched up by the powerful legs, and consists of insects and other invertebrates.

**SUPERB LYREBIRD** *Menura superba* SEE p. 7

Male, 80–90 cm; female, 45–50 cm. A large forest ground bird with lyre-shaped outer tail feathers and grey undertail coverts. **Male:** above, dark grey-brown, darker on crown and face, with bluish-black bare facial skin, and more rufous on wings and rump; tail, central feathers filamentous, blackish above and silver-grey below, and outer feathers lyre-shaped, blackish-brown above and white below with rufous notches; below, pale grey-brown, more rufous on throat and neck; undertail coverts, grey. **Female:** similar, but with dark-brown graduated tail feathers, lacking specialisation. Bill, black; eyes, blackish-brown; legs, black.

Southern Superb Lyrebirds have white lyre feathers on the undersurface; in northern New South Wales and southern Queensland they

Superb Lyrebird                    Albert Lyrebird

are grey (race *edwardi*). Distinguished from the Albert Lyrebird by the less rufous coloration, the notched lyre feathers, and the grey undertail coverts.

VOICE: The song, which includes mimicry, is probably the most remarkable of all birds; alarm call "kerwist;" "choo" and "nap" when feeding.

HABITAT: Mountain forests, particularly ferny gullies in the south; northern race *edwardi* is often found in open timber country among granite outcrops where there is profuse ground litter.

RANGE: South-eastern Australia, from Melbourne, Victoria, to south-eastern Queensland, introduced to Tasmania.

Sedentary.

### ALBERT LYREBIRD *Menura alberti* SEE p. 7

Male, 90 cm; female, 65 cm. A large forest ground bird without lyre-shaped outer tail feathers and with rufous undertail coverts. **Male:** above, rufous-brown, darker on crown, with bluish-black bare facial skin; tail, central tail feathers, filamentous, blackish above and silver-grey below, and outer tail feathers fan-shaped, blackish above and grey below; below, pale grey-brown tinged rufous; undertail coverts, rufous. **Female:** similar, but with dark rufous-brown graduated tail feathers lacking specialisation. Bill, black; eyes, blackish-brown; legs, black.

Distinguished from Superb Lyrebird by more rufous coloration, the unnotched outer tail feathers, and the rufous undertail coverts.

VOICE: Like the Superb Lyrebird, a remarkable mimic.

HABITAT: Rocky mountain forests.

RANGE: North-eastern New South Wales and south-eastern Queensland.

Sedentary.

## SCRUB-BIRDS — Atrichornithidae

Scrub-birds are found only in Australia. Although quite small and rather drab in appearance, they are allied to lyrebirds. They are ground birds, only rarely flying, preferring to creep or run with tail erect when disturbed. Because of the dense undergrowth and their habits they are very difficult to see. Their habitat requirements are so particular that they are extremely vulnerable to ecological disturbance, and the Noisy Scrub-bird has disappeared from much of the range occupied when Europeans arrived.

Their songs are rich and loud, and they mimic other species. The nest is on or near the ground, made from grass and rushes, domed with a side entrance, and lined with a plaster of woodpulp.

### RUFOUS SCRUB-BIRD *Atrichornis rufescens* SEE p. 5

16·5 cm. A finely-barred rufous bird with a white throat and two longitudinal black streaks down the breast and abdomen. **Male:** above, rufous-brown narrowly barred black; throat, white; upper breast black, and abdomen, rufous with a black streak on each side. **Female:** lacks black on breast. Bill, eyes, and legs similar in colour to Noisy Scrub-bird (below).

VOICE: Extremely powerful and rich song. Mimics other species.

HABITAT: Thickets in rain forest; normally very difficult to observe.

RANGE: South-eastern Queensland; north-eastern New South Wales. Sedentary.

### NOISY SCRUB-BIRD *Atrichornis clamosus* SEE p. 5

21 cm. A finely-barred brown bird with a white throat and black upper breast. **Male:** above, brown, finely-barred black; below, throat, white; upper breast, black; lower breast, white; abdomen, buff-brown. **Female:** lacks black breast markings. Bill, upper mandible, reddish-brown, lower mandible, pinkish-white; legs, pinkish-white.

The Brown Bristle-bird (p. 133) occurs in the same habitat, but may be identified by the smaller size, lack of white throat and black upper breast, and lack of fine bars in the upper plumage.

VOICE: A rich powerful "chip-chip-chip . . ." The female call is "tit-tit-tit-tit." Also mimics other species (Hutchinson 18).

HABITAT: Coastal rushes and densely-vegetated coastal gullies.

RANGE: South-western Australia (Two People Bay). Sedentary.

Rufous Scrub-bird

Noisy Scrub-bird

# LARKS—Alaudidae

Larks are long-legged, ground-dwelling birds. They are superficially similar to pipits. One native species and one introduced occur in Australia.

Larks are most easily distinguished from pipits by the rich fluting quality of the song, usually uttered while soaring high overhead. The nest is built on the ground, usually concealed by a tussock of grass.

**SINGING BUSHLARK** *Mirafra javanica* SEE p. 11

13 cm. A stout-billed, streaked brown or reddish-brown ground bird. Above back, brown with darker streaks; wing feathers edged rufous; tail, brown, with outer tail feathers white; below, cinnamon or buff, with dark streaks on throat and breast. Bill, stout, finch-like, brown; eyes, red-brown; legs, pink or grey-brown.

The coloration of this species is variable, depending to some extent on the prevailing colour of the ground. Where red soil is found, reddish birds occur, and very dark birds are found in areas of black soil. However, it is not unusual to see reddish birds on dark soil and vice versa.

The small size, lack of a crest, and darker underparts distinguish the bushlark from the introduced Skylark. The songs are rather similar, with the bushlark's being less powerful and rather more tinkling. The flight of the two is similar, on quivering wings, but the Skylark has a light trailing edge to the wings.

The pipit has a longer tail, a thin bill, wags its tail up and down when on the ground, and in the display flight gives a single trill with downward inflection.

VOICE: A rich melodious rather tinkling song uttered from a perch or while in flight; a single "chirrup" on the ground (Hutchinson 19).

HABITAT: Grassland.

RANGE: Northern and eastern Australia and South Australia in suitable grassland habitat.

Singing Bushlark

Skylark

**SKYLARK**  *Alauda arvensis*                                              <small>SEE</small> p. 11

19 cm. A stout-billed, streaked-brown ground bird with small crest. Above, brown, streaked darker; wings, brown; tail, brown, with outer tail feathers white; below, pale buff streaked black. Bill, dark brown above, pale below; eyes, dark brown; legs, pink-brown.

Larger and less rufous than the Singing Bushlark, the Skylark has a small crest (not always raised) and is paler on the underparts. The Skylark is also larger and more robust than the longer-tailed pipit, which has a thinner bill, and constantly wags the tail up and down.

<small>VOICE</small>: A rich melodious trilling usually uttered while flying, but also from a perch; the call while on the ground is a liquid "chirrup."

<small>HABITAT</small>: Grasslands.

<small>RANGE</small>: Introduced into south-eastern Australia.

# SWALLOWS—Hirundinidae

Swallows are small birds that spend much time on the wing chasing insects, or perched in small groups or flocks on telephone wires or dead trees. They are so common that they are often ignored, but flocks of Welcome Swallows in the north should be carefully studied for the presence of Barn Swallows. Two groups, swallows and martins, occur in Australia: swallows have deeply-forked tails and martins have square or only slightly forked tails. Most species build mud nests. Welcome Swallows commonly nest under house verandahs and even on shop fronts on busy streets; Fairy Martins nest colonially, building their bottle-shaped nests in clusters under bridges and culverts as well as in open caves and overhanging rocks. Tree Martins nest in hollow limbs of trees, often plastering the entrance with mud, while White-backed Swallows drill tunnels in sandy banks, using them as roosts as well as for nesting. In cold weather they remain in a torpid state in the burrows.

**WHITE-BACKED SWALLOW**  *Cheramoeca leucosterna*          <small>SEE</small> p. 9

15 cm. A fork-tailed swallow with white crown, throat, and back. Above, black, with white crown (grey in centre), and white upper back; throat, white; breast and abdomen, black. Bill, black; eyes, dark brown; legs, brown.

Distinguished from martins by the forked tail, pied appearance, and black rump.

<small>VOICE</small>: Loud "check" on the wing.

<small>HABITAT</small>: Open savannah with sandy banks used as nesting sites.

<small>RANGE</small>: Drier areas of Australia, avoiding forested regions except where extensive clearing has left suitable sandy banks.

Sedentary, perhaps migratory in south, but known to remain torpid in nesting burrows in cold weather.

**WELCOME SWALLOW** *Hirundo neoxena*                                      SEE p. 9

15 cm. A fork-tailed swallow with grey abdomen, rufous throat, and no throat band. Above, shining blue-black with dull black wings; forehead, rufous; tail, dull black with concealed white subterminal band; throat and upper breast, rufous; abdomen, grey. Bill, black; eyes, dark brown; legs, black.

Distinguished from the Barn Swallow by lack of black breast band and the grey abdomen.

VOICE: Single "seert" in flight; high-pitched twittering.

HABITAT: Cities and towns; most habitats except forests and deserts.

RANGE: Southern two-thirds of Australia, north to Port Hedland, Western Australia; Alice Springs, Northern Territory; and Cairns, Queensland.

Sedentary in Western Australia, migratory in south-east.

**BARN SWALLOW** *Hirundo rustica*                                         SEE p. 9

15 cm. A fork-tailed swallow with white abdomen, rufous throat, and black breast band. Above, shining blue-black; forehead, rufous; wing, dull black; tail, dull black, with concealed white subterminal band; throat and upper breast, rich rufous; breast band, black; abdomen, white. Bill, black; eyes, dark brown; legs, black.

When perched, the Barn Swallow appears bulkier than the Welcome Swallow; it is also shinier blue-black on the back, and the white abdomen is very obvious in flight. The best field character is the black breast band. As it moults while in Australia, the long tail feathers are often missing.

VOICE: Metallic "t-weet;" pleasant twittering.

HABITAT: Recorded so far only in or near towns, usually perching on telephone wires.

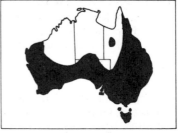

White-backed Swallow                          Welcome Swallow

RANGE: Recorded in Australia only at Derby, Western Australia; Innisfail, Queensland; and Darwin district, Northern Territory; widely spread in the Northern Hemisphere.

A non-breeding summer visitor, regular to Derby, Western Australia, but only rarely seen in north-eastern Australia.

**TREE MARTIN** *Petrochelidon nigricans* SEE p. 9

12·5 cm. A square-tailed swallow with greyish white rump and dark head. Above, glossy blue-black with dark-brown wings; forehead, rusty-brown; rump, greyish-white; tail, dull black; below, dull white, greyer on the breast, and faintly streaked black. Bill, black; eyes, dark brown; legs, black.

Distinguished from the swallows by the pale rump and square tail; from the Fairy Martin by the dark head and dull white rump.

VOICE: Quiet high-pitched chatter.

HABITAT: Open woodland.

RANGE: Australia, Tasmania, Bass Strait islands, Kangaroo Island, Melville Island; Timor, Sunda Islands, and New Guinea.

Sedentary in many areas, but migratory in south east, and appears to be a winter visitor to the west Kimberley, Western Australia.

**FAIRY MARTIN** *Petrochelidon ariel* SEE p. 9

11·5 cm. A square-tailed swallow with pure-white rump, rusty head and distinctive "chrrr" call. Above, shiny blue-black streaked white; head, rusty-brown; rump, pure white; wings and tail, dark brown; below, white, greyer on breast, finely streaked black. Bill, black; eyes, dark brown; legs, black.

Distinguished from the swallows by the white rump; from the Tree Martin by the rusty head, whiter rump and underparts, as well as the distinctive churring call.

Barn Swallow

Tree Martin

VOICE: Short "chrrr" or "prrrt-prrrt;" pleasant high-pitched chattering.

HABITAT: Open woodland, particularly near water and overhanging cliffs, culverts, and bridges where it builds its bottle-shaped nest.

RANGE: Australia, Tasmania.

Sedentary over much of its range, but migratory in both the southeast and the extreme north, the former as a breeding summer visitor, the latter as a non-breeding winter visitor.

# PIPITS AND WAGTAILS—Motacillidae

Small ground birds, many species of which wag the tail up and down. The pipits are rather like larks, but are more slender, have longer tail and thin bills. Only one pipit occurs in Australia. Three wagtails have been recorded as rare vagrants. Immatures look rather like pipits, but lack streaked upperparts.

### AUSTRALIAN PIPIT *Anthus novaeseelandiae*          SEE p. 11

15 cm. A streaked fuscous-brown ground bird with habit of bobbing the tail up and down. Above, fuscous-brown with paler edges to feathers; outer tail feathers, white; below, streaked and spotted black. Bill, above, brown, below, pink; eyes, brown; legs, pinkish-brown.

Distinguished from the Singing Bushlark and Skylark by its habit of bobbing the tail up and down. In flight it is noticeably longer-tailed, lacks both the quivering of the wings and the rich elaborate song. Distinguished from the Rufous Songlark by the lack of chestnut rump patch.

VOICE: A trilling "pirrit;" a downward trill while flying.

HABITAT: Grassland.

RANGE: Eastern Europe to Australia and New Zealand.

Sedentary.

Fairy Martin

Australian Pipit

## YELLOW WAGTAIL *Motacilla flava* SEE p. 11

15 cm. A yellow-breasted wagtail with olive-green back and blue-grey crown. **Adult:** above, olive-green; wings, black; tail, black with white edge; crown, blue-grey; eyebrows, white; below, bright yellow. **Immature:** above, olive-brown; wings, black, feathers edged white; crown, brown; eyebrows, buff; below, buff, with dark mottling on throat; often with scattered yellow feathers on breast and abdomen. Bill, black; eyes, brown; legs, black.

Wags tail up and down. Immature distinguished from pipit by lack of streaks in the plumage. Adult distinguished from the Yellow-headed Wagtail by the blue-grey crown, and from the Grey Wagtail by the lack of yellow rump and the olive-green back.

VOICE: "Tsweep."

HABITAT: Pasture, airfields, and grass around windmill overflows.

RANGE: Rare vagrant to northern Australia, with records from Bimbi, Dawson River, Queensland, to Derby, Western Australia.

Non-breeding summer visitor from Northern Hemisphere.


## YELLOW-HEADED WAGTAIL *Motacilla citreola* SEE p. 11

15 cm. A yellow-breasted wagtail with yellow head. Above, dark grey, with black nape; wings, dark grey, with two white bars; tail, blackish-grey, with white edges; head and underparts, bright yellow. Bill, black; eyes, brown; legs, black.

Bobs tail up and down. Distinguished from the Grey and the Yellow Wagtails by the yellow head.

VOICE: Shrill "chip" in flight.

HABITAT: Pasture.

RANGE: Rare vagrant, recorded once near Sydney.

Non-breeding summer visitor from Northern Hemisphere.

Yellow Wagtail

Yellow-headed Wagtail

**GREY WAGTAIL** *Motacilla cinerea*                    SEE p. 11

15 cm. A yellow-breasted wagtail with a yellow rump and a grey crown. Above, grey; rump, yellow; wings, black, with concealed white bar; tail, black, with white edges; crown, grey; eyebrows, white; throat, white; breast and abdomen, pale yellow. Bill, black; eyes, brown; legs, brown.

Wags tail up and down. In breeding plumage the Grey Wagtail has a black throat, but by the time any vagrants reach Australia this distinctive mark will most likely be lost with the moult. Distinguished in non-breeding plumage from Yellow Wagtail and Yellow-headed Wagtail by the yellow rump.

VOICE: "Te-seep" in flight.

HABITAT: Streams, grassy ponds, pasture, airports.

RANGE: Rare vagrant, recorded at Innisfail, Queensland; fairly regular migrant to New Guinea.

Non-breeding summer migrant from Northern Hemisphere.

# MAGPIE-LARKS—Grallinidae

The Magpie-lark is a ground-feeding pied bird widely spread throughout Australia wherever there is mud available to make its distinctive bowl-shaped nest. Because the nest is somewhat like those of the Apostle Bird and White-winged Chough the three are often grouped together, but they appear to have little in common. During the winter Magpie-larks often feed in large loose flocks of up to 300 birds.

**MAGPIE-LARK** *Grallina cyanoleuca*                    SEE p. 11

25–28 cm. A conspicuous, pied, white-bellied, ground-feeding bird. **Male:** above, black, with broad white patch in wing; rump, basal half of tail, and tail tip, white; head, throat, and upper breast, black, with eyebrows, small spot below eyes and cheek white; lower breast and

Grey Wagtail

Magpie-lark

abdomen, white. **Female:** similar, but with forehead and throat white, no eyebrows. Bill, white; eyes, creamy-white; legs, black. **Immature:** similar to male, but with throat as well as eyebrows white, and bill black.

VOICE: "Pee-o-wit" often sung as a duet; nasal "clut" (Hutchinson 44).
HABITAT: Open timber, open paddocks, water margins.
RANGE: Australia, rare in Tasmania.

Some are sedentary, but many form nomadic flocks in winter; possibly an extensive winter migration to Brigalow areas in Queensland.

# CUCKOO-SHRIKES — Campephagidae

Despite superficial similarities, cuckoo-shrikes have no affinities with either cuckoos or shrikes but form with minivets (not found in Australia) a quite distinctive family. The flight is generally undulating, and many species shuffle the wings on alighting. A number of species are migratory to southern Australia. Nests are usually small structures of grass bound by cobweb and placed in a horizontal fork.

Two groups occur in Australia. Trillers are small cuckoo-shrikes, with the males either pied or dark grey; in southern Australia the males arrive two or three weeks before the females. The cuckoo-shrikes are larger birds, predominantly grey in colour.

### GROUND CUCKOO-SHRIKE *Pteropodocys maxima*      SEE p. 13

35 cm. A pale grey bird with black wings, black forked-tail, and barred abdomen. **Adult:** above, pale grey; rump, white barred black; wings, grey; abdomen, white barred black. **Immature:** paler, with barred upperparts. Bill, black; eyes, pale yellow; legs, black.

Although it feeds on the ground, the Ground Cuckoo-shrike is most often seen in flight, when it appears white with black wings and tail.

Ground Cuckoo-shrike                    Black-faced Cuckoo-shrike

VOICE: A shrill "kree-el;" whistling "cheer-cheer;" harsh "cool-ook;" "hic-o-weeyit."

HABITAT: Sparsely-timbered country interspersed with grasslands, usually in drier country though it occasionally reaches the coast.

RANGE: Australia, avoiding denser forested areas.

Nomadic.

## BLACK-FACED CUCKOO-SHRIKE                          SEE p. 13
*Coracina novaehollandiae*

32·5 cm. A grey bird with a black face and throat: **Adult:** above, grey with black centres to wing and tail feathers; face and throat, black; below, grey and white. **Immature:** paler grey, with some faint barring on breast and back and black line through eyes. Bill, black; eyes, brown; legs, black.

Often perches on dead branches above trees, flicking wings after alighting.

Immature may be confused with Little Cuckoo-shrike, but is much bigger and has more extensive black through the eyes. Dark-phase Little Cuckoo-shrike has dark brown head and breast, but is much smaller.

VOICE: Plaintive "plee-urk;" a loud shrilling.

HABITAT: Open forest and savannah.

RANGE: Australia and Tasmania; migrating to Indonesia and Melanesia; accidental to New Zealand; islands north of Australia.

All eastern subspecies, including Tasmanian, have been collected in New Guinea, arriving in late May and leaving in September and early October. Generally, southern birds migrate north, but in the south-west they seem to be resident.

## LITTLE CUCKOO-SHRIKE *Coracina papuensis*          SEE p. 13

25–27·5 cm. A grey bird with black between eyes and bill or, rarely, with head and throat black and breast mottled-black. **Adult:** above, grey with black flight feathers edged white; throat and abdomen, white; breast, white in birds west of Normanton (race *hypoleuca*), pale grey between Normanton and Townsville (race *stalkeri*), and darker grey south of Townsville (race *robusta*), sometimes barred black and occasionally with head and throat black (dark phase). **Immature:** similar, but mottled with brown on breast and upperparts. Bill, black; eyes, brown; legs, black.

Dark phase *robusta* may be confused with Black-faced Cuckoo-shrike, but entire head is black, breast is mottled, and the call is pitched higher. The pale abdomen and generally untidy appearance distinguish the dark phase from the Cicada-bird. Adult light-phase birds may be confused with immature Black-faced Cuckoo-shrike, but the black mask does not extend behind the eyes.

VOICE: "Kisseek;" "quee-erk."

HABITAT: Forest, open woodland, and mangrove.

RANGE: Eastern and northern Australia, from Derby, Western Australia, to south-eastern South Australia.

Sedentary, with some nomadism in the south.

## BARRED CUCKOO-SHRIKE *Coracina lineata* SEE p. 13

22·5 cm. A dark grey bird with yellow eyes and boldly-barred abdomen, usually associated with native fig trees. Above, dark grey, darker round face; breast, grey, abdomen, barred black and white. Bill, black; eyes, yellow; legs, black.

VOICE: A plaintive whistling "whee" or "whee-uk."

HABITAT: Open forest and rain forest, particularly where there are native figs and fruit.

RANGE: Eastern Australia, Waigeu Island, New Guinea, Bismarck Archipelago, and Solomon Archipelago.

There is evidence of migration, and the Australian form has been collected in New Guinea.

## CICADA-BIRD (JARDINE TRILLER) SEE p. 13
*Coracina tenuirostris*

25·5 cm. A dark grey bird with a cicada-like call. **Male:** above and below, dark grey. **Female:** above, brown with pale eyebrows; below, buff, finely-barred black. **Immature:** above, strongly barred; below, streaked. Bill, black; eyes, brown; legs, black.

Male is unlike any other Australian bird. Female may be confused with the plumper female Varied Triller, differing in browner coloration, less white on wing, and larger size. Immature Oriental Cuckoo is not dissimilar in colour, but has much longer tail and wings, darker bars on underparts, and has a hawk-like flight.

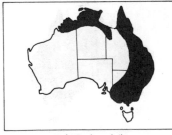

Little Cuckoo-shrike

Barred Cuckoo-shrike

VOICE: A loud cicada-like "kree-kree-kree-kree-kree-" which often continues for some time with a slight downward inclination. A rosella-like "Clewk clewk."

HABITAT: Forest.

RANGE: Northern and eastern Australia.

Migratory in southern Australia, arriving in September and October, males two to three weeks ahead of females.

## WHITE-WINGED TRILLER *Lalage sueurii*                          SEE p. 13

15–17 cm. A pied bird with a grey rump and black crown. **Male:** above, black with white shoulder and grey rump; below, white. **Male in eclipse:** (April to July approximately) head and back, brown. **Female:** above, brown, with paler marking on wings and eyebrows; below, pale grey. **Immature:** similar to female, but with streaked underparts and faintly-barred upperparts, usually lost by April. Bill, black; eyes, brown; legs, black.

The male may be confused with Varied Triller, but is much slimmer and more active, lacks white eyebrows and buff undertail coverts, and inhabits more open habitat. The female and male in eclipse may be confusing in northern Australia in winter to observers not aware that males lose their pied plumage. Often feed on eucalypt flowers in winter, and forehead may be yellow or orange with pollen.

VOICE: A rich vigorous song often uttered in flight by the male: "chi-chi-chi-joey joey joey" (Hutchinson 20).

HABITAT: Savannah and open forest; in winter in northern Australia often in flowering eucalypts and bauhinia; also feeds on the ground.

RANGE: Australia, Java to Lesser Sunda Islands, Celebes, and New Guinea.

Migrates to southern Australia in spring, males usually arriving in October two to three weeks ahead of females.

Cicada-bird

White-winged Triller

**VARIED TRILLER** *Lalage leucomela*                    SEE p. 13

17·5 cm. A pied bird with buff undertail coverts and white eyebrows. **Male:** above, black with white shoulder, greyish rump and white eyebrows; below, white with buff undertail coverts faintly barred. **Female:** above, grey-brown, with white wing markings and eyebrows; underparts, buff, finely barred black. **Immature:** similar to female, but barred on upperparts and streaked below. Bill, black; eyes, brown; legs, black.

Male may be confused with White-winged Triller, but is plumper, less active, and has white eyebrows and buff undertail coverts. The female may be confused with the female Cicada-bird, which is larger, browner, and lacks prominent white on shoulder. There is also a difference in habitat preferences, the Varied Triller preferring rain forest and the Cicada-bird open forest.

VOICE: A distinctive churring "chrrrr;" "drr-eea drr-eea drr-eea."

HABITAT: Rain forest, dense eucalypt forest, and mangroves.

RANGE: Northern and north-eastern Australia, Kei Islands, Aru Islands, eastern and southern New Guinea, Bismarck Archipelago.

Sedentary over most of its range, but migratory in New South Wales and southern Queensland.


# BULBULS—Pycnonotidae

Bulbuls are Old World, mainly tropical birds with fine bristles around the bill and on the nape. Many are crested and have loose, puff-like feathers on the rump. They are gregarious, searching in flocks for insects, fruit, and berries. The nest is cup-like, made from bark and grass, and well hidden. Two to four eggs, white spotted reddish-brown, form the clutch. The two species found in Australia are characterised by the crest, small in one species, and the red undertail coverts.

Varied Triller

Red-whiskered Bulbul

### RED-WHISKERED BULBUL *Pycnonotus jocosus*     SEE p. 15

20 cm. A crested bird with red behind the eyes and under the tail. Above, brown with crested crown; nape and sides of neck, black; patch behind eyes, red; cheek and throat, white; underparts, greyish-white; undertail coverts, red; tail, brown, tipped white. Bill, black; eyes, brown; legs, black.

VOICE: A jaunty whistling descending phrase, "wee-whit-h-h-h-h-h-who."

HABITAT: Suburban parks and gardens, particularly where there are fruiting shrubs and trees; rarely found far into surrounding bush.

RANGE: Introduced to Sydney, Melbourne, and Adelaide.

### RED-VENTED BULBUL *Pycnonotus cafer*     SEE p. 15

20 cm. A black-headed bulbul with scaled back and red undertail coverts. Above, smoky-brown, with each feather darker in the centre giving a scaled appearance; head and throat, black; below, whitish-grey, faintly scaled on the breast; undertail coverts, red; tail, brown, with broad white tip. Bill, black; eyes, dark brown; legs, grey.

VOICE: Cheerful rolling notes.

HABITAT: Open forest, suburban parks and gardens.

RANGE: Seen rarely in vicinity of Melbourne. (Introduced.)

## THRUSHES—Turdidae

Thrushes are mainly terrestrial birds, feeding on or near the ground. They have spotted young. The cup-shaped nests are often built on the ground, but some species build in trees and bushes. One typical, widely-distributed thrush, the Ground Thrush, occurs in dense, damp forests and thickets in eastern Australia, and a larger, more brightly-coloured form lives in the rain forests of the Atherton Tableland. Because it contradicts Bergmann's Rule (body size tends to be larger in cool

Red-vented Bulbul

Southern Scrub-robin

climates, smaller in warm climates) and because a smaller form has also been reported in the same area, some consider it a separate species. Others see it as a subspecies in a widespread and variable species.

The Blackbird and Song Thrush have been introduced. The scrub-robins have only recently been classified with the thrushes and are not typical at all of the family; they are sometimes placed with quail-thrushes in the babbler family, but are probably best retained in their old place with the Australian robins. They live almost entirely on the ground, moving with the tail half-cocked, and only occasionally climbing bushes, usually to sing. The nest is built in a small depression, and usually has a number of twigs radiating from the edge. The Southern Scrub-Robin lays one egg, the Northern usually two.

**SOUTHERN SCRUB-ROBIN** *Drymodes brunneopygia*        SEE p. 15

19–20 cm. A brownish-grey ground bird with rufous rump and two white bars on the wing. Above, brownish-grey with rufous rump; wings, darker with coverts tipped white forking two bars; eye-rings, white, with black spot above and below eyes; underparts, grey, with light-cinnamon undertail coverts; tail, dark brown, with rufous edges and white tip. Bill, black; eyes, dark brown; legs, black.

Most often observed walking on the ground with tail cocked at forty-five degrees, among undergrowth, or singing on a stick. The tail is often raised and lowered, and the wings are flicked. It is distinguished from quail-thrushes by the long cocked tail and the lack of white eyebrows. The Northern Scrub-robin is reddish-brown, has much more white about the face, and inhabits forest.

VOICE: A very loud "chip-por-wee," sometimes with an extra syllable added.

HABITAT: Mallee and scrubby sandplain.

RANGE: South-western Australia, avoiding the forested south-west; south-eastern South Australia; north-western Victoria; and south-western New South Wales.

Sedentary.

**NORTHERN SCRUB-ROBIN** *Drymodes superciliaris*        SEE p. 15

19–20 cm. A reddish-brown ground bird with two buff-white wing bars and a white face with a vertical black band through the eyes. Above, reddish-brown, with rufous rump; wings, black with two buff-white bars; face, whitish, with a vertical black band through the eyes; underparts, white, with buff suffusion on breast and flanks; tail, dark reddish-brown, edged rufous and tipped white. Bill, black; eyes, brown; legs, pinkish-brown.

VOICE: Thin, sharp whistle.

HABITAT: Forest, particularly edges.

RANGE: Cape York and eastern Arnhem Land, Northern Territory (Roper River), New Guinea, Aru Islands.

Sedentary.

## AUSTRALIAN GROUND-THRUSH *Zoothera dauma* SEE p. 15

25–27·5 cm. A boldly-scalloped ground bird found in forests and dense thickets. Above, bronze-brown; below, white, profusely scalloped with black tips to the feathers. Bill, black; eyes, dark brown; legs, dark grey.

VOICE: Flute-like warble heard mainly at dawn or dusk.

HABITAT: Forest and dense thickets, especially damp gullies, occasionally in drier and more open forest.

RANGE: Eastern Australia and Tasmania, north to Atherton district and possibly Cape York.

Sedentary.

## ATHERTON GROUND-THRUSH *Zoothera cuneata* SEE p. 15

28 cm. A boldly-scalloped ground bird found in rain forest on the Atherton Tableland. Above, bronze-brown, more richly-coloured on head and back; below, white, more buff on breast, profusely scalloped with black tips to the feathers. Bill, black; eyes, dark brown; legs, dark grey.

Very similar to the Australian Ground-thrush, but larger and rather more richly-coloured; it is probably not readily identifiable in the field.

VOICE: Unrecorded.

HABITAT: Rain forest.

RANGE: Atherton Tableland, North Queensland.

Sedentary.

Northern Scrub-robin

Australian Ground-thrush

**SONG THRUSH** *Turdus philomelos* SEE p. 15

22·5 cm. An introduced bird with heavily spotted breast. Above, brown; below, buff-white, heavily spotted black on breast and flanks. Bill, black; eyes, dark brown; legs, brown.

VOICE: Loud clear "did he do it did he do it, Judy did;" "come out, come out;" quiet "chick;" harsh "took took."

HABITAT: Suburban gardens.

RANGE: Vicinity of Melbourne.

Sedentary.

**BLACKBIRD** *Turdus merula* SEE p. 15

25 cm. An introduced bird either black with yellow bill and eye-rings (male) or mottled-brown (female). **Male:** all black, with yellow bill and eye-rings. **Female** and **immature:** above, brown, darker on tail and wings; below, mottled-brown, paler on throat. Bill, yellow (male) or brown (female); eyes, brown with yellow eye-rings (male); legs, black.

VOICE: Loud clattering cry, followed by protesting clucks; loud persistent "pink-pink." Loud melodious song.

HABITAT: Suburban gardens, dense undergrowth.

RANGE: Victoria; Tasmania; Adelaide, South Australia; and Sydney, New South Wales.

Sedentary.

# BABBLERS — Timaliidae

A diverse family of mainly ground-feeding birds with four distinct groups occurring in Australia. (a) The rail babblers live entirely on the ground. The nest is a cup-shaped structure in the quail-thrushes and dome-shaped in the log-runners. Quail-thrushes live in forests or savannah, often on stony ground, and take their name from the loud

Atherton Ground-thrush

Song Thrush

whirring of the wings as they take off when disturbed. The log-runners are confined to rain forest and have spinelike projections in the tail formed by the bare tips of the tail shafts. Some taxonomists place the two species in a family of their own, *Orthonycidae*. (b) The scimitar babblers have long down-curved bills, white eyebrows, build domed twig nests and move in small parties. One, Hall's Babbler, was discovered quite recently. Of particular interest is their social behaviour. (c) The whipbirds are longtailed crested ground birds which build cup-shaped nests in low bushes and lay blue eggs. They have distinctive calls, the whipcrack of the Eastern Whipbird and the "did-you-get-drunk" of the wedgebill being the best known. (d) The mud-nest builders build a nest rather like that of the Magpie-lark, but are social and behave like scimitar babblers.

## RAIL BABBLERS

The six species of rail babblers (four quail-thrushes, and two log-runners), live entirely on the ground. The quail-thrushes are fond of stony or rocky ground, particularly on ridges where there is plenty of vegetation cover. They lay their eggs in a depression in the ground lined with leaves or grass and usually placed at the base of a big rock or under an overhanging log. They are generally fairly difficult to observe unless they are nesting, but they reveal their location with loud, penetrating calls, particularly in the early morning and evening. The dry country species are variable in back colour, depending to some extent on the colour of the soil, but the underparts remain constant, so it is best to base identification on the pattern of the throat and breast. Some authorities ally the Nullarbor Quail-thrush with the Cinnamon Quail-thrush, others with the Chestnut Quail-thrush. Until a consensus of opinion is achieved it is preferable to keep it separate.

The log-runners are confined to rain forest, where they are fairly

Blackbird                                                    Southern Log-runner

easy to locate, as they are noisy birds, both in call and in their manner of feeding, scratching aside dead leaves. The nest is a large dome of sticks, usually placed at the base of a tree, on a tree stump, or on an earth bank.

## SOUTHERN LOG-RUNNER *Orthonyx temminckii*    SEE p. 15

17·5–20 cm. A mottled-brown ground bird with black patch on side of throat, which is white (male) or chestnut (female), found in rain forests. **Adult male:** above, mottled-brown and black; wings, black, with two buff bars; head, rufous-grey, with broad grey eyebrows; throat, white, with black patch on the side; abdomen, white, with rufous flanks; tail, dark brown, with stiff spines extending beyond tip. **Adult female:** similar, but with chestnut throat. **Immature:** mottled-brown. Bill, black; eyes, dark brown; legs, black.

VOICE: Loud resonant "be-kweek-kweek-kweek," sometimes in concert; soft "tweet" when feeding.

HABITAT: Sub-tropical rain forest.

RANGE: Rain forests of the south-east coast, from south-eastern Queensland to south-eastern New South Wales; other races occur in New Guinea.

Sedentary.

## NORTHERN LOG-RUNNER *Orthonyx spaldingi*    SEE p. 15

25–26·5 cm. A dark-brown ground bird with throat white (male) or chestnut (female), found in tropical rain forest. **Adult male:** above, blackish-brown; head, black; throat, breast, and abdomen, white; tail, dark brown, with extending spines. **Female:** smaller, with chestnut throat. **Immature:** mottled-brown. Bill, black; eyes, brownish-black surrounded by a conspicuous white circle; legs, black.

VOICE: "Chow-chilla," often followed by "chow-chow-chowy-chook-chook."

Northern Log-runner                    Spotted Quail-thrush

HABITAT: Tropical rain forest.
RANGE: North-eastern Queensland, from Ingham to Cooktown.
Sedentary.

## SPOTTED QUAIL-THRUSH *Cinclosoma punctatum*    SEE p. 17

26–30 cm. A spotted ground bird. **Male:** above, olive-brown and grey, spotted with black; shoulder, black, spotted white; wing, streaked black and chestnut; head, grey, with white eyebrows; face and throat, black, with white spot on side of neck; breast, grey; abdomen, white, spotted black; flanks and undertail, light chestnut; tail, tipped white. **Female:** similar, but lacking black throat and breast; chestnut patch on side of throat. Bill, black; eyes, light brown; legs, pinkish-brown.

Differs from other similar ground birds by the absence of conspicuous white bars on the wing coverts.

VOICE: Thin piping whistle; two-noted musical call at dawn.
RANGE: South-eastern Australia and Tasmania.
Sedentary.      *Pinaroo, S.A. - 10/72*

## CHESTNUT QUAIL-THRUSH *Cinclosoma castanotum*    SEE p. 17

20–22·5 cm. A chestnut-backed ground bird with brown head, black throat and breast, and grey-brown flanks. **Male:** above, brown with chestnut lower back and rump; shoulder, black with two white bars; white streaks above and below eyes; throat and centre of breast, black; sides of breast and flanks grey-brown bordered with black streaks; abdomen, white; central tail feathers and upper tail coverts, brown; outer tail feathers, black-tipped white. **Female:** duller, with grey throat and breast, and brown shoulder. Bill, black; eyes, reddish-brown; legs, grey-brown.

Distinguished from the Cinnamon Quail-thrush by the wholly black breast and preference for eucalypt habitat; from the Nullarbor Quail-thrush by habitat, grey-brown flanks, and brown head.

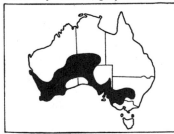

Chestnut Quail-thrush                     Nullarbor Quail-thrush

VOICE: A thin piercing whistle.

HABITAT: Dry woodlands and stony heaths, particularly in mallee woodland.

RANGE: South-western New South Wales; north-western Victoria; South Australia to south-western Australia as far north as the mulga-eucalypt line.

Sedentary.

## NULLARBOR QUAIL-THRUSH *Cinclosoma alisteri*     SEE p. 17

19 cm. A chestnut-backed ground bird with chestnut head, black throat and breast. **Male:** above, chestnut; shoulder, black with two white bars; white streaks above and below eyes; throat and breast, black; abdomen, buff-white spotted black at the sides; tail, central feathers chestnut, outer feathers, black-tipped white. **Female:** duller, with ear coverts and shoulders chestnut. Bill, black; eyes, reddish-brown; legs, grey-brown.

Distinguished from the Chestnut Quail-thrush by the chestnut head and buff flanks; from the Cinnamon Quail-thrush by the wholly black breast.

VOICE: A thin whistle.

HABITAT: Dongas (shallow vegetated depressions on the Nullarbor Plain).

RANGE: Nullarbor Plain.

Sedentary.

## CINNAMON QUAIL-THRUSH     SEE p. 17
*Cinclosoma cinnamomeum*

20 cm. A cinnamon-backed ground bird with a white and/or chestnut band between the black throat and breast. **Male:** above, cinnamon-brown; shoulder, black, with two white bars; white streaks above and

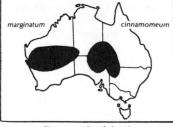

Cinnamon Quail-thrush

Chestnut-breasted Quail-thrush

below eyes; lower breast, black; abdomen, white, with cinnamon flanks.
**Female:** head, grey-brown; throat, cream or buff instead of black. Bill
black; eyes, dark brown; legs, dark grey.

Populations in the east (race *castaneothorax*) and west (race *margina-tum*) are darker than in the centre (race *cinnamomeum*). The race *castaneo-thorax*, regarded by some as a separate species, goes by the common
name of Chestnut-breasted Quail-thrush and has a complete band of
cinnamon on the upper breast.

Distinguished from the races of the Chestnut Quail-thrush by white
or cinnamon break between the black throat and breast and by the
preference for a mulga habitat.

VOICE: A plaintive whistle of five or six notes, "whee-wh-wh-wh-whee-whee," carrying for a considerable distance; usually dawn and
dusk; also a single piercing whistle.

HABITAT: Semi-desert scrub in sandy or stony localities, particularly
in mulga woodland along breakaways.

RANGE: Central Australia, from south-western Queensland and
north-western New South Wales to central Western Australia, south
to the mulga-eucalypt line.

Sedentary.

## CHESTNUT-BREASTED QUAIL-THRUSH                     SEE p. 17
*Cinclosoma cinnamomeum castaneothorax*

20 cm. A cinnamon-backed ground bird with a chestnut breast.
**Male:** above, cinnamon brown; shoulder, black with two white bars,
white streaks above and below eyes; throat, black; upper breast, chestnut;
lower breast, black continuing as black chevrons along the flank;
abdomen, white with greyish flanks; tail, black with outer feathers
tipped white. **Female:** similar to female Cinnamon Quail-thrush.

The white tips of the outer tail feathers protrude, giving the appearance
of white "tail-lights" as the bird walks away from the observer. The
chestnut breast distinguishes it from the other quail thrush. Where the
ranges of the Chestnut-breasted and Cinnamon Quail-thrushes meet,
hybrids occur.

VOICE: A five-noted, plaintive piping whistle, carrying for a consider-able distance.

HABITAT: Mulga and lancewood on stony hills, particularly where
there is abundant fallen mulga.

RANGE: South-western Queensland from the Grey Range to a point
midway between Cunnamulla and Eulo, and north-western New South
Wales.

Sedentary.

## SCIMITAR BABBLERS

The four species of babbler are quite similar to each other in appearance and behaviour, differing mostly for identification purposes in the shape and size of the eyebrows and the colour of the crown. They are usually observed in small parties of five to ten birds bouncing jerkily over the ground or hopping through trees in follow-the-leader fashion. Their large, dome-shaped stick nests are very obvious and are attended by the entire party. Sleeping nests are also constructed, and the entire group sleeps inside.

### GREY-CROWNED BABBLER *Pomatostomus temporalis*   SEE p. 19

23–25·5 cm. A grey-crowned babbler. Above, dark brownish-grey; rump and tail, black, broadly tipped white; wing, dark brownish-grey, with concealed pale cinnamon-brown patch (visible in flight); centre of crown, grey, shading into white forehead and eyebrows; throat, white, shading gradually to cinnamon-rufous abdomen and brownish-black flanks; undertail, black. Bill, black; eyes, pale lemon (adult) or brown (immature); legs, black.

Distinguished from White-browed and Hall's Babblers by the grey crown and pale wing patch visible in flight.

VOICE: Cat-like "meow;" churring and soft "tuk."

HABITAT: Woodland.

RANGE: Eastern and northern Australia, from Wooramel River, Western Australia, to south-eastern South Australia; southern New Guinea.

Sedentary.

### WHITE-BROWED BABBLER                                        SEE p. 19
*Pomatostomus superciliosus*

20 cm. A dark-crowned babbler with narrow white eyebrows and white throat, shading gradually to dark abdomen. Above, dark grey,

Grey-crowned Babbler

White-browed Babbler

with brownish wash; wing, dark brown, without concealed cinnamon patch; tail, black, broadly-tipped white; crown, dark grey; eyebrows, white; throat, white, shading gradually from dull-white breast to dark-grey abdomen. Bill, black, pale at base of lower mandible; eyes, reddish-brown; legs, dark grey.

Distinguished from Grey-crowned Babbler by dark crown and lack of wing-patch; from Hall's Babbler by the narrow white eyebrows and the gradual change from white throat to dark abdomen.

VOICE: Reedy "churr;" loud "tuk-tuk-tuk . . .;" cat-like "meow."

HABITAT: Dry woodland to arid country, interspersed with trees and bushes.

RANGE: Southern Australia, virtually exclusive of the Grey-crowned Babbler's range, although there is overlap in the mid-west and south-east.

Sedentary.

### HALL'S BABBLER *Pomatostomus halli*                         SEE p. 19

18 cm. A dark-crowned babbler with broad white eyebrows and white throat shading abruptly to dark breast and abdomen. Above, blackish-grey with brown wash on crown and nape; tail, black, broadly-tipped white; eyebrows, white; throat, white, shading abruptly to sooty-black breast and abdomen. Bill, black, with pale base to lower mandible; eyes, reddish-brown; legs, black.

Gives the impression of a blackbird with white brow, throat, and tail tip; juveniles look paler. Distinguished from White-browed Babbler by the broad eyebrows and white throat shading abruptly to dark breast; from the Grey-crowned Babbler by the overall darker appearance and dark crown.

VOICE: Loud "skeeyaah;" soft "tuk tuk tuk" when feeding.

HABITAT: Mainly mulga, lancewood, mineritchie, and similar trees growing in and among rocky hills.

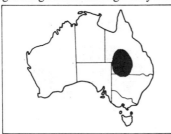

Hall's Babbler

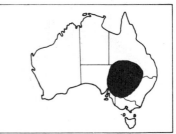

Chestnut-crowned Babbler

RANGE: South-western to south-central Queensland, north-central
New South Wales.

Sedentary.

## CHESTNUT-CROWNED BABBLER                           SEE p. 19
*Pomatostomus ruficeps*

21·5 cm. A chestnut-crowned babbler with two white wing bars.
Above, dark grey, scalloped pale grey; wings, brownish-black, with two
broad white bars on coverts; tail, black, tipped white; crown, chestnut,
with white margin; face and ear coverts, black; throat to centre of
abdomen, white; flanks, dark brownish-grey; undertail, black, with
feathers tipped white. Bill, black, with base of lower mandible bluish-
white; eyes, brown; legs, dark grey.

VOICE: Harsh "chat a chat."

HABITAT: Stands of timber, mostly casuarina, in saltbush country,
and vegetation along watercourses.

RANGE: Eastern South Australia, south-western Queensland, western
New South Wales, and north-western Victoria.

Sedentary.

# WHIPBIRDS

Whipbirds are crested ground birds ranging from rain forest to arid
mulga scrub. They build cup-shaped nests in low bushes or shrubs and
lay two greenish-blue eggs. The Eastern Whipbird is responsible for the
well-known whipcrack call heard in dense undergrowth. The Western
Whipbird is less well known, and inhabits mallee heaths. The two arid
country whipbirds are a sibling species, almost identical in plumage
but easily identifiable by call. The western species, the Chiming Wedgebill, has a bell-like descending call "did you get drunk;" the eastern
Chirruping Wedgebill has a completely different three-noted "tootsie
cheer" call.

*MT. Spec, Qu'land 5/70*

## EASTERN WHIPBIRD *Psophodes olivaceus*                  SEE p. 19

25–27·5 cm. A crested long-tailed ground bird with a white throat
patch and a loud whipcrack call. **Adult:** above, dark olive-brown; head,
black, with erectile crest; side of neck and throat, white; breast, black,
shading to dark grey-olive-brown, with mottled-white abdomen.
**Immature:** lacks white throat. Bill, black; eyes, brown; legs, reddish-
brown.

VOICE: Loud whipcrack; chuckles and whistles, sometimes in duet
between male and female.

HABITAT: Dense thickets in or near wet forests.
RANGE: Eastern Australia.
Sedentary.

## WESTERN WHIPBIRD *Psophodes nigrogularis*                SEE p. 19

22·5 cm. A crested long-tailed ground bird with black throat edged white. **Adult:** above, dark greenish-olive; head and crest, grey; throat, black, with white streak on each side; remainder of underparts, olive-grey, sometimes with white belly; tail, tipped white. **Immature:** lacks throat markings. Bill, dark brown; eyes, red; legs, dark brown.

VOICE: Harsh grating call; a sweeter song of four, five, or six notes, "it's for teacher."

HABITAT: Dense thickets in coastal sandhills and mallee scrub.

RANGE: South-western Australia; Eyre and Yorke peninsulas, Kangaroo Island, southern South Australia, and north-western Victoria.
Sedentary.

## CHIRRUPING WEDGEBILL *Psophodes cristatus*                SEE p. 19

20 cm. A drab, brown, crested ground bird of eastern arid areas, often seen singing "tootsie cheer" on top of a bush. Above, brown, darker on rump and crest; throat, dull white; underparts, dull buff; white streak in wing; tail, broadly tipped white. Bill, black; eyes, brown; legs, dark grey.

The lack of any black on throat or face distinguishes the wedgebills from other crested passerines in similar country. The western Chiming Wedgebill is similar in appearance but calls "did you get drunk" (Hutchinson 33).

VOICE: Incessant creaky "tootsie cheer."

HABITAT: Mulga, low arid scrub, and savannah.

RANGE: Arid areas of eastern Australia.
Sedentary.

Eastern Whipbird

Western Whipbird

**CHIMING WEDGEBILL**  *Psophodes occidentalis*          SEE p. 19

20 cm. A drab, brown, crested ground bird of western arid areas, often seen singing "did you get drunk" on top of a bush. Above, brown, darker on rump and crest; throat, dull white; underparts, pale buff; white streak in wing; tail, broadly tipped white. Bill, black; eyes, brown; legs, dark grey.

The lack of any black on throat or face distinguishes the wedgebills from other crested passerines in similar country. The eastern Chirruping Wedgebill is similar in appearance but calls "tootsie cheer."

VOICE: Incessant chime-like "did you get drunk," being rather creaky on the fourth note (Hutchinson 33).

HABITAT: Mulga, arid scrub, and savannah.

RANGE: Western arid areas of Australia, north of the mulga-eucalypt line.

Sedentary.

## MUDBUILDERS

Like the scimitar babblers, the mudbuilders live in small flocks. This habit has led to the vernacular naming of one as the Apostle Bird, an allusion to the belief by bushmen that twelve birds constitute a flock. The other species, the White-winged Chough, has a superficial resemblance to the European Chough, a member of the crow family. Because of their bowl-like mud nests, placed on a horizontal limb, the White-winged Chough and the Apostle Bird have been classified with the Magpie-lark which also builds a mud nest, although it is different in shape. Apart from the use of mud in the nest, the Magpie-lark seems to have nothing in common with the other two.

**WHITE-WINGED CHOUGH**  *Corvorax melanorhamphus*      SEE p. 19

45 cm. A social black ground-feeding bird with white patch in wings. Above and below, black, with large white patch in wing, visible in flight.

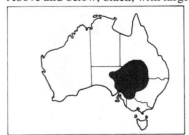

Chirruping Wedgebill

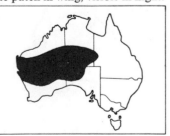

Chiming Wedgebill

Bill, black; eyes, red (often showing white eyeballs); legs, black.

VOICE: Harsh, grating, and piping.

HABITAT: Forest and woodland; often observed along country roadsides.

RANGE: South-eastern Australia, west of the Great Dividing Range; South Australia, except the north-east; and south-eastern Western Australia.

Sedentary, or locally nomadic.

### APOSTLE BIRD *Struthidea cinerea*                          SEE p. 19

33 cm. A social grey ground-feeding bird with long black tail. Above and below, dark grey, paler on head and breast, with each feather tipped lighter; wings, brown; tail, black, with green iridescence. Bill, black; eyes, white or brown; legs, black.

VOICE: Loud, harsh, grating, and scolding calls.

HABITAT: Open forest and woodland, often with particular vegetation, such as Callitris in central New South Wales, Casuarina in central Queensland, and Lancewood–Bulwaddi communities in Northern Territory.

RANGE: Inland eastern Australia, from south-eastern South Australia and north-western Victoria to the south-eastern corner of the Gulf of Carpentaria and west to Lawn Creek in north-western Queensland; an isolated population in central Northern Territory.

Sedentary or locally nomadic.

## AUSTRALIAN WRENS—Maluridae

A group of often beautifully-plumaged birds which carry the tail cocked. They feed on or near the ground and build domed nests close to the ground. There are four groups: (a) The fairy wrens, in which the

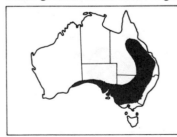

White-winged Chough

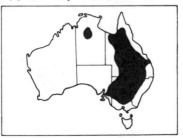

Apostle Bird

males are beautifully patterned in bright colours, predominantly blue, and the females are generally brown in colour. Many species live in family groups and as many as five fully-plumaged males have been seen visiting one nest. (b) The emu-wrens, which have unique barbless tail-feathers; they are among the smallest of local birds. The males have blue feathers on the throat. They live in dense cover, either heath or spinifex, and are fairly difficult to see except when the observer approaches a nest. (c) The grass-wrens, which feed almost entirely on the ground and are furtive in behaviour, making observation difficult. They are basically brown with white streaks, and most live in arid environments. (d) The bristle-birds, which feed on the ground and live in dense cover on heathlands and coastal sedge thickets. Although plainly-coloured, the feathers have a lacquered sheen.

## FAIRY WRENS

Thirteen species of fairy wrens are currently recognised. Blue predominates in the male colouring, but two species and one race lack blue entirely. The females are either brown or blue-grey and are much more difficult to identify than the males. One group of four species is characterised by largely blue and black males. Another more confusing group of six species is characterised by the chestnut shoulder patch. The males are closely similar and some degree of subjectivity must enter into their identification, particularly in distinguishing the Variegated and Purple-backed Wrens. In the north occur two very similar but isolated species with distinctive blue-grey females, the Lovely and Lavender-flanked Wrens. The Lavender-flanked is divided into two populations. In one of these the female has chestnut eye patches, but as they are lacking in the other, they may prove to be separate species. The remaining species, the White-winged, Red-backed, and Lilac-crowned Wrens, are quite distinctive.

Superb Blue Wren

Black-backed Wren

### SUPERB BLUE WREN *Malurus cyaneus*                    SEE p. 21

12·5 cm. The only white-bellied blue wren without a chestnut shoulder. **Coloured male:** crown, ear coverts, mantle, and tail, blue; remainder of upperparts, black; wings, brown; throat and breast, black, with purplish sheen; abdomen, white. **Uncoloured male:** above, grey-brown; tail, blue; underparts, dull white. **Female:** similar to uncoloured male, but with russet-brown face and brown bill; tail, brown. Bill, black (male) or reddish-brown (female); eyes, dark brown; legs, brown.

Voice: A trilling reel.

Habitat: Bushes and woodland; also in parks and gardens.

Range: Eastern Australia, from southern Queensland to South Australia, Kangaroo Island, and Tasmania.

Sedentary.

*Wyperfeld N.P. – 8/72*

### BLACK-BACKED WREN *Malurus melanotus*                    SEE p. 21

12·5 cm. A predominantly blue wren with blue throat and abdomen. **Breeding male:** crown, ear coverts, abdomen, mantle, and tail, violet-blue; remainder, black, with brown wings tinged violet. Bill, black; eyes, brown; legs, black. **Non-breeding male:** above, grey-brown; tail, blue; below, dull white. **Female:** similar but with bill and eye patch chestnut-brown.

The female is distinguished from the female Superb Blue Wren by the blue tail; from the female Purple-backed and Variegated Wrens by the smaller and paler chestnut face.

Voice: Rich reel.

Habitat: Dense shrubs, bushes, and grasses in woodland and savannah.

Range: Central western Queensland to north-western Victoria and Flinders Ranges, South Australia.

Sedentary.

### TURQUOISE WREN *Malurus callainus*                    SEE p. 21

12·5 cm. A predominantly blue wren with violet throat and blue abdomen. **Breeding male:** crown, ear coverts, mantle, and tail, caerulean-blue; throat, purple. Remainder, black, with wings brown tinged blue. Bill, black; eyes, brown; legs, black. **Non-breeding male:** above, brown; tail, blue; below, dull white. **Female:** similar, but with bill and eye patch chestnut-brown.

Distinguished from the Black-backed Wren by the richer throat colouring and paler blue upperparts. Female distinguished from female chestnut-shouldered wrens by smaller and paler chestnut face patch;

from female White-winged Wren by brighter blue tail and small chestnut face patch; indistinguishable from female Splendid and Black-backed Wrens.

VOICE: Gushing reel.

HABITAT: Dense shrubs, bushes, and grasses in arid woodland.

RANGE: Central Australia, from north of the Nullarbor Plain, Western Australia, to Ayers Rock, Northern Territory, and south to Spencer Gulf, South Australia.

Apparently less sedentary than other blue wrens.

## SPLENDID WREN *Malurus splendens*          SEE p. 21

12·5 cm. A predominantly blue wren with violet throat and abdomen, and with no black on lower back. **Breeding male:** crown, ear coverts, back, wings, and tail, violet-blue; throat and abdomen, violet; remainder, black. Bill, black; eyes, brown; legs, black. **Non-breeding male:** above, brown with blue in wings; tail, blue; below, dull white. **Female:** similar, but with chestnut eye-patch and bill.

Distinguished from Turquoise Wren (which may be a sub-species) by the violet abdomen and the violet-blue, instead of black, lower back. Female distinguished from female chestnut-shouldered wrens by smaller and paler chestnut face, and from female White-winged Wren by the brighter blue tail and chestnut face.

VOICE: Gushing reel.

HABITAT: Dense undergrowth in a variety of habitats from karri forest to mulga woodland.

RANGE: South-western Australia.

Sedentary.

## VARIEGATED WREN *Malurus lamberti*          SEE p. 23

14·5 cm. A chestnut-shouldered wren with black breast, bright-blue crown and back, and buff flanks; female, brown. **Coloured male:** crown

Turquoise Wren

Splendid Wren

and back, bright blue; ear coverts, caerulean-blue; shoulders, chestnut; throat and breast, black; flanks, buff; tail, dull blue-green, tipped white. **Uncoloured male:** above, fawn-brown; face, dull white; below, buff-white; sides of breast and flanks, buff; tail, dull blue-green. **Female:** similar to uncoloured male, but with chestnut face and brown bill. Bill, black (male) or reddish-brown (female); eyes, dark brown; legs, brown.

Male distinguished from Purple-backed Wren by the bright-blue rather than violet-blue crown and back, and the buff instead of white flanks; females are difficult to distinguish.

VOICE: Gushing reel, richer than Red-backed Wren and pitched higher than Superb Blue Wren; high pitched "tsree . . ."

HABITAT: Heath, forest undergrowth, thickets, mangroves.

RANGE: South-eastern Australia, from Fitzroy River, Queensland, to about Narooma, New South Wales. Sedentary.

**PURPLE-BACKED WREN** *Malurus assimilis*                    SEE p. 23

14·5 cm. A chestnut-shouldered wren with black breast, violet-blue crown and back, and white flanks; female, brown. **Coloured male:** crown and back, violet-blue; ear coverts, cobalt-blue; shoulders, chestnut; throat and breast, black, with small blue tuft on flank; flanks, white; tail, dull blue-green. **Uncoloured male:** above, fawn-brown; face, dull white; below, buff-white; tail, dull blue-green. **Female:** similar to uncoloured male, but with chestnut face and brown bill. Bill, black (male) or reddish-brown (female); eyes, dark brown; legs, brown.

Male distinguished from Variegated Wren by the violet rather than bright-blue crown and back, and the white instead of buff flanks; females are indistinguishable. Distinguished from Blue-breasted Wren and Red-winged Wren by the black rather than dark blue breast; and from the Lovely Wren and Lavender-flanked Wren by brown instead of blue-grey females.

Variegated Wren

Purple-backed Wren

VOICE: Gushing reel, not as rich as Turquoise, Black-backed, and Splendid Wrens, but richer than White-winged and Red-backed.

HABITAT: Dense low vegetation, including open forest undergrowth, mallee, cane grass, lignum, mangrove, spinifex, mulga, saltbush, and bluebush.

RANGE: Most of Australia, excluding the extreme north, south-east, south coast, and south-west.

Sedentary.


**BLUE-BREASTED WREN** *Malurus pulcherrimus*          SEE p. 23

14·5 cm. A chestnut-shouldered wren with dark-blue breast, violet-blue crown and back; female, brown. **Coloured male:** crown, ear coverts and back, violet-blue; shoulders, chestnut; throat and breast, dark violet-blue; flanks, white; tail, greenish-blue. **Uncoloured male:** above, fawn-brown; face, dull white; below, buff-white; tail, greenish-blue. **Female:** similar to uncoloured male, but with chestnut face and brown bill. Bill, black (male) or reddish-brown (female); eyes, dark brown; legs, brown.

Male distinguished from Purple-backed Wren by blue breast; from Red-winged Wren by violet-blue rather than pale greenish-blue crown and back.

VOICE: Gushing reel, not as rich as Splendid, Turquoise, and Black-backed Wrens, but richer than White-winged.

HABITAT: Dense low vegetation in open forest, mallee, heaths, and swamps. In the south-west the Blue-breasted Wren favours poison pea thickets.

RANGE: Southern Australia, from Eyre Peninsula, South Australia, to Shark Bay, Western Australia.

Sedentary.

Blue-breasted Wren

**RED-WINGED WREN** *Malurus elegans*                                        SEE p. 23

15 cm. A chestnut-shouldered wren with dark blue breast, pale greenish-blue crown and back; female, greyish-brown. **Coloured male:** crown, ear coverts and back, silvery greenish-blue; shoulders, chestnut; throat and breast, dark blue; flanks, white; tail, greyish-blue. **Uncoloured male:** above, greyish-brown, greyer on the head, and tinged chestnut on the wings; face, dull white; below, buff-white; tail, greyish-blue. **Female:** similar to uncoloured male, but with chestnut face and brown bill. Bill, black (male) or reddish-brown (female); eyes, dark brown; legs, brown.

Male distinguished from Purple-backed Wren by dark blue breast and pale greenish-blue crown; from the Blue-breasted Wren by the pale greenish-blue crown. The female has rather less chestnut about the eyes than the female Variegated and Blue-breasted Wrens.

VOICE: Gushing reel, usually shorter than other species.

HABITAT: Swampy undergrowth.

RANGE: South-western Australia.

Sedentary.

**LOVELY WREN** *Malurus amabilis*                                           SEE p. 23

14 cm. A chestnut-shouldered wren with black breast, violet-blue crown and back, and buff flanks; female, grey-blue, with white face. **Coloured male:** crown and back, violet-blue; ear coverts, bright blue; shoulders, chestnut; throat and breast, black; flanks, buff; tail, dark blue, tipped white. **Female:** above, grey-blue, brighter on the ear coverts and browner on the wings; face, white; below, white; tail, dark blue, tipped white. Bill, black; eyes, dark brown (male) or pale brown (female); legs, pinkish-brown.

Distinguished from Purple-backed Wren by the buff flanks and the lack of small blue patch on flank, and by the white-faced, grey-blue female.

Red-winged Wren                                          Lovely Wren

VOICE: Gushing reel, rather more tinny than Purple-backed Wren, but richer than Red-backed Wren.

HABITAT: Dense low tropical undergrowth on edges of rain forest, mangrove, melaleuca, and forests.

RANGE: Northern Queensland, south to the Edward River and Cardwell.

Sedentary.

## LAVENDER-FLANKED WREN *Malurus dulcis*           SEE p. 23

14 cm. A rock-haunting, chestnut-shouldered wren with black breast flanked with prominent lavender-blue patch, violet-blue crown and back, and white flanks; female, grey-blue with lores and feathers round eyes, white (Arnhem Land) or chestnut (Victoria River, Northern Territory, to Western Australia). **Coloured male:** crown and back, violet-blue; ear coverts, bright blue; shoulders, chestnut; throat and breast, black, with conspicuous lavender-blue patch on flank; remainder of flanks, white; tail, dark blue, tipped white. **Female:** above, grey-blue, brighter on the ear coverts and browner on the wings; face, white in Northern Territory, and chestnut in Western Australia; tail, dark blue, tipped white. Bill, black; eyes, dark brown (male) or light brown (female); legs, pinkish-brown.

Distinguished from the Purple-backed Wren by rock-haunting habit and by the grey-blue female.

VOICE: Gushing reel, tinnier than Purple-backed Wren, but richer than Red-backed Wren.

HABITAT: Rocky outcrops covered with vegetation.

RANGE: Two populations, one in north-western Arnhem Land, Northern Territory, and the other in the Kimberley Division, Western Australia.

Sedentary.

Lavender-flanked Wren

**WHITE-WINGED WREN** *Malurus leucopterus*          SEE p. 23

13·5 cm. A white-winged blue, or black, wren. **Coloured male:** above and below, cobalt-blue (mainland) or black (Dirk Hartog and Barrow islands) with white wings. **Uncoloured male:** above, pale reddish-brown; below, buff-white; tail, pale blue. **Female:** similar to uncoloured male, but with reddish-brown bill and brownish-blue tail. Bill, black (male) or reddish-brown (female); eyes, dark brown; legs, brown.

Male is unmistakable; female differs from female chestnut-shouldered wrens by lack of chestnut face patch and from female Superb Blue Wrens by the reddish-brown rather than greyish-brown back and the much paler blue tail; the female Red-backed Wren, which is virtually exclusive in range, lacks any blue in the tail.

VOICE: Tinkling reel, tinnier than any other wren.

HABITAT: Low vegetation, often on treeless plains in arid country; may be found on plains of scattered saltbush only centimetres high.

RANGE: Arid regions of Australia, mostly in areas less than 500 mm annual rainfall.

Sedentary, perhaps nomadic.


**RED-BACKED WREN** *Malurus melanocephalus*          SEE p. 23

12 cm. A red-backed black wren. **Coloured male:** above and below, black with back scarlet (east) or crimson (west). **Uncoloured male:** above, brown; below, buff-white; tail, brown. **Female:** similar to uncoloured male, but bill reddish-brown. Bill, black (male) or reddish-brown (female); eyes, dark brown; legs, brown.

Male unmistakable; female differs from all other female wrens in lack of blue in tail.

VOICE: Tinkling reel, more mechanical than other wrens.

HABITAT: Long grass in both wet and dry areas, especially where interspersed with low bushes.

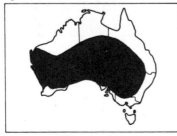

White-winged Wren                              Red-backed Wren

RANGE: Eastern and northern Australia, from Port Stephens, New South Wales, to Broome, Western Australia.

Sedentary.

## LILAC-CROWNED WREN *Malurus coronatus* SEE p. 21

15 cm. A mauve-crowned brown wren. **Coloured male:** above, cinnamon-brown; below, white, shading to buff on the flanks; crown, mauve, with central black streak; broad facial mask, black; tail, bright methyl blue. **Uncoloured male:** crown, brown; face, brown, with some black before the eyes, and separated from the crown by white eyebrows. **Female:** similar to uncoloured male, but with white face and chestnut ear patch. Bill, black; eyes, dark brown; legs, reddish-brown.

Male unmistakable; the bright-blue tail and chestnut ear patch of the female are distinctive.

VOICE: Shrill high-pitched "cheepa-cheepa-cheepa."

HABITAT: Closely associated with water in mangrove, cane grass, pandanus, and riverine vegetation.

RANGE: Northern Australia, from Derby, Western Australia, to O'Shannassy River, Queensland. Distribution is not continuous and is localised near watercourses.

Sedentary.

## EMU-WRENS

There are three distinct isolated populations of emu-wrens which are viewed differently by different taxonomists. Some treat them as separate species, others as sub-species. The diagnosis accepted here is that two species are involved, the Southern Emu-wren and the shorter-tailed Rufous-crowned Emu-wren, which has, as an isolated population, the Mallee Emu-wren. Because of their isolation from one another there is little chance of confusing the three forms.

Lilac-crowned Wren

**SOUTHERN EMU-WREN** *Stipiturus malachurus* SEE p. 21

19 cm including 10 cm tail. A heathland emu-wren. **Male:** above, cinnamon-brown, streaked darker; lores, throat, and upper breast, blue; below, buff. **Female:** lores, throat, and upper breast, cinnamon-brown, shading to buff. Bill, blackish-brown; eyes, reddish-brown; legs, light brown.

Lacks the bright forehead or crown of the two other forms, but confusion is unlikely if range and habitat are considered.

VOICE: A faint high-pitched version of the typical wren reel.

HABITAT: Heathland, swamp, and estuarine vegetation, sandplain, densely-covered coastal sand dunes, and in ranges up to 950 m in Blue Mountains.

RANGE: South-eastern Australia, from Lake Cooloola, Queensland, to St Vincent Gulf, South Australia; Tasmania; Kangaroo Island; and south-western Australia, from Israelite Bay to Shark Bay and Dirk Hartog Island.

Sedentary.

**MALLEE EMU-WREN** *Stipiturus ruficeps mallee* SEE p. 21

16·5 cm including 8 cm tail. A mallee-spinifex emu-wren, with a chestnut forehead. **Male:** above, olive-brown, streaked darker; forehead, chestnut; lores, eyebrows, throat, and upper breast, blue; below, greyish-buff. **Female:** lores, eyebrows, throat, and upper breast, buff. Bill, blackish-brown; eyes, reddish-brown; legs, light brown.

The chestnut forehead distinguishes it from the other emu-wrens, but confusion is unlikely if range and habitat are considered.

VOICE: Faint high-pitched version of the typical wren reel.

HABITAT: Spinifex in mallee scrub.

RANGE: North-western Victoria and south-eastern South Australia.

Sedentary.

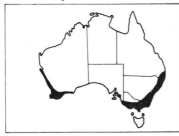

Southern Emu-wren

Mallee Emu-wren

**RUFOUS-CROWNED EMU-WREN** *Stipiturus ruficeps*      SEE p. 21

14·5 cm including tail 6 cm. A spinifex emu-wren with a rufous crown.
**Male:** above, reddish-brown, streaked darker; crown, rufous; lores,
eyebrows, ear coverts, throat and breast, blue; below reddish-buff.
**Female:** lacks blue colouring. Bill, blackish-brown; eyes, dark brown;
legs, reddish-brown.

The rufous crown distinguishes it from other emu-wrens, but range
and habitat should make confusion unlikely.

VOICE: A high silvery *malurus*-like reeling, also a series of four or
five extremely high notes, not audible to some observers.

HABITAT: Spinifex and other low-arid vegetation, particularly on
rocky ridges and sand dunes.

RANGE: Arid Australia, from mid-western Australia to central-
western Queensland and north-western South Australia.

Sedentary.


## GRASS-WRENS

Living as they do in arid or isolated environments, the grass-wrens
require the observer to make dedicated efforts to track them down.
Identification is not always easy, as some taxonomists with birds in the
hand have disagreed on the relationships of some populations. Ironically,
the Grey Grass-wren, the last species to be discovered (in 1967), is the
most distinctive. Fortunately some species occupy isolated ranges,
making identification easy. As for the others, by noting the basic colour
(either cinnamon-brown or reddish-brown), the amount of white on
the underparts, and the range and the habitat, confident identification
may be achieved. Two of the three cinnamon-brown species, the Thick-
billed and the Dusky Grass-wrens, are very similar, differing most in the
size of the bill and the choice of habitat. The other species, the Eyrean

Rufous-crowned Emu-wren

Grass-wren, is confined to a small area and has been seen by only a few people; almost the entire underparts of this bird are white. Also confined to a small area is the Grey Grass-wren, the most distinctively plumaged of all the grass-wrens. The two reddish-brown species, the widely spread Striated and the confined Dorothy's Grass-wren, are easily differentiated by range. The remaining two closely-related species differ from all the others in the broad tail feathers and blackish plumage. The White-throated lives on the Arnhem Land escarpment, and the Black Grass-wren in the west Kimberley area.

## THICK-BILLED GRASS-WREN SEE p. 25
*Amytornis textilis* (including *A. modestus*)

15–18 cm. A cinnamon-brown grass-wren with a thick bill. **Male:** above, cinnamon-brown with white streaks; lores, tinged rufous, with faint moustache; below, paler cinnamon, with white streaks; centre of abdomen, white; tail, dark brown. **Female:** similar, with rufous patch on flanks. Bill, black; eyes, brown; legs, dark grey-brown.

Perhaps best distinguished from the similar but darker Dusky Grass-wren by range and habitat preference, the Thick-billed preferring plains of saltbush and similar vegetation, and the Dusky preferring rocky hillsides covered with spinifex. The Eyrean Grass-wren has white underparts, and the Striated Grass-wren is much more rufous in colour.

VOICE: High-pitched squeak when disturbed; a high silvery song delivered from top of bush, with recurring phrases.

HABITAT: Plains of saltbush, bluebush, and cottonbush, and among flood debris along watercourses.

RANGE: Two populations, apparently separate, the first in southern Western Australia and South Australia, from Shark Bay to Eyre Peninsula, avoiding the forests of the south-west; and another population

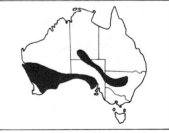

Thick-billed Grass-wren

in central-southern Northern Territory, north-eastern South Australia
and central-western New South Wales.

Sedentary, and nomadic in some areas.

### DUSKY GRASS-WREN *Amytornis purnelli*                SEE p. 25

15–18 cm. A cinnamon-brown grass-wren with a thin bill. **Male:**
above, cinnamon-brown, rather darker than *A. textilis*, streaked white;
crown, blackish-brown, streaked white; rump, tinged rufous; below,
pale cinnamon-brown, streaked white, with flanks greyish-brown
(Northern Territory) or pale grey (Mount Isa district, Queensland);
tail, dark brown. **Female:** similar, but with rufous flanks. Bill, black;
eyes, brown; legs, dark grey-brown.

Perhaps best distinguished from the similar but paler Thick-billed
Grass-wren by range and habitat, the Dusky inhabiting rocky hillsides covered with spinifex, and the Thick-billed inhabiting plains
covered with saltbush and similar vegetation, and debris-strewn watercourses. The Striated Grass-wren is much more rufous in colour.

VOICE: A song high and silvery, a rapid set of notes that usually
ends in silvery mangling or calandra (Parker).

HABITAT: Spinifex-covered rocky hills.

RANGE: Two populations, apparently separate; one (race *purnelli*)
in central Northern Territory, mid-eastern Western Australia, and
north-western South Australia; and another (race *ballarae*) in the
vicinity of Mount Isa, Queensland.

Sedentary.

### EYREAN GRASS-WREN *Amytornis goyderi*                SEE p. 25

14 cm. A cinnamon-brown grass-wren with white underparts. **Male:**
above, cinnamon-brown, greyish on crown and rufous on rump,
streaked white; moustache, indistinct black; underparts, white, with
cinnamon flanks; tail, dark brown, edged cinnamon. **Female:** not

Dusky Grass-wren

Eyrean Grass-wren

recorded. Bill, light grey-brown; eyes, unrecorded; legs, dark brown.

Distinguished from other grass-wrens in same area by the largely white underparts.

VOICE: Faint high-pitched "swi-it."

HABITAT: Dense cane grass (*Zygochloa paradoxa*) in sandhill country.

RANGE: Lower Macumba River north of Lake Eyre.

Sedentary.

## STRIATED GRASS-WREN *Amytornis striatus*          SEE p. 25

15–18 cm. A reddish-brown grass-wren with a white throat. **Male:** above, cinnamon-rufous, streaked white; moustache, black; throat, white; breast, dusky-buff, streaked white; abdomen, creamy-buff (southeast) or cinnamon-buff (elsewhere); wings and tail, blackish-brown, edged rufous. **Female:** similar, but with rufous flank. Bill, black; eyes, brown; legs, blue-grey.

Distinguished from other grass-wrens in same area by the more rufous coloration, except for *A. goyderi* which has the abdomen white.

VOICE: Loud "tew-tew;" pleasant rippling song; plaintive high-pitched "peep."

HABITAT: Mainly *Triodia*, on sandhills, sandplains, and among mallee.

RANGE: Arid regions of Australia, from mid-western Western Australia to central-western Queensland, central-western New South Wales, and north-eastern Victoria.

Sedentary.

## DOROTHY'S GRASS-WREN *Amytornis dorotheae*          SEE p. 25

15–18 cm. A reddish-brown grass-wren with white throat and breast. **Male:** above, cinnamon-rufous, streaked white; moustache, black; throat and breast, white; flanks, cinnamon-buff, streaked white; tail

Striated Grass-wren                              Dorothy's Grass-wren

and wings, dark brown, edged rufous. **Female:** not recorded. Bill, black; eyes, brown; legs, blue-grey.

Restricted range is outside the range of any other grass-wren.

VOICE: Unknown.

HABITAT: Spinifex-covered sandstone ranges.

RANGE: Sandstone plateaus of the lower McArthur River, Northern Territory.

Sedentary.

## WHITE-THROATED GRASS-WREN SEE p. 25
*Amytornis woodwardi*

20 cm. A blackish grass-wren with a white throat. **Male:** above, black, streaked white; rump, chestnut; throat, white; abdomen, chestnut, streaked white; tail and wings, black. **Female:** similar, but with cinnamon abdomen. Bill, blackish-grey; eyes, brown; legs, dark brown.

Range is outside that of any other grass-wren.

VOICE: A soft "chrrr" (Crawford); a sharp buzzing "zzzt zzzt zzzt," sometimes breaking into short, rich song as in *A. textilis* (Parker).

HABITAT: Rocky outcrops covered with spinifex.

RANGE: North-western Arnhem Land plateau, Northern Territory, from the King River to the upper Mary River.

Sedentary.

## BLACK GRASS-WREN *Amytornis housei* SEE p. 25

20 cm. A blackish grass-wren. **Male:** above, black, streaked white; rump, chestnut; below, black, streaked white; tail, black. **Female:** similar, but with breast and abdomen light chestnut. Bill, black; eyes, dark brown; legs, brownish-black.

Range is outside that of any other grass-wren.

VOICE: A harsh version of the Blue Wren's reel; loud ticking interspersed with grating sounds accompanied by tail flicking.

White-throated Grass-wren          Black Grass-wren

HABITAT: Rocky gorges covered with spinifex.

RANGE: West Kimberley division, Western Australia, in the vicinity of Mount House and the Charnley River.

Sedentary.

**GREY GRASS-WREN** *Amytornis barbatus* SEE p. 25

18 cm. A grey-brown grass-wren with white underparts. Above, light grey-brown, with broad white streaks edged black; face, white, with black band through the eyes and on side of throat; underparts, white, but lightly streaked black on the breast; wings and tail, blackish, edged pale brown. Bill, black; eyes, reddish-brown; legs, black.

VOICE: Double or triple "tsit-tsit-tsit" often given repetitively from a dead stick.

HABITAT: Cane grass (*Eragrostis australasica*) and lignum clumps on swamp plains.

RANGE: The overflow of the Bulloo River in north-western New South Wales and south-western Queensland.

Sedentary.

## BRISTLE-BIRDS

Two species of bristle-birds occur in the south-east and extreme south-west of Australia, living in dense heaths and thickets where they are difficult to observe. The eastern and western populations of the Brown Bristle-bird are sometimes regarded as separate species, but they are so similar that here they are considered conspecific. The Rufous Bristle-bird also has eastern and western populations; the western form inhabits an extremely small area and has been sighted only a few times, the last in 1940.

Grey Grass-wren

### BROWN BRISTLE-BIRD *Dasyornis brachypterus* SEE p. 5

21–22 cm. A long-tailed, dark grey-brown ground bird with scalloped dark brown breast, found in dense coastal and mountain heaths. Above, dark grey-brown with lacquered appearance; centre of wing and rump, rufous; inconspicuous pale buff eyebrows; throat, pale grey; breast, brown, scalloped darker; flanks, dark brown; belly, pale grey-brown. Bill, dark brown above, pale below; eyes, reddish-brown; legs grey-brown. The western form (race *longirostris*) has a longer bill, is faintly mottled-grey on the back, and has a blacker crown.

Feeds on the ground over which it moves with cocked tail.

Differs from the Rufous Bristle-bird in smaller size, dark brown instead of rufous crown, dark brown scalloped breast instead of grey scalloped breast; found in coastal thickets. The Rufous Bristle-bird has a pale patch around and before the eyes. The ranges do not overlap. Darker than the scrub birds, which have finely barred plumage and reddish-brown flanks (male scrub birds have dark patches on the sides of the throat).

VOICE: Loud musical variable "it-wooa-weet-sip;" sharp "zip;" soft "tuck."

HABITAT: Dense heathlands of coast and mountain.

RANGE: South-eastern Australia, in suitable localities from Cunningham's Gap, Queensland, to Mallacoota, Victoria.

Sedentary.

### RUFOUS BRISTLE-BIRD *Dasyornis broadbenti* SEE p. 5

23–25 cm. A long-tailed, dark grey-brown ground bird with rufous crown, scalloped grey breast, and a pale patch around and before the eyes. Above, dark grey-brown with lacquered appearance; crown and ear coverts, rufous; rump and centre of wing, cinnamon; throat, and centre of breast and abdomen, pale grey; sides of breast, grey, scalloped

Brown Bristle-bird

Rufous Bristle-bird

brown; flanks, brown. Bill, dark brown above, pale below; eyes, reddish-brown; legs, dark brown.

In coastal thickets in Victoria the crown of this species is rather brown, becoming more rufous in South Australia, and brightest in south-western Australia (where it has not been observed for many years). It lives in the densest thickets, often moving on the ground with cocked tail.

Distinguished from the Brown Bristle-bird by the pale eye patch, more rufous crown and greyer scalloped breast. The ranges do not overlap.

VOICE: Loud "chip-chip-chew-cheweeee;" sharp "tweek."

HABITAT: Dense coastal thickets, particularly in tangled sedges.

RANGE: Coastal south-western Victoria and south-eastern South Australia; Western Australia between Cape Leeuwin and Cape Naturaliste.

Sedentary.

## OLD WORLD WARBLERS—Sylviidae

The Old World warblers are generally small birds with thin pointed bills fringed at the base with rictal bristles; many are exceptional songsters. Their habits are varied. Australian species may be found in reeds, spinifex, or long grass. The nest may be cup-shaped or domed, and in the case of the cisticolas, it is encased in leaves or grass sewn together.

**REED-WARBLER** *Acrocephalus australis*                SEE p. 27

16–17 cm. A brown unstreaked reed bird with pale eyebrows and wing less than 8 cm. Above, brown, darker on head; eyebrows, buff-white; below, buff-white, more cinnamon on flanks. Bill, brown on upper mandible, pale on lower; eyes, pale yellow; legs, blackish-brown.

Reed-warbler

Can only be distinguished from the extremely rare Great Reed-warbler by measurements.

VOICE: Rich melodious "twitchy-twitchy-twitchy quarty-quarty-quarty;" a loud sharp "chut."

HABITAT: Reed beds, mangroves, and sometimes introduced willows.

RANGE: Australia and Tasmania.

Migratory in the south, nomadic or sedentary in the north.

## GREAT REED-WARBLER *Acrocephalus arundinaceus*     SEE p. 27

17–18 cm. A brown unstreaked reed bird with pale eyebrows, wing more than 8 cm. Above, brown, darker on head; eyebrows, buff-white; below, buff-white, more cinnamon on flanks. Bill, dark above, pale below; eyes, pale yellow; legs, blackish-brown.

Can only be distinguished from the common reed-warbler by hand measurement.

VOICE: Similar to Reed-warbler.

HABITAT: Reed beds.

RANGE: Once recorded, Melville Island, 1912.

Migratory.

## GOLDEN-HEADED CISTICOLA *Cisticola exilis*     SEE p. 27

10 cm. A small streaked grass bird with golden crown (breeding male) or streaked crown and unstreaked nape (female and non-breeding male); call is a buzzing "zzzt," often followed by a sharp "plik." **Breeding male:** above, cinnamon-brown, streaked black; crown, golden-buff, often raised in display; below, white, with face, sides of neck, and flanks, pale cinnamon-rufous; tail, blackish-brown, with rufous edges, and shorter than in non-breeding plumage. **Non-breeding male and female:** similar, but with crown cinnamon-brown streaked black, and with an unstreaked cinnamon-rufous nape and narrow band on rump.

Great Reed-warbler

Golden-headed Cisticola

Bill, black above, pale below; eyes, brown or golden; legs, pinkish-brown.

Usually observed in tangled grass or on top of tussocks or bushes, but in breeding season male has a distinctive butterfly-like display flight, and often perches on telephone wires, etc. Distinguished from the Streaked Cisticola by the golden crown (breeding) or unstreaked nape (non-breeding and female) and the distinctive call.

VOICE: A buzzing "zzzt," often followed by a sharp "plik;" a buzzing "keart-keart-keart-keart;" a nasal sneezing "chew."

HABITAT: Long grass and other tangled vegetation usually in moist situations.

RANGE: Eastern and northern Australia, extending to central India and southern China.

Sedentary.

## STREAKED CISTICOLA *Cisticola juncidis*          SEE p. 27

10 cm. A small streaked grass bird with streaked crown and nape. **Breeding:** above, cinnamon-brown, streaked black; crown and nape, brown, lightly streaked black; eyebrows, buff-white; rump, more rufous; underparts, white, with pale cinnamon-rufous face, neck, and flanks; tail, broadly tipped white. **Non-breeding:** more heavily streaked, particularly nape and rump. Bill, black above, pale below; eyes, brown or golden; legs, pinkish-brown.

Usually observed in the grassy margins of coastal flood plains. Distinguished from the Golden-headed Cisticola by the streaked nape and the distinctive call.

VOICE: A loud, metallic "lik-lik."

HABITAT: Grassy margins of coastal flood plains.

RANGE: Northern Australia, extending to southern Asia, southern Europe, and Africa.

Sedentary.

Streaked Cisticola

**LITTLE GRASSBIRD** *Megalurus gramineus*          SEE p. 27

14 cm. A streaked reed-and-grass bird with a long, graduated tail and streaked crown. Above, brown, broadly streaked brownish-black; broad white stripe through eyes; crown, streaked black; underparts, whitish, speckled brown on the throat, and light buff on the flanks. Bill, pinkish-brown, paler below; eyes, pale brown; legs, brown.

Distinguished from Tawny Grassbird by streaked crown and plaintive call; from cisticola by long tail. Usually furtive and difficult to observe.

VOICE: Plaintive three-noted "pee-pee-peeee."

HABITAT: Reed beds and long grass on swamps; inland *Typha* and lignum swamps.

RANGE: Australia and Tasmania.

Sedentary on permanent swamps, but visiting temporary swamps.


**TAWNY GRASSBIRD** *Megalurus timoriensis*        SEE p. 27

19 cm. A streaked grassbird with a long graduated tail and unstreaked crown. Above, brown broadly streaked blackish-brown; broad white stripe through eyes; crown, rufous and unstreaked; underparts, whitish. Bill, brown, paler below; eyes, pale brown; legs, brown.

Distinguished from the Little Grassbird by the larger size, unstreaked rufous crown, and song. Less furtive in behaviour, and more obvious during breeding season.

VOICE: Rich song in display flight "ch-ch-ch-zzzzzzzt lik lik;" loud chirping "see-lick," high-pitched downward trill; metallic "chuck chuck chuck chuck."

HABITAT: Grassland, generally in drier areas than Little Grassbird; herbage in swamps and along watercourses.

RANGE: Northern and eastern Australia, extending to the Philippines. Sedentary.

Little Grassbird                    Tawny Grassbird

**RUFOUS SONGLARK** *Cinclorhamphus mathewsi*                SEE p. 11

15–18 cm. A streaked grassy-ground bird with rufous rump. Above, pale brown, streaked darker; rump, rufous; eyebrows, pale buff; underparts, pale buff, with upper breast spotted (male) or grey (female). Bill, black; eyes, brown; legs, grey.

Feeds on the ground among grasses, but perches in trees, and sings on the wing or on a perch.

VOICE: A rich melodious song uttered in flight or on a perch; a sharp "ter-lick;" a short trill (Hutchinson 23).

HABITAT: Grassy areas in savannah woodland.

RANGE: Australia.

Migratory in southern Australia, arriving in September and leaving in March, but individuals may stay through winter; resident or nomadic in northern Australia.

**BROWN SONGLARK** *Cinclorhamphus cruralis*               SEE p. 11

18–24 cm. A dark grassy-ground bird with dark belly. **Male:** above, dark brown, streaked paler; indistinct pale eyebrows; underparts, brownish-black. Bill, black; eyes, brown; legs, pinkish-brown. **Female:** similar, but smaller and with paler upperparts and underparts, light buff, with blackish-brown belly. Bill, pinkish-brown.

The dark underparts, creaky song, display flight on quivering wings, and habit of sitting on fence posts with crown and tail raised, are distinctive. Feeds on the ground among grasses, usually prefers shorter grass than Rufous Songlark.

VOICE: A loud creaky "twitchy tweedle" like an unoiled wheel.

HABITAT: Grassland, dry scrub, and lightly-timbered savannah.

RANGE: Australia.

Migratory in southern Australia arriving in September and leaving in March, but not always regular; probably if inland conditions are suitable, it does not migrate south.

Rufous Songlark

Brown Songlark

**SPINIFEX-BIRD** *Eremiornis carteri*                     SEE p. 27

15 cm. A rufous-brown ground bird with long graduated tail. Above, rufous-brown; forehead, rufous; underparts, buff-white, more cinnamon on flanks and undertail coverts; tail, dark brown, tipped light buff. Bill, black above, blue-grey below; eyes, light brown; legs, dark grey.

Flies with tail drooping, but sometimes hops on ground with half-cocked tail. When perching, tail looks too heavy, drooping straight down.

VOICE: A pleasant warble "te-tee-te-too;" sharp "tik;" grating "chuk;" high-pitched almost inaudible ventriloquial "see."

HABITAT: Spinifex (*triodia*) particularly where there are low bushes; in Northern Territory partial to tall spinifex in dry creek beds.

RANGE: Central Australia, north-western Australia, and north-western Queensland.

Sedentary.

# AUSTRALIAN WARBLERS—Acanthizidae

Australian warblers have many characteristics in common with Old World warblers, due perhaps to the nature of their ecological requirements rather than to closer relationships. All Australian warblers have thin pointed bills with bristles at the base; most have a dark, subterminal band in the tail, and all build domed nests. There are several groups: (a) Fairy warblers, which feed among the outer foliage of trees mainly in higher rainfall areas. (b) Thornbills, which more or less replace the fairy warblers in drier habitats. (c) Whitefaces, which are distinguished by the white forehead. (d) Scrub-wrens, which feed mainly on the ground. (e) Sandstone warblers. One of these, the Rock Warbler, is associated with the Hawkesbury sandstones; the other lives in rain forest and often feeds with the lyrebird.

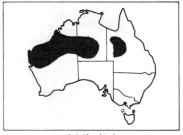

Spinifex-bird

## FAIRY WARBLERS

Fairy warblers are dainty birds, rather more active than their allies the thornbills. They differ further in being strictly arboreal and lack the streaks on ear coverts and breast, and the contrasting rump colour found in so many thornbills. Also different is their feeding habit of fluttering at a clump of leaves looking for insects. Nine species are currently listed, but further field study may prove some of them to be only subspecifically distinct. Many of the species now recognised favour mangrove as a habitat. Most are rather similar in coloration and the observer must rely on the amount of white in the tail, the presence or absence of an eyebrow stripe, and range as aids to identification. Three species have yellow underparts and are probably best distinguished on throat colour and range, but immatures and females are confusing, particularly as the young of some other species have yellowish underparts. The northern form of the Weebill and the Little Thornbill both add to likely confusion, so they should be kept in mind.

### WHITE-THROATED WARBLER *Gerygone olivacea*     SEE p. 29

11 cm. A yellow-breasted warbler with white throat and grey-brown back. **Adult:** above, grey-brown sometimes with golden-brown tinge on rump; white patch before eyes; throat, white; breast and abdomen, yellow; tail, blackish-brown, each outer feather white at base and with a white spot near tip. **Immature:** throat, yellow. Bill, black; eyes, red; legs, black.

Distinguished from female Black-throated Warbler by presence of white in tail tip, greyish instead of dark green upperparts, and habitat; from the Fairy Warbler by the greyish upperparts, habitat, and lack of black chin spot. The immature is very like the immature Fairy Warbler, but is paler on the back. Other species which may be confused with the

White-throated Warbler

immature are the Little Thornbill (dull olive-green back, brown eyes, "tizz-tizz" call); northern form of Weebill (short pale bill, white eyes, yellowish-green back, black subterminal band, and no white in tail).

VOICE: A liquid descending trill "wh-wh-whee-hoo-whee-hoo whee-hoo whee hoo whee hoo whee hoo . . . whee-youuuuu" (Hutchinson 24).

HABITAT: Open forest, woodland, and trees bordering watercourses.

RANGE: Eastern and northern Australia, south-eastern New Guinea (Port Moresby).

Partly migratory in south-east, elsewhere resident or nomadic.

## BLACK-THROATED WARBLER *Gerygone palpebrosa*    SEE p. 29

10 cm. A yellow-breasted warbler with throat, blackish-brown (male) or white (female), and tail without white tip. **Adult male:** above, bright olive with white patch before eyes; face and throat, blackish-brown with white moustache; breast and abdomen, yellow; tail, brown with no white tip. Bill, black; eyes, reddish-orange; legs, black. **Adult female:** similar but without black throat. **Immature:** pale yellow below, from throat to tail.

Female and immature distinguished from White-throated Warbler and Fairy Warbler by lack of white in tail.

VOICE: Undulating warble.

HABITAT: Rain forest, dense river vegetation, and mangroves.

RANGE: North-eastern Queensland, from Cape York to Herbert River; New Guinea, western Papuan islands, Aru Islands, and Japen Island.

Sedentary.

## FAIRY WARBLER *Gerygone flavida*    SEE p. 29

10 cm. A yellow-breasted warbler with white throat, black chin, and brownish-green back. **Adult male:** above, brownish-green with white

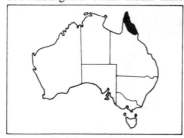

Black-throated Warbler                          Fairy Warbler

patch before eyes; chin, black; throat, dull white or pale yellow; moustache, white; breast and abdomen, yellow; tail, brown with white spots at tip. **Adult female:** similar but lacking the white moustache. **Immature:** lacks black chin; throat, breast, and abdomen, pale yellow. Bill, black; eyes, red; legs, black.

Distinguished from female Black-throated Warbler (ranges only just meet) by white in tail. Immature may be confused with immature White-throated Warbler (paler back, open forest habitat), Little Thornbill (brown eyes, generally outside rain forest, "tizz tizz" call), or Weebill (short pale bill, white eyes, black subterminal band, and no white in tail, and open forest habitat).

VOICE: "Whitty whit you;" bright chattering.

HABITAT: Rain forest and thickly-vegetated rivers; mangroves.

RANGE: Central-eastern Queensland, from the Atherton Tableland to just south of Mary River.

Sedentary.

## GREEN-BACKED WARBLER *Gerygone chloronota*     SEE p. 29

10 cm. A green-backed mangrove warbler with white underparts. Above, dull green; crown, grey-brown; underparts, white, with flanks and vent olive-yellow; tail, brown. Bill, grey-green above, white below; eyes, reddish-brown; legs, dark grey.

A bird of somewhat similar range, habitat, and colour is the white-breasted form of the Lemon-breasted Flycatcher. It has quite different habits, flying from a perch at passing insects and possesses indistinct eyebrows, upright stance, and tail-wagging habit.

VOICE: A high reeling three-noted descending cadence (Parker).

HABITAT: Mangroves and dense river vegetation; tends to move in the upper and middle foliage.

RANGE: Coastal northern Australia, from Yirrkala, Northern Terri-

Green-backed Warbler

tory, to Derby, Western Australia; southern New Guinea, Aru Islands, and Waigeu Island.

Sedentary.

### LARGE-BILLED WARBLER *Gerygone magnirostris*      SEE p. 29

12 cm. A brown-backed mangrove warbler with white eye-rings and buffy-white underparts. Above, olive-brown; eye-rings, white; underparts, buffy-white; tail with broad blackish subterminal band. Bill, black; eyes, reddish-brown; legs, dark grey.

Differs from Dusky Warbler (ranges do not meet) in dark forehead, lack of striped eyebrows, and dark eyes; from the Mangrove Warbler by the lack of eyebrows and absence of white in the tail tip.

VOICE: Rich melodious song rather like White-throated Warbler.

HABITAT: Mangrove and contiguous scrub, and along forest streams.

RANGE: Coastal northern Australia, from Suttor River, Queensland, to Anson Bay, Northern Territory.

Sedentary.

### DUSKY WARBLER *Gerygone tenebrosa*      SEE p. 29

11·5 cm. A brown-backed mangrove warbler with pale forehead and eyebrows, and dusky-white underparts. Above, pale rufous-brown; forehead, white; eyebrows, pale buff; underparts, dusky-white, with yellowish flanks; tail with faint subterminal bar. Bill, black; eyes, white; legs, black.

Differs from Large-billed Warbler (ranges do not meet) in white forehead, pale buff eyebrows and white eyes; from the Mangrove Warbler and White-tailed Warbler by dark-tipped tail.

VOICE: A sleepy plaintive melody rather like the White-tailed Warbler.

HABITAT: Mangrove and contiguous vegetation; along creeks and streams and in rocky gorges.

Large-billed Warbler

Dusky Warbler

RANGE: Coastal north-western Australia, from Carnarvon, Western Australia, to about Wyndham, Western Australia.

Sedentary.

## MANGROVE WARBLER *Gerygone levigaster*          SEE p. 29

10 cm. A brown-backed mangrove warbler with white eyebrows, dull white underparts, and white tail tip. **Adult:** above, brown (greyer along the north coast); eyebrows, white; underparts, dull white, whitest on throat and undertail coverts; tail, brown, with broad indistinct blackish subterminal band, and white spots in the tail tip. **Immature:** underparts, yellowish, particularly eye-rings and throat; no eyebrows. Bill, black; eyes, red; legs, black.

Very similar to the Brown Warbler which normally has a different habitat (rain forest), but occasionally enters mangroves, but has a different call and looks smaller. Other mangrove-dwelling warblers distinguished by: Dusky Warbler (white forehead, dark tail tip); Large-billed Warbler (no white eyebrows, dark tail tip); and Green-backed Warbler (green back, dark tail tip).

VOICE: A plaintive warble, rather like the White-tailed Warbler.

HABITAT: Mangrove and contiguous vegetation.

RANGE: Coastal eastern and northern Australia, from Hunter River, New South Wales, to Derby, Western Australia.

Sedentary.

## BROWN WARBLER *Gerygone mouki*          SEE p. 29

9 cm. A brown-backed rain forest warbler with white eyebrows, white underparts, and white tail tip. Above, brown; face, violet-grey; eyebrows and narrow band on forehead, white; underparts, white, tinged with light buff; tail, brown with broad indistinct blackish subterminal band, and white spots in the tail tip. Bill, black; eyes, reddish-brown; legs, black.

Mangrove Warbler                              Brown Warbler

The Brown Warbler seeks its food in more deliberate fashion than other warblers.

Very similar to the larger-looking Mangrove Warbler which lives in or near mangroves (although the Brown Warbler sometimes enters mangroves), and has a different song. Other warblers which may be occasionally seen in or near Brown Warbler range are: Large-billed Warbler (lacks white eyebrows and has dark tail tip); White-tailed Warbler (paler colour, more extensive white in tail, different song, and drier habitat).

VOICE: Repetitive three-noted ascending song "what-is-it, what is it."

HABITAT: Rain forest particularly on mountains; occasionally in other dense vegetation and mangrove.

RANGE: Three isolated populations: north-eastern Queensland from Atherton Tableland to Mount Spec; Mackay district, central eastern Queensland; south-eastern Queensland, eastern New South Wales, and north-eastern Victoria.

Probably sedentary with some seasonal altitudinal movement.

## WHITE-TAILED WARBLER *Gerygone fusca* SEE p. 29

10 cm. A pale-brown backed warbler with white eyebrows, white underparts, and extensive white in tail; found in drier woodland. Above, pale grey-brown; eyebrows, white; underparts, white, tinged grey on throat and breast; tail, blackish, with base of each outer feather and a large spot at the tip white. Bill, black; eyes, red; legs, black.

The large amount of white in the tail and the pale upperparts distinguish the White-tailed Warbler from other species, but it is found outside the range of most other *Gerygones*. It occurs in mangroves over some of the range of the Dusky Warbler, and just contacts the Mangrove Warbler at Derby, Western Australia.

VOICE: A plaintive, sleepy, unfinished cadence.

White-tailed Warbler

HABITAT: Dry forest and woodland; on the north-west coast, mangrove.

RANGE: Inland Victoria, New South Wales, Queensland, Northern Territory, and southern Western Australia, but extending as far north as Derby in mangroves.

May have inland winter movement in west.

## THORNBILLS

Thornbills have a largely undeserved reputation for being difficult to identify. This reputation has been handed down from the days when bird books described many more species than are recognised today. Part of the problem is due to confusion with fairy warblers. In general thornbills are less active than fairy warblers, and have streaks on the ear coverts and often on the breast. Many have contrasting rump colour, and many species feed on the ground.

Basically thornbills can be divided into three groups: (a) Three small species rather like fairy warblers in behaviour. The Weebill, Striated Thornbill, and Little Thornbill are active, very vocal birds (three or four individuals can give the observer the impression that the bush is "full of birds"). They are strictly arboreal and often feed in the fairy warblers' manner of hovering near a clump of leaves, inspecting the foliage for insects. They can be distinguished by the prominent streaks on the ear coverts. (b) The pale-eyed thornbills have yellowish or reddish rumps and have a tendency to feed on the ground. Only one, the Mountain Thornbill, has a streaked breast. They generally nest in hollow branches, behind loose bark, or in dense grass, grass trees, or samphire. (c) The dark-eyed thornbills have reddish rumps. All, except for the Slate-backed, are streaked on the breast. They rarely if ever feed on the ground, and the nest is usually built among leaves or twigs. In the south-east three very similar species occur. Two of these, the Brown and Tasmanian, are found together in Tasmania. The Brown and Broad-tailed occur on the mainland, but are exclusive in range. Elsewhere in Australia the Broad-tailed is variable in colour and was once divided into several species. The immense task of studying these populations in detail may result in a resurrection of some of these forms, or may prove that the Brown and Broad-tailed Thornbills are conspecific.

**WEEBILL** *Smicrornis brevirostris*                        SEE p. 31

8–9 cm. A tiny, short-billed, olive-backed warbler with yellow underparts, pale eyes, and loud vigorous call. Above, yellowish-olive (brighter in the north); eyebrows, pale buff; underparts, yellow (more buff in the south and brighter in the north); wings and tail, dark brown, with dull white spots on tail tip. Bill, brown above, pale below (yellower in north); eyes, pale yellow or white; legs, brown.

Often in small parties, and often accompanies other foliage-feeding warblers and thornbills.

Similar to immature Little Thornbill, but pale eyebrows and loud call are distinctive.

VOICE: "Wee-willy-weet-weet;" throaty "tchik."

HABITAT: Dry forests to semi-desert, wherever there is leafy foliage.

RANGE: Australia, except dense forests, treeless desert, coastal south-east and south-west.

Sedentary or nomadic.

*Lake Alexandrina, S.A. 3/72*

## LITTLE THORNBILL (YELLOW THORNBILL) SEE p. 31
*Acanthiza nana*

9 cm. A dark-eyed thornbill with yellow underparts. Above, olive-green (southern) to buff-olive (northern); ear coverts streaked dark brown and buffy-white; underparts, yellow; tail, brown, with broad black subterminal band. Bill, black; eyes, dark brown; legs, black.

Distinguished from Weebill by dark longer bill, lack of pale eyebrows, streaked ear coverts, and call; from the Fairy Warbler on the Atherton Tableland by different habitat; from immature White-throated Warbler by the streaked ear coverts, lack of pale eyebrows, and call.

VOICE: Constant "zit-zit," harsher and louder than Striated Thornbill.

HABITAT: Dry forests and woodland, including brigalow and some mallee.

RANGE: South-eastern Australia; an isolated population on the Atherton Tableland.

Sedentary.

Weebill

Little Thornbill

Portland Vic, 11/72

## STRIATED THORNBILL *Acanthiza lineata*    SEE p. 31

7 cm. A pale-eyed thornbill with streaked forehead and breast. Above, dull greenish-olive; head and face, brown streaked white on forehead; throat and breast, pale buff, with diffuse dark streaking; belly and flanks, yellowish-buff; tail, dark brown, with broad black subterminal band. Bill, dark brown; eyes, grey; legs, dark grey.

VOICE: "Zit-zit," softer than Little Thornbill.

HABITAT: Dry forests and woodland, usually favouring denser timber than the Little Thornbill, but often found together.

RANGE: South-eastern Australia.

Sedentary.

Portland Vic. 9/72

## BROWN THORNBILL *Acanthiza pusilla*    SEE p. 31

10 cm. A dark-eyed thornbill with rufous scalloped forehead, streaked throat and breast, rusty-brown rump, and buff flanks. Above, olive-brown, with rusty-brown rump; forehead, rufous, with pale scallops; throat and breast, white, streaked black; flanks, vent, and undertail coverts, buff; tail, brown, with rusty-brown base, dark subterminal band and whitish tip. Bill, black; eyes, reddish-brown; legs, black.

Feeds in low foliage to about 5 m; carries tail half-cocked. Distinguished from Tasmanian Thornbill by the scalloped forehead, buff flanks, and bolder striations on the throat and breast; from the Broad-tailed Thornbill by the more rufous forehead, with less obvious freckles, tail only half-cocked, and duller rufous rump.

VOICE: Musical warble; harsh alarm notes; accomplished mimic.

HABITAT: Rain forest, dense moist eucalypt forest particularly along creeks, usually observed in the lower story but not on the ground.

RANGE: South-eastern Australia, from Eungella Range, Queensland, to St Vincent Gulf, South Australia; Kangaroo Island, Tasmania, and Bass Strait Islands.

Sedentary.

## BROAD-TAILED THORNBILL *Acanthiza apicalis*    SEE p. 31

10 cm. A dark-eyed thornbill with brown scalloped forehead, streaked throat and breast, rufous rump, and buff flanks. Above, pale olive-brown with rufous rump; forehead, brown or ashy-brown, with white scallops; throat and breast, buffy-white, with black streaks; flanks, buff; tail, rufous at base, with dark subterminal band and white tip. Bill, black; eyes, red; legs, black.

Over its wide range the Broad-tailed Thornbill varies slightly in colour, being darkest in the east (race *albiventris*) and south-west (race *apicalis*), and palest in the arid centre (race *whitlocki*). In the extreme south-west is a form (race *leeuwinensis*) very like the Brown Thornbill.

Distinguished from the Brown Thornbill by the browner, more conspicuously scalloped forehead, richer rufous rump, stronger voice, and habit of cocking the tail completely.

VOICE: Pleasant, but rather soulless warble; harsh scolding notes; mimics other birds, including such unlikely species as Brown Goshawk.

HABITAT: Undergrowth in mulga, mallee, and dry low scrub.

RANGE: Southern Australia, from inland New South Wales and Queensland to south-west.

Sedentary.

## TASMANIAN THORNBILL *Acanthiza ewingi*             SEE p. 31

10 cm. A dark-eyed thornbill with tawny-brown dappled forehead, dappled throat and breast, and white flanks. Above, olive-brown, with rusty rump; forehead, tawny-brown, dappled darker; throat and breast, light grey, dappled dark grey; flanks and undertail coverts, white; centre of wing, cinnamon-brown, with black margins. Bill, black; eyes, reddish-brown; legs, black.

Distinguished from Brown Thornbill by dappled brown forehead, dappled breast, and white flanks and undertail coverts; also tends to frequent denser forest.

VOICE: Similar to Brown Thornbill.

HABITAT: Dense forest.

RANGE: Tasmania.

Sedentary.

## SLATE-BACKED THORNBILL *Acanthiza robustirostris*     SEE p. 31

9 cm. A dark-eyed thornbill with pale grey forehead, streaked black, pinkish-rufous rump, and unstreaked whitish underparts. Above, slaty-

Striated Thornbill

Brown Thornbill

grey, with pinkish-rufous rump; head, blue-grey, paler on forehead which is streaked black; underparts, whitish; tail, pinkish-cinnamon at base, remainder blackish, with dull white tip. Bill, black; eyes, reddish-brown; legs, black.

Similar to Chestnut-tailed Thornbill, but differs in having dark eyes, and forehead streaked, not scalloped.

VOICE: "Tseep;" harsh "tchrit;" three-noted call "wi-pu-chew."

HABITAT: Mulga country, particularly in association with *Eremophila* bushes.

RANGE: Southern arid Western Australia, from Shark Bay, south to Yalgoo and Broad Arrow, north to Peak Hill and east to north-western South Australia and south-western Northern Territory.

Sedentary or nomadic.


## CHESTNUT-TAILED THORNBILL                       SEE p. 31
*Acanthiza uropygialis*

9 cm. A white-eyed thornbill with whitish underparts and chestnut rump. Above, drab brown, with chestnut rump; forehead, reddish-brown, freckled paler; underparts, white, greyish on the breast and tinged buff elsewhere; tail, chestnut at base, remainder black, tipped white.

The white eyes and ground-feeding habits distinguish it from other reddish-rumped thornbills in similar habitat (Broad-tailed Thornbill and Slate-backed Thornbill).

VOICE: "See-ti-ti-ti-ti seeee;" harsh "teu;" short pleasant warble.

HABITAT: Dry savannah, mulga, and mallee woodland.

RANGE: Arid southern Australia, north to Fortescue River, Western Australia, south-western Queensland; avoiding south-west and south and south-east coastal regions.

Sedentary.

Broad-tailed Thornbill

Tasmanian Thornbill

## YELLOW-TAILED THORNBILL SEE p. 31
*Acanthiza chrysorrhoa*

10 cm. A pale-eyed thornbill with bright-yellow rump and spotted forehead. Above, yellowish-olive, with bright yellow rump; forehead, black, spotted white; underparts, white, with yellowish or buff suffusion; tail, whitish at base, with black subterminal band and white or pale-yellow tip. Bill, black; eyes, pale grey; legs, black.

Feeds predominantly on the ground. Often falls backwards on the perch, hanging almost upside down.

VOICE: A pleasant reeling warble; "chip-chip" in flight or when feeding; tinkling "tsit tsit tsit tsit."

HABITAT: Open woodland, cultivated paddocks, pastures, and orchards; parks and gardens.

RANGE: Southern Australia, extending through the Channel country in western Queensland, to the Gulf of Carpentaria; Tasmania. Sedentary.

## BUFF-TAILED THORNBILL *Acanthiza reguloides* SEE p. 31

9 cm. A pale-eyed thornbill, with rump and basal half of tail buff. Above, pale olive-brown, with buff rump; forehead and face, freckled white; underparts, dull white, with creamy throat; tail, pinkish-buff at base, with black subterminal band and dull white tip. Bill, black; eyes, white or pale cream; legs, black.

On the Atherton Tableland occurs an isolated population, the Varied Thornbill (race *squamata*) with bright-yellow underparts, and yellower rump.

Differs from the Samphire Thornbill in habitat and the pinkish-buff basal half of the tail.

VOICE: A pleasant warble rather like Yellow-tailed Thornbill, but more metallic.

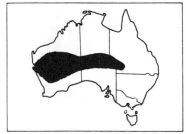

Slate-backed Thornbill

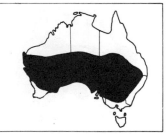

Chestnut-tailed Thornbill

HABITAT: Open woodland, particularly where the ground is covered with fallen leaves, branches, and short grass. Arboreal and terrestrial feeder.

RANGE: South-eastern Australia, from Fitzroy River, Queensland, to Mount Lofty Ranges, South Australia; an isolated population of the Atherton Tableland, Queensland.

Sedentary.

## SAMPHIRE THORNBILL *Acanthiza iredalei* SEE p. 31

9 cm. A pale-eyed thornbill with buffy-yellow rump. Above, greyish-olive to dark olive, with buff-yellow to yellowish-olive rump; forehead and face, freckled white; underparts, creamy-buff, with darker flanks; tail, blackish-brown, with black subterminal band and dull white tip. Bill, black; eyes, white or pale cream; legs, black.

Eastern birds (race *hedleyi*) are darker than western, particularly north of Adelaide (race *rosinae*).

Similar to Buff-tailed Thornbill, but with yellowish rump and entirely dark tail; the samphire habitat is distinctive. Western birds are rather similar to female Orange Chats in colour and habitat, but are more olive above, have pale eyes, and call differently.

VOICE: Warbling song; "chip chip" when flying.

HABITAT: Samphire bordering salt lakes, salt flats, and associated vegetation. It feeds mostly on the ground.

RANGE: Arid southern Australia, from mid-west Victoria to Carnarvon, Western Australia. Much of its range is concentrated around salt country in mulga.

Sedentary.

## WESTERN THORNBILL *Acanthiza inornata* SEE p. 31

10 cm. A pale-eyed thornbill, with rump only faintly paler than the greyish-olive back. Above, greyish olive-brown; rump, faintly tinged

Yellow-tailed Thornbill

Buff-tailed Thornbill

yellow; forehead and face, freckled pale brown; underparts, pale buff; tail, brown, with indistinct subterminal black band. Bill, black; eyes, white or pale grey; legs, grey-brown.

VOICE: Metallic warble very like Buff-tailed Thornbill; loud "wh wh wh wh-whit." Mimics other species.

HABITAT: Woodland particularly jarrah, karri, and marri forest. Arboreal and terrestrial feeder.

RANGE: South-western Australia.

Sedentary.

## MOUNTAIN THORNBILL *Acanthiza katherina* SEE p. 31

10 cm. A pale-eyed rain forest thornbill with dull rufous rump. Above, olive-green, with dull rufous rump; forehead, buff-olive, freckled pale buff; underparts, pale yellow, shading to greenish-yellow on flanks; tail with black subterminal band and tipped white. Bill, black; eyes, white; legs, black.

The only thornbills in similar locality (but different habitat) are the Varied Thornbill, which is olive-brown above and has a buff rump, and the Little Thornbill which is bright yellow below and has no rump patch; both of these inhabit open forest.

VOICE: Not recorded.

HABITAT: Rain forest.

RANGE: Atherton Tableland, Queensland.

Sedentary.

# WHITEFACES

Whitefaces are easily distinguishable by the band of white feathers on the forehead. They are rather similar to thornbills, but the beak is stouter.

Samphire Thornbill

Western Thornbill

They feed mostly on the ground and nest in a variety of situations, from knot-holes in hollow branches to crevices in eagle nests.

## SOUTHERN WHITEFACE *Aphelocephala leucopsis* SEE p. 33

10 cm. A whiteface with buff (east) or chestnut (west) flanks. Above, drab brown; forehead, white; underparts, white with flanks varying from buff in the east to chestnut in the west; tail, blackish-brown, tipped white. Bill, black; eyes, white; legs, black.

Distinguished from other whitefaces by the absence of any bands on the breast.

VOICE: Tinkling bell-like twitter; soft "tik-tik-tik."

HABITAT: Woodland and savannah to dry grasslands. Arboreal and terrestrial feeder.

RANGE: Southern Australia, generally avoiding the south-east and south-west coastal area.

Sedentary.

## BANDED WHITEFACE *Aphelocephala nigricincta* SEE p. 33

10 cm. A whiteface with black breast band. Above, cinnamon-brown, more rufous on rump; crown, grey-brown; forehead, white, with vertical black band before eyes; underparts, white, with narrow black breast band and rufous blotches on the flanks. Bill, black; eyes, white; legs, black.

VOICE: Bell-like twitter, more musical than Southern Whiteface; liquid "pee-pee-pee."

HABITAT: Mulga woodland; saltbush and spinifex; sandhills and gibber.

RANGE: Central Australia, from south-western Queensland to central Western Australia.

Nomadic or sedentary, mainly terrestrial feeder.

Mountain Thornbill

Southern Whiteface

## CHESTNUT-BREASTED WHITEFACE SEE p. 33
*Aphelocephala pectoralis*

10 cm. A whiteface with broad chestnut breast band. Above, rusty-brown; crown, grey; forehead, white; underparts, white, with broad chestnut breast band and flanks blotched rufous. Bill, black; eyes, white; legs, black.

VOICE: Weak chatter.

HABITAT: Gibber plains and desert tablelands with scattered bushes and mulga.

RANGE: Central South Australia.

# SCRUB-WRENS

Scrub-wrens are ground-feeding birds usually found in dense under-growth, from arid heaths and bluebush to rain forest. Most are tame and can be called quite close to the observer, but some are very shy and difficult to view. Generally the nests are well hidden and built on or near the ground, but the Large-billed and Yellow-throated Scrub-wrens build obvious bulky football-shaped structures suspended from hanging vegetation, particularly lawyer cane tendrils. The White-browed Scrub-wren has four distinct forms which are here treated separately, as each is easily distinguishable in the field. The two heath-wrens also have pale yellow eyes but differ in the habit of cocking the tail. The Large-billed Scrub-wren is found in the rain forests and dense forests of the east, rarely feeding on the ground. On the Atherton Tableland occurs a similar form, the Atherton Scrub-wren, which does feed on the ground. The Red-throat is the dry country representative of these two. Of some interest is the Field-wren; it has several forms, but as they intergrade imperceptibly into each other they are treated here as one. The other scrub-wrens, Speckled Warbler and Scrub-tit, are easily identifiable.

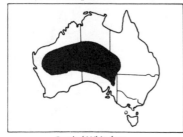

Banded Whiteface                    Chestnut-breasted Whiteface

## WHITE-BROWED SCRUB-WREN SEE p. 35
*Sericornis frontalis frontalis*

11·5 cm. A pale-eyed scrub-wren with white brow, white spot below
the eyes, and unspotted breast. **Male:** above, olive-brown with chestnut-
brown rump; white stripe on alula and wing coverts; eyebrows and spot
below eyes, white; lores, black; throat, white, faintly streaked black;
remainder of underparts, light buffy-yellow, with buff-olive flanks; tail,
dark brown, with indistinct subterminal band and pale tip. **Female:**
lores, grey-brown; throat unstreaked. Bill, blackish-brown, paler below;
eyes, pale buff; legs, pink-brown.

In Queensland the race *laevigaster* differs from southern birds in the
darker ear coverts, unstreaked throat, distinct dark tail band, and white
tail tip.

VOICE: Loud chattering rattle.

HABITAT: Dense undergrowth in forest; along creeks, in gullies, and
around tidal inlets.

RANGE: South-eastern Australia, from McPherson Range, northern
New South Wales, to Adelaide.

Sedentary.

## BUFF-BREASTED SCRUB-WREN SEE p. 35
*Sericornis frontalis laevigaster*

11·5 cm. A pale-eyed scrub-wren with white brow, white spot below the
eyes, black behind the eyes, and buff-lemon breast. **Male:** above, olive-
brown with chestnut-brown rump; white stripe on alula and wing
coverts; eyebrows and spot below eyes, white; lores and ear coverts,
black; throat white and unstreaked; remainder of underparts, buff-
lemon with buff flanks; tail, dark brown with dark subterminal band and
white tip. **Female:** similar but with some grey on the largely black ear
coverts.

White-browed Scrub-wren

Buff-breasted Scrub-wren

Differs from the White-browed Scrub-wren in the black behind the eyes, paler underparts with unstreaked throat, and white tip to tail.

VOICE: Similar to White-browed Scrub-wren.

HABITAT: Dense undergrowth in forest, along creeks and gullies.

RANGE: Eastern Queensland from McPherson Range to Atherton Tableland.

Sedentary.

## SPOTTED SCRUB-WREN *Sericornis frontalis maculatus* SEE p. 35

11·5 cm. A pale-eyed scrub-wren with spotted breast. Above, greyish-brown; white stripe on alula and wing coverts; eyebrows and spot below eyes, white; underparts, white or lemon-yellow, spotted black on the breast. Bill, dark brown above, pale below; eyes, pale buff; legs, pink-brown.

VOICE: Ascending musical "tee-taree-tee," often rapidly repeated. Harsh "zit-zit."

HABITAT: Dense undergrowth in forest, along creeks, and coastal sand dunes; sandplain heaths.

RANGE: Southern and south-western Australia, from Kangaroo Island and Adelaide to Shark Bay.

Sedentary.

## BROWN SCRUB-WREN *Sericornis frontalis humilis* SEE p. 35

13·5 cm. A pale-eyed, dark scrub-wren, with indistinct eyebrows, dark lores, and white on the alula. Above, dark cinnamon-brown with chestnut rump; white stripe on alula and very faint stripe on wing coverts; eyebrows, indistinctly white; throat, grey, spotted darker; breast, yellowish; flanks, olive; tail, brown. Bill, dark brown above, pale below; eyes, pale buff; legs, pink-brown.

Distinguished from the Scrub-tit by the dark face, larger size, and pale eyes.

Spotted Scrub-wren

Brown Scrub-wren

VOICE: Rather less musical than other scrub-wrens, with a creaky quality; also "chip chip" alarm call.

HABITAT: Dense undergrowth in forest; suburban gardens.

RANGE: Tasmania, Flinders Island, and King Island, Kent Group. Sedentary.

## LITTLE SCRUB-WREN *Sericornis beccarii* SEE p. 35

11·5 cm. A dark-eyed scrub-wren, with a pale spot on the forehead, pale broken eye-rings, and two white bars on the wing coverts. Above, brown, with chestnut rump; wing, with two white bars on the alula and wing coverts; crown and ear coverts, bright brown; forehead and lores, black, with white spot on forehead (race *minimus*); broken eye-rings, white or buff; underparts, pale yellow, greyish-buff on flanks; tail, brown, without dark band. Bill, pinkish-brown; eyes, orange-red; legs, pale pink-brown.

Distinguished from the two other scrub-wrens that approach its range by the unique face pattern and the two wing bars.

VOICE: Unknown.

HABITAT: Dense undergrowth in forest.

RANGE: Eastern Cape York north of Cooktown. Sedentary.

## LARGE-BILLED SCRUB-WREN *Sericornis magnirostris* SEE p. 35

13 cm. A dark-eyed arboreal scrub-wren with pale forehead and face. Above, dark buff-olive with rump more tawny; wing without any pale bars; forehead and face, light buff, without any white markings; underparts, pale olive-buff, more buff on throat and undertail coverts; tail, dark brown. Bill, black; eyes, dark reddish-brown; legs, pale yellowish-brown.

The virtual lack of any distinctive markings and arboreal habits

Little Scrub-wren

Large-billed Scrub-wren

distinguish it from other scrub-wrens, except the Atherton Scrub-wren, which has a darker forehead and face and is often seen feeding on the ground. The dark tail tip and pale legs distinguish it from thornbills and warblers in similar habitat; probably the closest is the Large-billed Warbler, which has a dark tail tip but has black legs, virtually white underparts, and is considerably more dainty.

Voice: Mostly silent, but an occasional soft musical twitter or harsh alarm note when disturbed.

Habitat: Dense undergrowth and lower story of forest.

Range: Eastern Australia, from Cooktown, Queensland, to Melbourne, Victoria.

Sedentary.

## ATHERTON SCRUB-WREN *Sericornis keri*          SEE p. 35

13·5 cm. A dark-eyed terrestrial scrub-wren with dark forehead and face. Above, olive-brown; forehead and face, rather more rufous, but not distinctly paler than crown; throat, whitish; remainder of underparts, pale olive-buff; tail, brown. Bill, black; eyes, reddish-brown; legs, pale yellowish-brown.

Very similar to the Large-billed Scrub-wren, but with the face and forehead not distinctly paler than the crown, and contrasting with the whitish throat. It is more terrestrial in behaviour.

Voice: Not recorded.

Habitat: Rain forest.

Range: Atherton Tableland, above 600 m.

Sedentary.

## YELLOW-THROATED SCRUB-WREN          SEE p. 35
*Sericornis lathami*

14 cm. A black-faced scrub-wren with yellow throat and eyebrows. Above, olive-brown; face and ear coverts, black, with long yellow and

Atherton Scrub-wren

Yellow-throated Scrub-wren

white eyebrows; throat, yellow; breast and flanks, olive-brown, tinged yellow; abdomen, white; tail, rufous at base. Bill, black; eyes, pale brown; legs, pinkish-brown.

VOICE: A clear melodious whistle of four or five notes, usually included in exceptional mimicry of other species.

HABITAT: Rain forest.

RANGE: North Queensland to Mount Dromedary, New South Wales. Sedentary.

## SCRUB-TIT *Sericornis magna* SEE p. 35

11·5 cm. A dark-eyed scrub-wren with white face and wing bar. Above, dark cinnamon-brown; lores and area about eyes, white; throat, white; remainder of underparts, pale yellow, with buff flanks; tail with broad subterminal band and white tips to outer feathers. Bill, black; eyes, dark brown; legs, pinkish-brown.

Distinguished from the Brown Scrub-wren by the white face, dark eyes, and prominent wing bar.

VOICE: Difficult to differentiate from Brown Scrub-wren and Brown Thornbill.

HABITAT: Dense undergrowth in forest, along creeks and swamps, particularly where there are ferns; feeds on the ground, and also on tree trunks.

RANGE: Tasmania. Sedentary.

*Pinaroo, S.A.*
*10/70*

## CHESTNUT-TAILED HEATH-WREN SEE p. 33
*Hylacola pyrrhopygia*

14 cm. A chestnut-rumped heath-wren without white patch on shoulder. Above, brown, greyer on head, and chestnut on rump; eyebrows, white; underparts, whitish, with dark streaks on the throat

Scrub-tit

Chestnut-tailed Heath-wren

and breast, and yellowish wash on flanks; tail, dark brown, with broad dark subterminal band and white tip carried in cocked position. Bill, blackish-brown; eyes, pale yellow; legs, fleshy-brown.

Distinguished from Shy Heath-wren by lack of white patch on shoulder; and from the Field-wren by the unstreaked upperparts.

VOICE: A most beautiful varied song, including mimicry.

HABITAT: Woodland thickets, low scrub, and open heath; feeds on or near ground.

RANGE: South-eastern Australia, from north-eastern New South Wales to Mount Lofty Ranges and Flinders Ranges, South Australia. Sedentary.

*Pinaroo, SA. 10/70*

**SHY HEATH-WREN** *Hylacola cauta*                    SEE p. 33

12 cm. A dark chestnut-rumped heath-wren with a white patch on the shoulder. Above, dark brown, with dark chestnut rump; patch on shoulder, white; eyebrows, white; underparts, whitish, without yellow wash and streaked with black on throat and breast; tail, dark brown, with dark subterminal band and white tip, carried in cocked position. Bill, blackish-brown; eyes, pale yellow; legs, fleshy-brown.

Distinguished from Chestnut-tailed Heath-wren by white patch on shoulder, darker chestnut rump, more heavily streaked throat and breast, and lack of yellowish tinge on underparts; habitat also is rather different where the ranges meet. Distinguished from the Field-wren by the unstreaked upperparts.

VOICE: Melodious "chee-chee-chick-a-dee;" mimics other species.

HABITAT: Bushes and low vegetation in mallee woodland; sandplain in Western Australia.

RANGE: Southern Australia, from Wyalong, central-western New South Wales, to the Murchison River, Western Australia.

Sedentary.

Shy Heath-wren

**FERN-WREN** *Oreoscopus gutturalis*                    SEE p. 35

13 cm. A scrub-wren with black patch on the breast. Above, dark bronze-brown; forehead, slightly scaled white; eyebrows, white; chin, white; throat and breast, black; remainder of underparts, grey-brown. Bill, black; eyes, dark brown; legs, pale pinkish-brown.

The black throat is distinctive, as also is its habit of "burrowing" for food under leaves on the rain forest floor.

VOICE: A wide range of musical notes; accomplished mimic; harsh chatter; soft "chick-ick."

HABITAT: Rain forest.

RANGE: North-eastern Queensland.

Sedentary.

**REDTHROAT** *Pyrrholaemus brunneus*                    SEE p. 33

11·5 cm. A greyish-brown, dry-country scrub-wren with chestnut throat (lacking in female). Above, greyish-brown; forehead, faintly freckled-white; throat, pale chestnut; breast, pale grey-brown; tail, blackish-brown, with outer feathers broadly tipped white. Bill, black; eyes, red; legs, blackish-brown.

The female may be confused with some thornbills, but the lack of any contrasting colour on the rump, the broad white tips to the outer tail feathers, and the fluttering noise made by the wings in flight should help identification.

VOICE: Rich varied song based on "wheet wheet widda widda wheet whee;" mimics other species.

HABITAT: Semi-arid scrub; mulga and mallee woodland; saltbush and lignum.

RANGE: Arid southern Australia, from western Queensland, New South Wales, and Victoria (Wyperfeld) to Fortescue River, Western Australia.

Sedentary.

Fern-wren

Redthroat

**FIELD-WREN** *Calamanthus fuliginosus* ) SEE p. 33

13 cm. A variable, olive, or reddish, scrub-wren streaked above and below. Above, olive-brown (in the south) to reddish-brown (further north) streaked darker; rump, same colour as back (in the south) or chestnut (further north); eyebrows, white; underparts, yellowish-buff (in the south) to whitish (further north) streaked darker; tail, reddish-brown, with dark subterminal band and white tip, carried in cocked position. Bill, grey-brown to pinkish-brown; eyes, pale yellow; legs, pinkish-brown.

Although variable in colour, the Field-wren is easily identified by the streaked back and underparts, cocked tail, and scantily timbered habitat.

VOICE: "Whirr-whirr-chick chick whirr-ree-ree."

HABITAT: Open country with dense ground cover; heath, grassland, tussock grass, sandplain, samphire, and saltbush. Terrestrial.

RANGE: Southern Australia, from south-eastern New South Wales to North West Cape, Western Australia (avoiding the moist south-west), Tasmania, and Bass Strait islands.

Sedentary.

**SPECKLED WARBLER** *Chthonicola sagittata* SEE p. 33

11·5 cm. A streaked ground warbler with white face and white speckled crown. Above, grey-brown, streaked darker, brighter on the rump; crown, dark brown, speckled and streaked white; lores, face, and ear coverts, white; above the white eyebrows are other dark "eyebrows," sometimes partly concealed, black in males and reddish-brown in females; underparts, yellowish-white, streaked black; tail, dark brown, tipped white. Bill, dark grey-brown; eyes, brown; legs, pinkish-brown.

Feeds on the ground often in the company of other birds.

Distinguished from the Field-wren by the paler white face, uncocked tail, confiding habits, and timbered habitat.

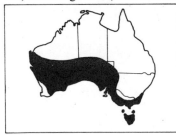

Field-wren                    Speckled Warbler

VOICE: Sweet musical chatter; harsh grating twitter when disturbed.
HABITAT: Open timbered woodland, particularly where leaf strewn and sparsely grassed.
RANGE: South-eastern Australia, from the Connor River to south-western Victoria.
Sedentary.

## SANDSTONE WARBLERS

Two species of ground-feeding warblers, which are probably not closely related, are grouped for convenience. The Rock Warbler is closely associated with the Hawkesbury sandstones and is confined to a relatively small area in central eastern New South Wales. It suspends its nest in a cave or from an overhanging rock. The Pilot-bird takes its name from its frequent association with the Superb Lyrebird when feeding. It inhabits dense forests, particularly on rocky gullies and creeksides. The nest is placed on the ground and is well hidden.

### ROCK WARBLER *Origma solitaria* SEE p. 33

14 cm. A dark rock-haunting warbler with greyish-white throat. Above, blackish-brown, more reddish on forehead and face; throat, greyish-white, faintly speckled black; remainder of underparts, reddish-brown; tail, sooty-black. Bill, blackish-brown; eyes, reddish-brown; legs, blackish-brown.

VOICE: A shrill melancholy "good-bye" repeated several times; rasping alarm call.
HABITAT: Rocky gullies and ravines in Hawkesbury sandstone and associated limestone.
RANGE: Central-eastern New South Wales, from Scone to Pigeon House Mountain.
Sedentary.

Rock Warbler

**PILOT-BIRD**  *Pycnoptilus floccosus*                    SEE p. 33

17 cm. A dark ground bird with reddish-brown face and throat and speckled white centre to abdomen. Above, dark brown; forehead, face, and throat, reddish-brown; breast, reddish-brown, scalloped darker; centre of abdomen, speckled white; tail, dark brown, flicked up and down when feeding. Bill, dark brown above, pinkish below; eyes, red; legs, reddish-brown.

Often associated with the Superb Lyrebird when feeding.

VOICE: Distinctive "guinea-a-week" from male; "whit a witchee-too" from female.

HABITAT: Moist leaf-strewn floor of dense forest.

RANGE: Extreme south-eastern Australia, from Dandenongs, Victoria, to Port Hacking, New South Wales, and Mount Wilson, New South Wales.

Sedentary.

# FLYCATCHERS — Muscicapidae

Flycatchers are small insect-eating birds with a tendency, more developed in some than others, to take prey on the wing. They have rather flat bills with five stiff bristles on each side of the broad gape. The nest is a small, cup-shaped structure, often well-camouflaged with strips of bark or lichen. There are two groups: (a) Australian robins, which have no relationship with the Old World robins. (b) Fantails, sometimes placed in a separate family, *Rhipiduridae*.

## AUSTRALIAN ROBINS

In general Australian robins are not efficient flycatchers, preferring to take their prey on the ground after sighting it from a prominent perch. Many of them are characterised by brilliant breast colour, either

Pilot-bird

red or yellow. Three species, the Brown, Lemon-breasted, and Yellow Flycatchers, do take prey in the air and their bills are rather flatter than most. They build very small nests, the smallest of any Australian bird, usually placed in a horizontal fork, often on a dead branch. The males of the five species of red-breasted robins are easy to identify, each having a distinctive feature, but the grey-brown females are more similar, and the identification of several of these requires some care. Their nests are beautiful cup-shaped structures often decorated with lichens and placed in a vertical fork, behind loose bark, or occasionally in a cavity in a vertical earth bank. Most of the other robins are easy to distinguish, but some mention should be made of the yellow-breasted robins, which are very tame and usually allow a close approach. They decorate their nests with strips of bark. Three forms, the Southern, Northern, and Western, are often regarded as one species; but in general each form occupies exclusive territory. The Southern Yellow Robin occurs far north of the southern limit of the Northern Yellow Robin, so here they are kept separate. One species, the White-breasted Robin of the south-west, has lost yellow pigment altogether. Two species occur in the rain forests: the Pale Yellow Robin, which has two distinctive forms, and the White-faced Robin of Cape York.

**BROWN FLYCATCHER** *Microeca leucophaea*          SEE p. 37

12·5 cm. A brown-backed flycatcher with white-edged black tail. Above, grey-brown, with white edges to wing feathers; eyebrows, dull white; underparts, white, with greyish or buff clouding on the breast; tail, black, with outer tail feathers white. Bill, blackish-brown; eyes, brown; legs, black.

Wags tail from side to side in slightly figure-of-eight movement.

VOICE: Prolonged musical "peter-peter . . ."

HABITAT: Open timbered, mostly eucalypt, country, particularly where there are large fallen branches.

Brown Flycatcher

RANGE: Northern, eastern, and south-western Australia; south-eastern New Guinea (Port Moresby).

Sedentary.

## LEMON-BREASTED FLYCATCHER SEE p. 37
*Microeca flavigaster*

11·5 cm. A yellowish-olive-backed flycatcher with yellow underparts. **Adult:** above, yellowish-olive, with buffy-yellow edges to wing feathers; eyebrows, buffy-white and indistinct; throat, white; breast and abdomen, yellow, more dusky on breast; tail, blackish-brown, tips of outer feathers pale buff. **Immature:** similar, but with whitish underparts. Bill, blackish-brown; eyes, dark brown; legs, dark grey.

The north-western race *tormenti* (often referred to as the Brown-tailed Flycatcher, *M. brunneicauda*) differs in having the underparts white.

Distinguished from Yellow Flycatcher by wholly dark bill, dark legs, and yellowish-olive head.

VOICE: Whistling musical phrase of about six notes "chew-chew-swee so-wu-chew."

HABITAT: Mangrove, forest, paperbark swamps, and woodland.

RANGE: Northern Australia, from Ord River, Western Australia, to Bowen, Queensland; New Guinea.

Sedentary.

## YELLOW FLYCATCHER *Microeca griseoceps* SEE p. 37

11·5 cm. A yellowish-olive-backed flycatcher with yellow underparts, blue-grey head, and yellow legs. Above, yellowish-olive, blue-grey on head; throat, white; breast and abdomen, yellow, more dusky on breast; tail, blackish-brown, tipped pale buff. Bill, black above, yellow below; eyes, brown; legs, yellow.

Lemon-breasted Flycatcher

Yellow Flycatcher

Distinguished from Lemon-breasted Flycatcher by blue-grey head, bi-coloured bill, and yellow legs.

VOICE: Loud double whistle; sibilant "zzt-zzt-zzt;" musical trill.

HABITAT: Rain forest, particularly around the edges.

RANGE: Cape York; southern New Guinea.

Sedentary. *Portland Vic.*                              *8/72*

## SCARLET ROBIN *Petroica multicolor*                    SEE p. 37

13 cm. A red-breasted robin with black throat and large white cap (male) or a greyish-brown robin with breast tinged red and small white forehead spot (female). **Male:** above, black, with white streak on wing; forehead, white; throat, black; breast, red; abdomen, white; tail, black, with white outer edges. **Female:** above, grey-brown, with buffy-white streak in wing; forehead, white; throat, grey; breast, tinged red; abdomen, white; tail, edged white. Bill, black; eyes, brown; legs, black.

Male distinguished from Flame Robin by black throat, larger white forehead, less orange and more scarlet breast. Female distinguished from all other female robins by pink breast.

VOICE: Trilling warble "ch-ch-char-weeya."

HABITAT: Dry forest, woodland parks, and gardens.

RANGE: South-eastern Australia, south-western Australia; Tasmania, and Bass Strait islands.

Some local movements to more open habitat after breeding. *Portland Vic, 3/72*

## FLAME ROBIN *Petroica phoenicea*                       SEE p. 37

13–14 cm. A red-breasted robin with red throat and small white cap (male) or a greyish-brown robin with creamy streaks in wing (female). **Male:** above, dark grey with white streak in the wing; small spot on forehead, white; throat and breast, orange-red; abdomen, white; tail,

Scarlet Robin

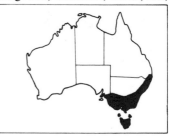

Flame Robin

dark grey, edged white. **Female:** above, grey-brown, with creamy streak in wing; underparts, pale buff, whiter on belly. Bill, black; eyes, blackish-brown; legs, black.

Distinguished from the Scarlet Robin by the paler upperparts, smaller white cap, and orange-red breast extending to the throat. Female distinguished from Scarlet Robin by grey breast and dark forehead; from female Red-capped Robin by lack of reddish forehead; from female Pink and Rose Robins by lack of white forehead spot; and from female Hooded Robin by lack of extensive white at the base of the tail.

VOICE: Thin piping trill "you-may-come-if-you-will-to-the-sea."

HABITAT: Dry forest and woodland when breeding, more open country after breeding.

RANGE: South-eastern Australia; Kangaroo Island; Tasmania, and Bass Strait islands.

Some individuals are sedentary, others are migratory or nomadic, moving to and from Tasmania, from high to low country, and from heavy to light timber. A winter visitor to South Australia and Kangaroo Island.

**RED-CAPPED ROBIN** *Petroica goodenovii* SEE p. 37

11·5 cm. A red-breasted robin with a red cap (male) or a grey-brown bird with small creamy streak in wing and reddish forehead (female). **Male:** above, black, with white streak in the wing; forehead, red; throat, black; breast, red; abdomen, white; tail, black, with white edges. **Female:** above, grey-brown, with small creamy streak in the wing; forehead, reddish; underparts, dull white. Bill, black; eyes, dark brown; legs, black.

Female distinguished from all other female robins by reddish forehead.

VOICE: "Toc-toc," like tapping two stones together; reeling warble "trr-trr-derra dee dee" or "dik-dik- chau yau yau."

Red-capped Robin

HABITAT: Variable from forest to semi-arid desert scrub; particularly associated with Callitris pines, mulga, and low scrubby *Melaleuca* (e.g. *M. glomerata*).

RANGE: Southern Australia, generally avoiding moist coastal areas; Flinders Island, and Rottnest Island. Has been observed in the west Kimberley, Western Australia.

Migratory in south; may also move to west Kimberley in winter.

**ROSE ROBIN** *Petroica rosea* SEE p. 37

10 cm. A pink-breasted robin with white in the tail (male) or a greyish-brown robin with small white forehead spot and white in the tail (female). **Male:** above, dark grey, without white in the wing; small white spot on forehead; throat, dark grey; breast, rose-pink; abdomen, white; tail, dark grey with white outer feathers. **Female:** grey-brown with two buff bars in the wing; small white spot on forehead; underparts, pale grey-brown, darker on breast and sometimes tinged red; tail, grey-brown, with white in outer tail feathers. Bill, black; eyes, dark brown; legs, dark brown; soles, yellow.

Rather more aerial than other robins, taking insects in the air rather than on the ground.

Male distinguished from male Pink Robin by less extent of pink on the breast, and white in the tail. Female distinguished from female Pink Robin by white in tail; from female Flame and Red-capped Robins by small white spot on forehead; and from female Scarlet Robin by lack of extensive reddish suffusion on breast.

VOICE: Soft musical "tick-a-tick-a-tick-pee-pee;" harsh churring notes.

HABITAT: Forest, mainly wet forests when breeding and open forests at other times.

RANGE: South-eastern Australia, from south-eastern South Australia to central-eastern Queensland.

Some seasonal altitudinal movement and also from wet to dry forest.

Rose Robin

**PINK ROBIN** *Petroica rodinogaster* SEE p. 37

13·5 cm. A pink-breasted robin without any white in the tail (male) or a grey-brown robin with two pale buff wing bars and no white in the tail (female). **Male:** above, very dark grey, without white in the wing; small white spot on forehead; throat, very dark grey; breast and belly, pink; lower abdomen, white; tail, dark grey, with no white. **Female:** above, dark grey-brown, with two buff-white bars in the wing; forehead, usually without pale spot; underparts, pale pinkish-brown, greyer on breast; no white in tail. Bill, black; eyes, dark brown; legs, black.

Lack of white in tail distinguishes both male and female from other similar robins.

VOICE: Slight warble; "tick tick" like snapping twig.

HABITAT: Lower stages of wet forest, sometimes in dry forest.

RANGE: Extreme south-eastern Australia, concentrated in Victoria and Tasmania; winter visitor to Australian Capital Territory.

Sedentary; or regular seasonal altitudinal movements, and from wet to dry forest.

**HOODED ROBIN** *Petroica cucullata* SEE p. 39

16·5 cm. A pied robin (male) or grey-brown robin with white in wing and at base of tail (female). **Male:** above, black, with white patches on mantle and wing; head and throat, black; underparts, white; tail, basal two-thirds of outer tail feathers, white. **Female:** above, grey-brown, with white patch in the wing; throat and foreneck, grey; abdomen, white; tail, basal two-thirds of outer tail feathers, white. Bill, black; eyes, dark brown; legs, black.

Distinguished from other robins by white in base of tail, except Mangrove Robin which has no obvious white on the wing while at rest and lives in or near mangroves.

VOICE: Long twittering trill, but usually rather quiet.

Pink Robin

Hooded Robin

HABITAT: Open forest to arid savannah.

RANGE: Australia, except north and east of line from Rockhampton to Normanton.

Generally sedentary, but some may have seasonal migration in south.

## DUSKY ROBIN *Petroica vittata* SEE p. 39

16·5 cm. A brown Tasmanian robin. Above, dull brown, with small white patch in wing and white on shoulder edge; underparts, pale brown, with white throat; tail, brown, with tips and outer feathers edged white. Bill, black; eyes, brownish-black; legs, brownish-black.

VOICE: "Choo-wee, choo-we-er."

HABITAT: Relatively open areas in forest and woodland, particularly where fallen timber and debris litter the forest floor; around clearings and homesteads.

RANGE: Tasmania and Bass Strait islands.

Sedentary.

## MANGROVE ROBIN *Peneoenanthe pulverulenta* SEE p. 39

16·5 cm. A dark grey mangrove robin, with underparts and basal half of tail white. Above, dark grey, with concealed white stripe in wing (obvious only in flight); dark streak through eyes; underparts, white, greyish on the breast; tail, blackish-brown, with basal half of outer tail feathers white. Bill, black; eyes, dark reddish-brown; legs, black.

VOICE: Varied musical song; short clear whistle.

HABITAT: Mangroves.

RANGE: Northern Australia, from Exmouth Gulf, Western Australia, to Rockingham, Queensland; New Guinea and Aru Islands.

Sedentary.

Dusky Robin

Mangrove Robin

**GREY-HEADED ROBIN** *Heteromyias cinereifrons* SEE p. 39

17 cm. A grey-headed, tortoise-shell-coloured robin with a rufous rump. Above, olive-brown, with white patch in the wing; rump, rufous; crown, grey; lores, black; black patch behind eyes, shading to olive-brown ear coverts; throat, white; breast, pale grey; belly, white, with flanks and vent pale reddish-brown; tail, rufous. Bill, blackish-brown; eyes, dark brown; legs, pinkish-brown.

VOICE: Loud whistle followed by several lower notes.

HABITAT: Rain forest, particularly around clearings and along roadsides.

RANGE: North-eastern Queensland, from Cardwell to Bloomfield River; New Guinea.

Sedentary.


**WHITE-BROWED ROBIN** *Poecilodryas superciliosa* SEE p. 39

14 cm. A brown-backed robin with white brow and white flanks; often cocks tail. Above, olive-brown, with white patch in the wing; eyebrows and streak below eyes, white; underparts, white, greyer on breast; tail, olive-brown, tipped white. Bill, black; eyes, brown; legs, blackish-brown.

Distinguished from Buff-sided Robin by white flanks and more arboreal habits; from White-eared Flycatcher by brown back and dark ear coverts.

VOICE: Loud clear whistle "tit toee-toee, tit-toee toee tit toe."

HABITAT: Wet forests and dense vegetation along creeks in drier country.

RANGE: North-eastern Queensland, from Cape York to Burdekin River.

Sedentary.

Grey-headed Robin

White-browed Robin

**BUFF-SIDED ROBIN** *Poecilodryas cerviniventris*          SEE p. 39

15 cm. A brown-backed robin with white brow and buff flanks. Above, olive-brown, with white patches in the wing, darker on the head; brow and spot below eyes, white; underparts, white, greyer on the breast, with flanks and undertail orange-buff; tail, olive-brown, tipped white. Bill, black; eyes, brown; legs, blackish-brown.

Distinguished from White-browed Robin by buff flanks and more terrestrial habits (ranges are exclusive).

VOICE: Four-noted piping whistle.

HABITAT: Mangrove; dense vegetation along rivers.

RANGE: Northern Australia, from Derby, Western Australia, to Gregory River, Queensland.

Sedentary.

**SOUTHERN YELLOW ROBIN** *Eopsaltria australis*          SEE p. 39

15 cm. A yellow-breasted robin with olive rump. Above, dark ash-grey; rump, yellowish-olive to olive; chin, white; underparts, bright yellow, sometimes tinged olive (south). Bill, black; eyes, dark brown; legs, blackish-brown.

Distinguished from Northern Yellow Robin by olive rump.

VOICE: A mournful single note; scolding alarm "chuck-chuck."

HABITAT: Mainly dry forest and woodland, parks, and gardens.

RANGE: South-eastern Australia, from Millicent, South Australia, to north-eastern New South Wales, then inland further north to Dawson River, Queensland.

Sedentary; may be some seasonal altitudinal movement.

**NORTHERN YELLOW ROBIN** *Eopsaltria chrysorrhoa*          SEE p. 39

15 cm. A yellow-breasted robin with yellow rump. Above, dark ash-grey, with bright yellow rump; chin, white; underparts, rich yellow. Bill,

Buff-sided Robin

Southern Yellow Robin

black; eyes, dark brown; legs, blackish-brown.

Distinguished from Southern Yellow Robin by yellow rump, denser habitat.

VOICE: Single, sometimes double, or triple, piping note; harsh alarm "chuck chuck-a-churr."

HABITAT: Rain forest and dense forest.

RANGE: North-eastern Australia, from north-eastern New South Wales to Cooktown, Queensland, usually not far inland.

Sedentary.

## WESTERN YELLOW ROBIN *Eopsaltria griseogularis*     SEE p. 39

15 cm. A grey-breasted robin with yellow abdomen. Above, dark ash-grey with yellow (Western Australia) or olive-yellow (South Australia) rump; throat, white; breast, grey; abdomen, yellow. Bill, black; eyes, dark brown; legs, blackish-brown.

VOICE: Single piping whistle; harsh alarm "chuck chuck."

HABITAT: Dry forest and woodland, favouring casuarina.

RANGE: Eyre Peninsula, South Australia; south-western Australia from about Eucla to the Murchison River, Western Australia.

Sedentary.

## WHITE-BREASTED ROBIN *Eopsaltria georgiana*     SEE p. 39

15 cm. A dark blue-grey robin with white underparts and white-tipped tail. Above, dark blue-grey, paler over eyes, sometimes white patch obvious on shoulder; underparts, white; tail, blackish, with white tips on outer feathers. Bill, black; eyes, dark brown; legs, blackish-brown.

VOICE: Whistling "whee-oh;" harsh alarm "whit whit churr."

HABITAT: Dense gully thickets, karri forest, and coastal acacia scrub.

RANGE: South-western Australia.

Sedentary.

Northern Yellow Robin

Western Yellow Robin

**PALE YELLOW ROBIN** *Eopsaltria capito*          SEE p. 39

15 cm. A pale-yellow-breasted rain-forest robin with whitish or buff face and brownish-olive head. Above, greenish-olive, browner on head; lores and ring around eyes, white (south) or buff (north); throat, white; underparts, pale yellow, more olive on sides of breast and flanks; tail, brownish-olive. Bill, black; eyes, reddish-brown; legs, pinkish-brown.

Distinguished from the Northern Yellow Robin by paler colour, uncoloured rump, greenish-olive back, pale legs, and pale face; from the White-faced Robin (which is outside its range) by the much less definite facial pattern and brownish-olive rather than black head.

VOICE: Low twitter; harsh alarm "churr churr."

HABITAT: Rain forest, associated with lawyer vine.

RANGE: North-eastern Australia, from Dungog, New South Wales, to Bloomfield River, Queensland.

Sedentary.


**WHITE-FACED ROBIN** *Eopsaltria leucops*          SEE p. 39

13 cm. A yellow-breasted rain-forest robin with white face and black head. Above, greenish-olive, black on head; face, eye-rings, and throat, white; underparts, yellow, more olive on sides of breast and flanks; tail, dark greenish-olive. Bill, black; eyes, reddish-brown; legs, dull yellow.

It is outside the range of other yellow-breasted robins; the black crown contrasting with the white face is distinctive.

VOICE: Musical five-noted song; harsh alarm "chee-chee."

HABITAT: Rain forest.

RANGE: Cape York; southern New Guinea lowlands, and mountains to 1,500 m.

Sedentary.

White-breasted Robin

Pale Yellow Robin

# FANTAILS

Fantails take their name from the habit of constantly opening the tail, probably as an aid in flushing insects which are collected in flight. They are very active and quite aggressive towards hawks, kookaburras, etc. The nest is a neat, cup-shaped structure built from spiderweb and grass, often with a "tail" hanging below the branch on which it is placed. The largest of the four species is the Willie Wagtail; the name derives from the constant sideways movement of the tail, not from any relationship with the true wagtails, which wag their tails up and down. Of the remaining species, two are grey and one is brown and rufous.

### GREY FANTAIL *Rhipidura fuliginosa* SEE p. 41

15 cm. An active grey fantail with white eyebrows, white streak behind eyes, and two white bars on wing coverts. Above, grey, with two white bars on the brown wing coverts; eyebrows, streak behind eyes, and throat, white; breast, dark grey, sooty-black in centre; abdomen, pale cinnamon; undertail coverts, white; tail feathers, dark grey with white shafts and white edges and tips to outer feathers. Bill, black; eyes, dark brown; legs, black.

Distinguished from Northern Fantail by white line behind eyes, two white wing bars, and white shafts in tail.

VOICE: High-pitched musical twitter.

HABITAT: Forest and woodland, gardens, parks, and mangroves.

RANGE: Australia, Tasmania, Bass Strait islands, Kangaroo Island; New Zealand to Solomon Islands; New Guinea in vicinity of Hall Sound.

Apparently regular seasonal movements, a partial exodus from southern range in winter.

### NORTHERN FANTAIL *Rhipidura rufiventris* SEE p. 41

16·5 cm. A relatively inactive grey fantail with no white streak behind eyes, no distinct wing bars, and no white shafts in tail. Above, grey, with

White-faced Robin

Grey Fantail

no distinct bars on the wing coverts; eyebrows and throat, white; breast, grey and streaked white; remainder of underparts, buffy-white; tail, dark grey, edged and tipped white on outer feathers. Bill (discernibly longer than Grey Fantail), black; eyes, dark brown; legs, black.

Distinguished from Grey Fantail by lack of white streak behind eyes and on wing coverts, and the lack of white shafts in the tail feathers; much more inactive, sitting upright on the perch with little tail fanning.

VOICE: Musical "doo doo deed a day doo;" "chuck chuck."

HABITAT: Mainly open forest, particularly paperbark; rarely wet forest and mangrove.

RANGE: Northern Australia, from Derby, Western Australia, to Burnett River, Queensland; New Guinea, Solomon Islands, Moluccas, and Lesser Sunda Islands.

Sedentary.

### RUFOUS FANTAIL  *Rhipidura rufifrons*                      SEE p. 41

15 cm. A brown fantail with rufous forehead and rump. Above, brown, with rufous rump; forehead, rufous; throat, white; upper breast, black with white freckling on lower edge; abdomen, creamy-white, with buff flanks and undertail coverts; tail, rufous basal half, remainder black with white tips to outer feathers. Bill, black; eyes, brown; legs, black.

VOICE: Thin metallic call "tst-tst-tseeyou-tst;" sharp "tsit tsit."

HABITAT: Wet forest and mangroves during breeding season; more open forest at other times.

RANGE: Eastern and northern Australia.

Regular migration from southern range, arriving spring and leaving early autumn, moving as far as New Guinea.

### WILLIE WAGTAIL  *Rhipidura leucophrys*                      SEE p. 41

20 cm. A black-and-white fantail with black throat. Above, black; eyebrows, white; throat, black; breast and abdomen, white. Bill, black; eyes, dark brown; legs, black.

Northern Fantail

Rufous Fantail

Distinguished from Restless Flycatcher by black throat and white eyebrows; from male Satin Flycatcher by white eyebrows.

VOICE: "Sweet pretty creature;" harsh chatter.

HABITAT: From edge of rain forest to edge of desert.

RANGE: Australia, Kangaroo Island; southern New Guinea and neighbouring islands; Solomon Islands, Micronesia, and Lesser Sunda Islands.

Some regular movement from south-eastern Australia in winter.

# MONARCH FLYCATCHERS — Monarchidae

Like the flycatchers of family *Muscicapidae*, the monarch flycatchers have flat bills and five stiff bristles on each side of the wide gape, acting as "scoops" for catching insects in flight. Many of them have flat crests which, when raised, give the crown a broad appearance. The cup-shaped nests are even more elaborately decorated with lichen and moss than those of the muscicapids. Immature monarchs are not spotted as are the immatures of the muscicapids. Many monarch flycatchers are migratory, particularly in south-eastern Australia. In general the calls are harsh and frog-like, but some species have sweet whistles. In most cases there are no problems in identification. However, the Broad-billed Flycatcher and the females of the Leaden and Satin Flycatchers, all species which constantly "shiver" the tail, are very similar, and some care is required to separate them.

### LEADEN FLYCATCHER *Myiagra rubecula*      SEE p. 41

16 cm. A tail-shivering flycatcher with dark grey upperparts and throat (male) or with brownish-grey upperparts, throat and breast cinnamon-buff, and all-dark tail (in the female). **Male:** above, dark grey, glossed blue-green on head; throat, dark grey; breast, abdomen, white. **Female:**

Willie Wagtail

Leaden Flycatcher

above, brownish-grey, lacking gloss; throat and breast, cinnamon-buff; abdomen, white; tail, dark brownish-grey. Bill, blue-grey; eyes, blackish-brown; legs, black.

Male distinguished from Satin Flycatcher by dark grey rather than black upperparts and less extensive dark throat. Female distinguished from female Satin Flycatcher by more extensive cinnamon-buff on breast; from Broad-billed Flycatcher by rather duller colouring and all-dark tail.

VOICE: "Peter-peter;" frog-like "queeark."

HABITAT: Forest, mangrove, and woodland.

RANGE: Eastern and northern Australia; south and eastern New Guinea, and adjacent islands.

Regular migrant to southern range (September–March, Sydney) moving as far as New Guinea in winter; probably sedentary in tropics.

## SATIN FLYCATCHER *Myiagra cyanoleuca*  SEE p. 41

15 cm. A tail-shivering, black-and-white flycatcher (male) or one with brownish blue-grey upperparts, cinnamon-buff throat, and all-dark tail. **Male:** above, throat and breast, glossy bluish-black; abdomen, white. **Female:** above, brownish blue-grey, lacking gloss; throat, cinnamon-buff; breast and abdomen, white; tail, all dark. Bill, slaty blue-grey, black at tip; eyes, blackish-brown; legs, black.

Female distinguished from female Leaden Flycatcher by the rather bluer upperparts and the less extensive cinnamon-buff on the underparts, in contrast to the male which has a more extensive dark throat and breast than the male Leaden. Female distinguished from the Broad-billed Flycatcher (range meets only on Cape York) by the lack of white in the tail, the upperparts not so greenish-blue and rather darker, and the smaller amount of cinnamon-buff on the throat.

VOICE: "Chew-ee;" harsh rasping "queeark."

Satin Flycatcher

HABITAT: Forest and woodland, more allied to upland and mountain forest than the Leaden Flycatcher.

RANGE: Eastern Australia, from Tasmania to Cape York; southern New Guinea, adjacent islands, and New Britain.

Regular migration to southern range arriving in September and leaving most of eastern Australia in March or April; there may be some altitudinal movement in the northern parts of its Australian range.

## BROAD-BILLED FLYCATCHER *Myiagra ruficollis* SEE p. 41

15 cm. A tail-shivering, mangrove flycatcher with steely blue-grey upperparts, cinnamon-buff throat, and tail narrowly edged and tipped white. Above, steely blue-grey (rather more glossy for the male); throat and breast, cinnamon-buff; abdomen, white; tail, edged and tipped white. Bill, slaty blue-grey above, grey below; eyes, blackish-brown; legs, black.

Distinguished from female Leaden and Satin Flycatchers by the white in the tail. The male is also brighter in colour, and the tail is not shivered to the same extent. The broad bill is not a character that can be used as the sole criterion in field identification, as all the *Myiagra* flycatchers have broad bills.

VOICE: Frog-like "queeark."

HABITAT: Mangrove and contiguous vegetation.

RANGE: Northern Australia, from Derby, Western Australia, to Cape York, Queensland; southern New Guinea to Timor.

Sedentary.

## SHINING FLYCATCHER *Myiagra alecto* SEE p. 41

16 cm. A shining black flycatcher (male) or a chestnut-backed fly-catcher with black head (female). **Male:** shining black, with red inside the mouth. **Female:** above, chestnut; head, black; underparts, white;

Broad-billed Flycatcher

Shining Flycatcher

tail, chestnut. Bill, dark blue-grey; eyes, reddish-brown; legs, black.

VOICE: Long soft whistle; harsh alarm "creeek."

HABITAT: Mangrove, swamp vegetation, and dense river margins, particularly pandanus.

RANGE: Northern Australia, from Derby, Western Australia, to Noosa Heads, Queensland.

Sedentary.

### RESTLESS FLYCATCHER *Myiagra inquieta* SEE p. 41

20 cm. A black-and-white flycatcher with white throat. Above, black; underparts, white; female has rust-coloured breast. Bill, black; eyes, dark brown; legs, black.

Distinguished from Willie Wagtail and Satin Flycatcher by white throat.

VOICE: Musical "tu-whee, tu-whee;" harsh metallic grating, like scissors being ground (Hutchinson 26).

HABITAT: Open forest and woodland.

RANGE: Northern, eastern, and south-western Australia; southern New Guinea (Merauke).

Sedentary or nomadic.

### BLACK-FACED FLYCATCHER *Monarcha melanopsis* SEE p. 43

16·5 cm. A rufous-bellied, black-faced flycatcher with grey breast and grey wings. **Adult:** above, slate-grey, paler on head and around eyes; face and throat, black; breast, grey; abdomen, rufous; tail, grey. **Immature:** lacks black face. Bill, blue-grey; eyes, dark brown; legs, blue-grey.

Distinguished from Pearly (Black-winged) Flycatcher by grey wings and tail and by black of face not reaching eyes; from Spectacled Flycatcher by different face pattern, grey breast, and lack of white in the tail.

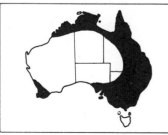

Restless Flycatcher                          Black-faced Flycatcher

VOICE: Rich whistle "why-you-which-ye-ou;" harsh grinding note.

HABITAT: Forest and woodland, more usually in secluded gullies and dense forest.

RANGE: Eastern Australia; eastern New Guinea, Fergusson, Goodenough, Tagula, and Trobriand islands.

Migratory in southern range, arriving September, leaving March, moving as far as New Guinea.

## BLACK-WINGED (PEARLY) FLYCATCHER SEE p. 43
### *Monarcha frater*

15 cm. A rufous-bellied, black-faced flycatcher with grey breast and black wings. **Adult:** above, slate-grey with black wings; face (to front edge of eye) and throat, black; breast, grey; abdomen, rufous; tail, black. **Immature:** lacks black face. Bill, blue-grey; eyes, dark brown; legs, blue-grey.

Distinguished from Black-faced and Spectacled Flycatchers by black wings and tail.

VOICE: Same as Black-faced Flycatcher.

HABITAT: Rain forest and adjoining woodland.

RANGE: Eastern Cape York, Queensland, north of Claudie River.

May be regular migrant, or resident population of New Guinea species.

## SPECTACLED FLYCATCHER *Monarcha trivirgata* SEE p. 43

16·5 cm. A white- or buff-bellied, black-faced flycatcher with rufous breast. Above, dark blue-grey; forehead, throat, and band through eyes, black; sides of throat and neck, breast and flanks, rufous, shading to buff-white on abdomen; tail, black and broadly tipped white on outer feathers. Bill, dark blue-grey; eyes, dark brown; legs, dark blue-grey.

Distinguished from Black-faced and Black-winged (Pearly) Flycatchers by the rufous breast.

Black-winged Flycatcher

Spectacled Flycatcher

VOICE: Repeated "pree-eet, pree-eet;" "phew-ew-weet;" frog-like "croak-croak;" rasping chatter.

HABITAT: Wet forest, mangroves, and adjacent woodland.

RANGE: Eastern Australia, from south-eastern New South Wales to Cape York, Queensland; southern New Guinea, Louisiade Archipelago, Salawati Island (Papua), Moluccas, and Timor.

Sedentary in north; migratory in southern range arriving in September, leaving in February or March.

## WHITE-EARED FLYCATCHER *Monarcha leucotis* SEE p. 43

13·5 cm. A pied flycatcher with white rump and white patches on the head and wing. Above, black, with white bars on the wing; eyebrows, small spot before eyes, and ear coverts, white; underparts, white, with greyish breast and flanks; tail, black, with outer tail feathers tipped white. Bill, black, bluish-grey at base; eyes, dark brown; legs, black.

Distinguished from White-browed Robin by white ear patch, white rump, and darker upperparts.

VOICE: Plaintive "doo-dee-doo," middle note higher than others; harsh alarm "chrrk-chrrk-chrrk;" also flute-like whistle.

HABITAT: Wet forest and mangrove.

RANGE: Coastal north-eastern Australia, from Murwillumbah, New South Wales, to Cape York, Queensland.

Probably migrant in southern range.

## PIED FLYCATCHER *Arses kaupi* SEE p. 43

15 cm. A white-collared, pied flycatcher with black breast band and erectile frill on nape. **Male:** above, black, with white rump and collar; head, black, with pale blue wattle around the eyes; underparts, white,

White-eared Flycatcher

Pied Flycatcher

with black spot on chin and black band on the breast. **Female:** similar, but white collar narrower and separated from white throat. Bill, blue-grey; eyes, dark brown, bare skin around eyes, pale blue; legs, dark grey-blue.

Distinguished from Frill-necked Flycatcher (ranges are exclusive) by black breast band.

VOICE: Soft "chrr chrr;" harsh grating; deep drawn-out "zzzreeee-zzzreeee zzzreeee."

HABITAT: Rain forest and adjacent open forest; mangrove.

RANGE: North-eastern Queensland, from Herbert River to Bloomfield River.

Sedentary.

## FRILL-NECKED FLYCATCHER SEE p. 43
*Arses telescopthalmus lorealis*

14 cm. A white-collared pied flycatcher with erectile frill on nape and without black breast band. **Male:** above, black with white rump and collar; head, black with bright blue wattle around eyes; chin, black; underparts, white. **Female:** similar, but with white lores, no black on chin, and sometimes a rusty-brown tinge on the breast. Bill, blue-grey; eyes, dark brown, bare skin around eyes, bright blue; legs, dark grey-blue.

Distinguished from the Pied Flycatcher (ranges are exclusive) by lack of black breast band.

VOICE: Same as Pied Flycatcher.

HABITAT: Rain forest and adjacent open forest.

RANGE: Cape York, south to Peach River north of Coen, Queensland; New Guinea and nearby western islands.

Possibly sedentary.

Frill-necked Flycatcher

## BOAT-BILLED FLYCATCHER SEE p. 43
*Machaerirhynchus flaviventer*

13 cm. A broad-billed flycatcher with yellow eyebrows and underparts. **Male:** above, black, with olive suffusion in southern range; wings, black, with two white bars and feather edges, white or yellow; eyebrows, yellow; throat, white; breast and abdomen, bright yellow; tail, black, thinly edged and broadly tipped white. **Female:** above, yellowish-olive, with brownish-black wings barred and edged white; eyebrows, yellow; throat, white; breast and abdomen, pale yellow. Bill, broad and flat, black; eyes, blackish-brown; legs, dark blue-grey.

VOICE: Melodious trill; soft "tizzz-tizzz."

HABITAT: Rain forest.

RANGE: North-eastern Queensland, from Rockingham Bay and Mount Spec to Cape York; New Guinea and nearby western islands. Sedentary.

# THICKHEADS—Pachycephalidae

Thickheads are rather robust birds with relatively large heads. The bill is thick and slightly hooked at the end. Most are excellent songsters. The nest is cup-shaped and made from grass, leaves, and/or bark. There are three groups: (a) Whistlers, which inhabit between them most habitats in Australia, from mangrove and rain forest to mallee and mulga. (b) Shrike-thrushes, which are rather like large whistlers and are notable for their beautiful songs. (c) Shrike-tits, crested strong-billed birds that feed mainly by stripping loose bark from trees in search of invertebrates.

## WHISTLERS
Whistlers are rather inactive, often strikingly plumaged birds with clear melodious songs. They tend to be stoutly built and feed on insects,

Boat-billed Flycatcher

usually taken in vegetation; although one, the White-breasted Whistler, often feeds on the ground among mangroves taking small crabs. Males are generally more colourful than females. In most species the diagnostic features are clear-cut, but some cause confusion. The males of the Golden and Mangrove Golden Whistlers are very similar, but apart from habitat differences the former has yellow edges to the wing feathers and the latter grey. Females are easily separated by the presence or absence of yellow underparts. More confusing, however, are the two similar northern whistlers, the Brown and the Grey. They cannot be confused with each other, as they inhabit exclusive ranges, but being un-whistler-like in form and behaviour they are often confused with other birds, notably the white-breasted form of the Lemon-breasted Flycatcher (the "Brown-tailed Flycatcher") in the case of the Brown, and the Yellow Flycatcher in the case of the Grey.

### RUFOUS WHISTLER *Pachycephala rufiventris* SEE p. 45

17 cm. A rufous-breasted whistler with white throat and black breast band (male) or a pale buff-breasted whistler with streaked throat and breast (female). **Male:** above, dark olive-grey; black band extending from beak through eyes and across breast; throat, white; breast and abdomen, rufous; tail, blackish-brown. **Female:** above, olive-grey; throat, white, streaked black; breast and abdomen, pale buff, streaked black. **Immature male:** similar to female, but more concentrated streaking on upper breast. Bill, black; eyes, reddish-brown; legs, dark grey-brown.

Female distinguished from female White-breasted Whistler in mangroves by heavier streaking, particularly on the throat; from Bower Shrike-thrush by habitat, smaller size, and paler underparts.

VOICE: Rich melodious phrase; "ee-chong;" "joey-joey . . ." (Hutchinson 27).

Rufous Whistler

HABITAT: All kinds of forest and woodland, mostly dry, but including mangrove.

RANGE: Australia, except areas without woodland; south-eastern New Guinea and Rossel Island, Moluccas, New Caledonia; most extra-Australian races lack rufous underparts.

Sedentary over much of its range, but nomadic and migratory in the south-east.

## WHITE-BREASTED WHISTLER SEE p. 45
*Pachycephala lanioides*

20 cm. A white-breasted whistler with white throat, black head and breast band, and chestnut collar (male) or a pale buff-breasted Whistler with streaked breast and abdomen (female). **Male:** above, dark grey, with black wings and chestnut collar; head, black, joining black breast band; throat and abdomen, white; tail, black. **Female:** above, brownish-grey; underparts, pale buff, whiter on throat, greyer on breast, streaked black. Bill, black; eyes, reddish-brown; legs, dark grey.

Female distinguished from female Rufous Whistler, which occasionally enters mangroves, by lighter streaking, particularly on throat; larger, more robust build; and particularly the large bill.

VOICE: A richer song than Rufous Whistler, though similar; whistling "per-weet" and "twit" (Hutchinson 28).

HABITAT: Mangroves, particularly along tidal creeks.

RANGE: Northern Australia, from Carnarvon, Western Australia, to Normanton, Queensland.

Sedentary.

## GOLDEN WHISTLER *Pachycephala pectoralis* SEE p. 45

16·5 cm. A forest-dwelling, yellow-bellied whistler (male) or an unstreaked grey-breasted whistler, with yellow, buff, or white, under-tail coverts (female). **Male:** above, olive-yellow, with wing feathers

White-breasted Whistler

Golden Whistler

black, edged greyish-yellow; collar, yellow; head, black, joining black breast band; throat, white; breast and abdomen, yellow; tail, grey in Tasmania and becoming blacker further north. **Female:** above, olive-grey to olive-brown; throat and breast, greyish and slightly mottled on breast; abdomen, buff (mainland) or white (Tasmania); undertail coverts, white in Tasmania, buff in southern and south-western Australia, and yellow in northern Australia. **Immature:** rufous edges to wing-feathers. Bill, black; eyes, reddish-brown; legs, black.

Male difficult to distinguish from male Mangrove Golden Whistler, but is larger and has different habitat. Female distinguished from female Mangrove Golden Whistler by greyish, buff, or white, breast and abdomen, brownish tail, and different habitat.

VOICE: "Wi-wi-wi-wiyou-wit;" plaintive "seep."

HABITAT: Forest and woodland.

RANGE: Australia, Tasmania, Bass Strait islands, and Kangaroo Island; from Java through New Guinea lowlands to Pacific Islands.

Generally sedentary, but some local nomadism.

## MANGROVE GOLDEN WHISTLER SEE p. 45
*Pachycephala melanura*

15 cm. A mangrove-dwelling, yellow-bellied whistler. **Male:** above, olive-yellow, with black wing feathers edged greyish-yellow; broad collar, yellow; head, black extending to black breast band; throat, white; breast and abdomen, yellow; tail, black in eastern range, and greenish-yellow at base in western range. **Female:** above, olive-brown; throat, white; breast and abdomen, yellow; tail, black. Bill, black; eyes, reddish-brown; legs, black.

Male is difficult to distinguish from the Golden Whistler, but is smaller, has rather larger yellow collar, and has different habitat; female is distinguished by the yellow belly and black tail.

Mangrove Golden Whistler

VOICE: Similar to Golden Whistler.

HABITAT: Mangrove and contiguous vegetation.

RANGE: Islands and coastal northern Australia, from 35 km north-west of Mackay, Queensland, to Carnarvon, Western Australia; southern New Guinea.

Sedentary.

## OLIVE WHISTLER *Pachycephala olivacea* SEE p. 45

18–20 cm. An olive-brown whistler with a mottled-white throat. **Male:** above, olive-brown, slightly reddish on rump; head, dark grey, joining light grey breast; throat, white, mottled with grey; abdomen, reddish-buff. **Female:** similar, but with olive-brown head, and breast brown like abdomen. Bill, blackish-brown; eyes, dark brown; legs, blackish-brown.

VOICE: Musical whistles "I'll-get-you;" "you're cranky;" and slow "whee-too."

HABITAT: Forest and thickets, particularly Beech forest north of Sydney.

RANGE: South-eastern Australia, from south-eastern Queensland to Millicent, South Australia; Tasmania and Bass Strait islands.

Sedentary.

## GILBERT'S WHISTLER *Pachycephala inornata* SEE p. 45

19 cm. A grey whistler with cinnamon throat and black lores (male) or an all-grey whistler (female). **Male:** above, brownish-grey; lores, black; throat, cinnamon; breast and flanks, pale grey; belly and under-tail coverts, buffy-white. **Female:** above, dark grey; below, light greyish-buff, darker on breast. Bill, dark olive-grey; eyes, reddish-brown; legs, dark olive-grey.

Male distinguished from Red-lored Whistler by black lores. Female is like a small shrike-thrush.

Olive Whistler

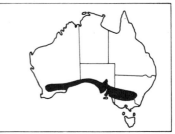

Gilbert's Whistler

Voice: Musical "er-whit-er-whit;" loud "pooo-eee;" harsh "chook."
Habitat: Dry woodlands such as mallee and mulga.
Range: Southern Australia, from Cowra and Nymagee, New South
Wales, to Eyre Peninsula, South Australia; south-western Australia.
Sedentary. *Pinaroo, S.A. 10/72*

### RED-LORED WHISTLER *Pachycephala rufogularis*   SEE p. 45

20 cm. A grey whistler with cinnamon throat and lores. **Male:** above,
brownish-grey; lores and throat, cinnamon; breast and flanks, pale grey;
abdomen, brownish-buff. **Female:** similar, but the cinnamon areas paler.
Bill, dark olive-grey; eyes, reddish-brown; legs, dark olive-grey.

Distinguished from Gilbert's Whistler by the cinnamon lores, rather
paler (much paler in female) cinnamon colouring and browner belly.

Voice: Loud clear whistle followed by sound like in-drawn breath.
Habitat: Whipstick mallee and porcupine grass.
Range: North-western Victoria and Murray mallee in South Aus-
tralia; Pulletop National Park, Griffith, New South Wales.
Sedentary.

### BROWN WHISTLER *Pachycephala simplex*   SEE p. 45

16 cm. A pale grey-brown whistler with dull white belly. Above, pale
grey-brown; below, dull white, tinged buff on breast, which is faintly
streaked. Bill, black; eyes, light brown; legs, black.

Distinguished from Grey Whistler by white belly (ranges are exclusive).
Voice: Similar to Grey Whistler.
Habitat: Mangrove and wet forest.
Range: Coastal Northern Territory.
Sedentary.

### GREY WHISTLER *Pachycephala griseiceps*   SEE p. 45

14 cm. A pale grey-brown whistler tinged greenish-olive above, with
pale yellow belly. Above, pale grey-brown, tinged greenish-olive on the

Red-lored Whistler

Brown Whistler

back, darker on the head; throat, white to pale buff; breast, darker buff, faintly streaked; abdomen, pale lemon-yellow. Bill, brown; eyes, brown; legs, bluish-grey.

Distinguished from Brown Whistler by the yellowish belly.

VOICE: Whistling "dum dum dee da dum."

HABITAT: Rain forest.

RANGE: North-eastern Queensland, from Rockingham Bay to Cape York; Moluccas; New Guinea and adjacent islands.

Sedentary.

## SHRIKE-THRUSHES

The name "shrike-thrush," a conjugation of the names of two dissimilar families, is not an ideal one for these birds, but until a more suitable alternative becomes popular (perhaps "gudilang" from the Aboriginal) it is preferred here to the alternative "thrush," which suggests even more strongly an untrue relationship. Shrike-thrushes, though plain in plumage, are remarkable for the richness and purity of their songs. Of particular note in this respect is the tropical Brown-breasted (or Sandstone) Shrike-thrush, whose liquid notes are heightened by echoes among the sandstone gorges. Four of the five species are found only in the north. The remaining species occurs over the whole of Australia; it forms two distinct populations, one in the west, and the other in the north and east. Apart from where they hybridise over a small area the two forms are easily separable in the field, so they are kept separate here. Also included here is the Crested Bell-bird, which is in essence a terrestrial shrike-thrush with a crest; its bell-like ventriloquial whistle is a feature of the inland.

**GREY SHRIKE-THRUSH** *Colluricincla harmonica*          SEE p. 47

24 cm. A grey thrush with brown back. Above, dark grey, with brown back; lores, white; underparts, pale grey, darker on breast which is more

Grey Whistler

Grey Shrike-thrush

or less streaked darker. Bill, black; eyes, brown; legs, dark grey. In the north, rather greyer on the back (race *brunnea*).

Distinguished from the Western Shrike-thrush by the pale grey undertail coverts.

VOICE: Wide range of melodious calls based on "pip pip pip pip ho-ee;" harsh "yor-ick."

HABITAT: Forest and woodland, parks, and gardens.

RANGE: Eastern and northern Australia, from Broome, Western Australia, to Spencer Gulf, South Australia; Kangaroo Island, Tasmania, and Bass Strait islands; eastern New Guinea.

Sedentary.


## WESTERN SHRIKE-THRUSH                    SEE p. 47
*Colluricincla harmonica rufiventris*

24 cm. A greyish thrush with cinnamon-buff undertail coverts. Above, dark grey, tinged olive; underparts, pale grey, shading to cinnamon-buff undertail coverts. Bill, black; eyes, brown; legs, dark grey.

Distinguished from the Grey Shrike-thrush by the cinnamon-buff undertail coverts.

VOICE: "Pip pip pip poee;" harsh "yor-ick" (Hutchinson 30).

HABITAT: Forest and woodland.

RANGE: Western and central Australia, from Eyre Peninsula, South Australia, to Alice Springs, Northern Territory, west to Fortescue River, Western Australia.

Sedentary.


## RUFOUS SHRIKE-THRUSH *Colluricincla megarhyncha*    SEE p. 47

19 cm. A reddish-brown thrush with pale bill. Above, olive-brown; throat, white, or pale cinnamon-buff; remainder of underparts, reddish-

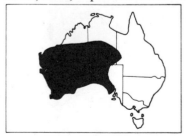

Western Shrike-thrush

Rufous Shrike-thrush

cinnamon, with dark streaks on the throat and breast. Bill, pale pinkish-brown; eyes, grey-brown; legs, purplish-grey.

VOICE: "Tu whee, wet wet;" rasping sneeze.

HABITAT: Rain forest, mangrove and contiguous woodland.

RANGE: Eastern Australia, from Cape York, Queensland, to Hasting River, New South Wales; Sangihe Island (near Celebes) to New Guinea and adjacent islands.

Sedentary.

## LITTLE SHRIKE-THRUSH *Colluricincla parvula*   SEE p. 47

19 cm. A reddish-brown thrush with dark bill. Above, buff-brown; face and throat, white; breast and flank, cinnamon-buff, with faint streaking on throat and breast; centre of abdomen, dull white. Bill, blackish-brown; eyes, reddish-brown; legs, bluish-grey.

VOICE: Similar to Rufous Shrike-thrush.

HABITAT: Mangrove, swamp woodland, and riverine thickets.

RANGE: Coastal Northern Territory; inland in wet north-western corner of Northern Territory; Melville Island.

Sedentary.

## BOWER SHRIKE-THRUSH *Colluricincla boweri*   SEE p. 47

21·5 cm. A cinnamon-breasted thrush with blue-grey back. Above, dark blue-grey; lores and throat, whitish; breast and abdomen, pinkish-cinnamon, with throat and breast streaked dark grey. Bill, black; eyes, dark chestnut-brown; legs, dark slate-grey.

VOICE: "To-whee-to-wet."

HABITAT: Rain forest, usually above 300 m.

RANGE: North-eastern Queensland, from Cairns to Cardwell.

Some seasonal altitudinal movement.

Little Shrike-thrush                        Bower Shrike-thrush

## BROWN-BREASTED (SANDSTONE)
**SHRIKE-THRUSH** *Colluricincla woodwardi* SEE p. 47

21·5 cm. A reddish-brown terrestrial thrush of sandstone cliffs. Above, dark brown, greyish on the head; lores and throat, buffy-white; breast and abdomen, pinkish-cinnamon, streaked on throat and breast. Bill, blackish-brown; eyes, reddish-brown; legs, dark brown.

VOICE: A most beautiful pure variable song often heightened by echoes (Hutchinson 31).

HABITAT: Cliffs, gorges, and tumbled boulders in sandstone ranges.

RANGE: Sandstone areas of northern Australia, from the Kimberleys to north-western Queensland.

Sedentary.

## CRESTED BELL-BIRD *Oreoica gutturalis* SEE p. 47

23 cm. A crested bird with white face and black breast band (male) or a grey-brown bird with black patch on crown (female). **Male:** above, buff-brown, greyer on the crown; crest and line through eyes joining breast band, black; face and throat, white; lower breast and abdomen, buffy-white; flanks and undertail coverts, light cinnamon-buff. **Female:** lacks crest; has white face and black breast band; in place of the crest is a black patch on the crown. Bill, black; eyes, orange (male), reddish-brown (female); legs, dark grey.

VOICE: Haunting ventriloquial "pan-pan-pallela" (Hutchinson 32).

HABITAT: Dry woodland to arid scrub with scattered trees.

RANGE: Arid Australia.

Sedentary or nomadic.

# SHRIKE-TITS

The endemic shrike-tit has three isolated forms, an eastern, a western, and a northern. All are similar, but as there is some disagreement as to

Brown-breasted Shrike-thrush

Crested Bell-bird

their status, they are treated here separately. With their large crested heads strikingly patterned in black and white, and their yellow underparts, they cannot be mistaken for any other birds. The nest is quite different from that of any other thickhead, being a deep cup-shaped structure placed among thin upright branchlets.

### EASTERN SHRIKE-TIT *Falcunculus frontatus*     SEE p. 47

19 cm. A shrike-tit with yellow breast and abdomen and grey edges to wing feathers. **Male:** above, yellowish-green with black wings and tail having each feather edged grey; crested head, black with prominent white streaks; throat, black; breast and abdomen, yellow. **Female:** similar, but throat and foreneck yellow, mottled-black. Bill, black; eyes, red; legs, grey.

Voice: Chuckling "knock on the door jack;" long single whistle.

Habitat: Dry forest and woodland.

Range: Eastern Australia, from Atherton Tableland, Queensland, to southern Flinders Ranges, South Australia.

Sedentary, with some nomadism.

### NORTHERN SHRIKE-TIT *Falcunculus frontatus whitei*     SEE p. 47

16·5 cm. A small shrike-tit with yellow breast and abdomen and yellow edges to wing feathers. **Male:** above, greenish-yellow, with black wings and tail having each feather edged yellow; crested head, black with prominent white streaks; throat, black; breast and abdomen, yellow. **Female:** throat and foreneck, yellow, mottled-black. Bill, black; eyes, red; legs, grey.

Voice: Not recorded.

Habitat: Dry forest, particularly stringybark on ridges.

Range: Northern Australia, apparently isolated populations: Drys-

Eastern Shrike-tit

Northern Shrike-tit

dale River and Deception Range, Western Australia; Larrimah, Borroloola, and McArthur River, Northern Territory.

Sedentary.

## WESTERN SHRIKE-TIT SEE p. 47
*Falcunculus frontatus leucogaster*

18 cm. A shrike-tit with yellow breast and white abdomen. **Male:** above, bright yellowish-green, with black wings having greenish-yellow edges; crested head, black, with prominent white streaks; throat, black; breast and undertail coverts, yellow; abdomen, white. **Female:** throat, greenish-yellow, mottled-black. Bill, black; eyes, red; legs, grey.

VOICE: Whistling "poo-wee-er."

HABITAT: Wandoo and karri forest (generally white smooth-barked trees).

RANGE: South-western Australia.

Sedentary.

# AUSTRALIAN CHATS—Ephthianuridae

A small endemic family (chat-warblers) of five brightly-coloured species that feed on the ground. The females are generally duller in plumage than the males. They often move in flocks and nest in loose colonies. The nests are cup-shaped and are usually placed in bushes close to the ground.

Some are particularly well-adapted to conditions in the drier areas, and there is a general preference for samphire as a habitat.

*nelson, Vic. 3/72*

## WHITE-FRONTED CHAT *Ephthianura albifrons* SEE p. 49

11 cm. A small white and grey bird with a black band on the breast. **Male:** above, grey; wings and tail, brown; head and upper breast, white;

Western Shrike-tit

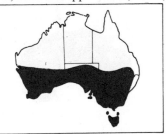

White-fronted Chat

nape and band across breast, black; abdomen, white. **Female:** above, brown; below, white, with faint band on breast. Bill, black; eyes, white (male), brown (female); legs, black.

Usually seen in samphire, perched on top of the bushes or walking jerkily on the ground.

VOICE: Metallic "tang."

HABITAT: Samphire, saltbush, paddocks, and plains with stunted bushes.

RANGE: Southern Australia and Tasmania.

Nomadic in drier areas but sedentary when conditions are suitable.

## CRIMSON CHAT *Ephthianura tricolor* SEE p. 49

11 cm. A chat with crimson cap, breast, and rump. **Male:** above, brown, with white edges to wing feathers; crown and rump, crimson; throat, white; breast and abdomen, crimson. **Female:** above, brown; rump, red; breast, cream, with red patches. **Immature:** similar to female, but lacking red breast patches. Bill, black (male), black above pink below (female); eyes, yellow; legs, brown.

It is believed to have an eclipse plumage, but fully-plumaged males have been seen in winter near Yalgoo in Western Australia and near Derby, Western Australia.

VOICE: Metallic "tang" rather like White-fronted Chat; a whistling "tsee tsee tsee."

HABITAT: Favours saltbush and samphire, and in mulga country prefers trichinium bushes.

RANGE: Australia, except the wetter forested areas.

Migrates through flowering shrub savannah, feeding in part from nectariferous flowers.

## ORANGE CHAT *Ephthianura aurifrons* SEE p. 49

11 cm. An orange chat with a black mask. **Male:** above, brown with yellow edging to the feathers; head and rump, orange; below, orange

Crimson Chat                                          Orange Chat

with black face and throat. **Female:** above, yellowish-brown; rump, yellow; below, yellowish-white. Bill, black; eyes, red-brown; legs, black.

In the western half of its range, the female may be mistaken for the Samphire Thornbill as it lives in much the same habitat, but is paler in colour and has a clearer yellow rump. Both share the habit of sitting atop samphire bushes, then disappearing from view to the ground, bobbing up again on another bush, perhaps a hundred metres away.

VOICE: Metallic "tang."

HABITAT: Samphire and saltbush, particularly in saltpans and around salt lakes.

RANGE: Southern Australia, avoiding the wetter areas; southern Northern Territory.

Nomadic to some extent, but sedentary in favourable areas, e.g. the salt flats near the mouth of the Wooramel River, Western Australia.

**YELLOW CHAT** *Ephthianura crocea*                          SEE p. 49

10·5 cm. A yellow chat with black breast band. **Male:** above, yellowish-brown; head and rump, yellow; below, yellow, with black breast band. **Female:** rather duller and lacking the breast band. Bill, black; eyes, red-brown; legs, black.

VOICE: A musical call of three descending syllables.

HABITAT: Saltbush, samphire, and grasses on lagoons and river flats; cumbungi swamps along bore drains of the interior.

RANGE: An unusual distribution, recorded to date from the Fitzroy and Ord rivers, Western Australia; Alligator and Victoria rivers, Northern Territory; Norman and Fitzroy rivers, Queensland; Coorabulka, south-western Queensland.

Sedentary.

**GIBBER CHAT** *Ashbyia lovensis*                            SEE p. 49

12·5 cm. A yellow-breasted chat found on gibber plains. **Male:** above, yellowish-brown; eyebrows and face, yellow; below, yellow.

Yellow Chat

Gibber Chat

**Female:** similar, but rather paler yellow. Bill, black; eyes, pale yellow; legs, black.

Rather Pipit-like in behaviour, it is one of the few birds found on gibber plains.

VOICE: "Wheat wheat wheat."

HABITAT: Gibber plains.

RANGE: South-western Queensland, south-eastern Northern Territory, north-western New South Wales, and north-eastern South Australia.

Locally migratory.

## SITTELLAS — Sittidae

Sittellas are small, large-footed, short-tailed birds that feed on insects found in tree bark. Their strong claws enable them to move up and down tree trunks and branches. They generally move in small flocks of up to a dozen birds, noisily moving from tree to tree. The cup-shaped nest is placed in a vertical fork, and is camouflaged with small strips of bark so that it looks, from below, like a knot in the branch.

The five forms are of doubtful status as in general they replace each other geographically, and there tends to be some intergradation where they meet. As typical examples of each are easily recognisable in the field, they are treated separately here.

Tropical forms have white "windows" in the wings; southern forms have orange "windows."

**ORANGE-WINGED SITTELLA** *Neositta chrysoptera*     SEE p. 51

10–12 cm. A sittella with streaked underparts, dark head, and an orange patch in the wing. **Male:** above, brown, streaked darker; rump, white; wing, black, with orange "window" obvious in flight; below, white, streaked dark grey; throat, white; undertail coverts, barred black. **Female:** similar, but with black throat. **Immature:** head and throat,

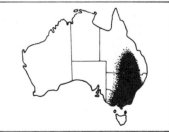

Orange-winged Sittella

white, streaked black. Bill with dark tip and yellow base; eyes, red-brown, eye-rings, yellow; legs, yellow.

The streaked underparts and darker appearance of the head distinguish it from the Black-capped Sittella at the western edge of its range. Adults are easily told from the White-headed Sittella by the dark head, but immatures are more similar, and it is best to base identification on the flock rather than the individual.

VOICE: Twittering "wit-it-it, wit-it-it . . ."

HABITAT: Trees, feeding on the outer branches.

RANGE: South-eastern Australia, inland of the White-headed Sittella in north-eastern New South Wales and south-eastern Queensland.

Sedentary.

## WHITE-HEADED SITTELLA *Neositta leucocephala* SEE p. 51

10–12 cm. A sittella with streaked underparts, white head, and orange patch in the wing. **Male:** above, grey-brown, streaked darker; rump, white; wings, black, with orange "windows" obvious in flight; head, white; below, white, streaked darker; undertail coverts, barred. **Female:** similar. **Immature:** head, streaked darker. Bill with black tip and yellow base; eyes, red-brown; legs, yellow.

The white head of the adult distinguishes it from adults of other forms, but immatures are similar, and identification should be based on the flock rather than the individual.

VOICE: Twittering "wit-it-it, wit-it-it . . ."

HABITAT: Trees, feeding on outer branches.

RANGE: North-eastern New South Wales, south-eastern Queensland.

Sedentary.

## STRIATED SITTELLA *Neositta striata* SEE p. 51

10–12 cm. A sittella with striated underparts, dark head, and white patch in the wing. **Male:** above, brown, streaked darker; rump, (white?);

White-headed Sittella

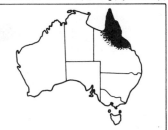

Striated Sittella

wing, black, with white "window" obvious in flight; head, black; below, grey, streaked darker; paler on throat. **Female:** similar, but with black throat. **Immature:** grey head, streaked darker. Bill with black tip and yellow base; eyes, red-brown, with yellow eye-rings; legs, yellow.

The streaked underparts distinguish it from the White-winged Sittella. Immature is similar to immature White-headed Sittella and should be identified on the flock rather than the individual.

VOICE: Twittering "wit-it-it, wit-it-it . . ."

HABITAT: Trees, feeding on outer branches.

RANGE: Northern Queensland, from Inkerman north to Cape York. Sedentary.

## WHITE-WINGED SITTELLA *Neositta leucoptera* SEE p. 51

10–12 cm. A white-breasted sittella with a black cap and a white patch in the wing. **Male:** above, pale grey-brown; rump, white; wings, black, with white "windows" obvious in flight; head, white, with a black cap; below, white; barred undertail coverts. **Female:** similar, but black cap extending below the eyes. **Immature:** streaked head and back. Bill with black tip and yellow base; eyes, red-brown, with yellow eye-rings; legs, yellow.

Distinguished from its southern counterpart, the Black-capped Sittella, by the white instead of orange "window" in the wing; from its eastern counterpart the Striated Sittella by the streaked underparts. Immatures are streaked on the head and back, but not to the same extent as the Striated Sittella.

VOICE: A rapid loud tinkling "Tsit-it-it . . ." (Hutchinson 34).

HABITAT: Trees, feeding mostly along outer branches.

RANGE: Northern Australia south to Broome and Mount Alexandra, Western Australia; Tanami, Banka Banka, and Alexandria, Northern Territory; and east to western Queensland.

Sedentary.

White-winged Sittella

**BLACK-CAPPED SITTELLA** *Neositta pileata*                    SEE p. 51

10–12 cm. A white-breasted sittella with a black cap and an orange patch in the wing. **Male:** above, grey-brown, streaked darker; rump, white; wing, black with orange "window" obvious in flight; head, white, with a black cap; below, white; barred undertail coverts. **Female:** similar, but black cap extending below the eyes. **Immature:** streaked head and back. Bill, black at tip, base yellow; eyes, brown, with yellow eye-rings; legs, yellow.

Distinguished from its northern counterpart, the White-winged Sittella, by the heavier streaks on the back and the orange instead of white "window" in the wing; from the Orange-winged Sittella by the white rather than streaked underparts. Immatures are streaked on head and back, but not to the same extent as the Orange-winged Sittella.

VOICE: A rapid loud tinkling "tsit-tsit-tsit . . ."

HABITAT: Trees, feeding mostly along the outer branches.

RANGE: Southern Australia north to the Pilbara, Western Australia, and south-western Queensland, avoiding eastern Australia.

Sedentary.

# AUSTRALIAN TREE-CREEPERS — Climacteridae

Although birds of the tree trunks and branches, tree-creepers differ from sittellas in being larger, having longer tails, and always progressing upwards when feeding in trees. In contrast with sittellas, they often visit dead and fallen trees. The eggs are laid in a tree hollow, sparsely lined with leaves, grass, rabbit or kangaroo droppings, or charcoal. Some species feed on the ground, particularly the Brown, White-browed, and Rufous. Flight is purposeful, with rapid beats on "windowed" wings interspersed with undulating glides.

The females of most species have a small orange-buff spot on the cheek.

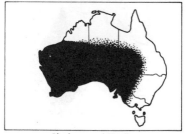

Black-capped Sittella

**BROWN TREE-CREEPER** *Climacteris picumnus*                SEE p. 51

15 cm. A grey-brown tree-creeper with a white brow and streaked abdomen. Above, grey-brown; wings with buff "windows;" broad buff-white eyebrows; cheek, faintly freckled grey-white; throat, greyish-white; breast, grey; abdomen, striped longitudinally black and white. Bill, black; eyes, dark brown; legs, black.

Distinguished from the White-throated Tree-creeper by the pale eyebrows; the White-browed Tree-creeper is smaller and has much more prominent stripes on the underparts extending to the breast and cheeks, and has chestnut rather than buff "windows" in the wings.

VOICE: A loud "pink pink;" a loud penetrating descending series of whistles.

HABITAT: Open forest where it feeds on bark insects; also feeds on the ground; riverine woodland in the interior.

RANGE: Southern Queensland, New South Wales, Victoria, and eastern South Australia.

Sedentary.

**BLACK TREE-CREEPER**                                       SEE p. 51
*Climacteris picumnus melanota*

15 cm. A darker northern version of the Brown Tree-creeper. **Male:** above, dark brown wing, with pale buff "window;" broad buff-white eyebrows; below, grey brown, streaked black and white on the abdomen. **Female:** small rufous patch on throat.

Although called the Black Tree-creeper, it has a much paler appearance than the Black-tailed Tree-creeper.

VOICE: Loud "weet-weet-weet-wit-wit-wit-wit."

HABITAT: Open forest, where it feeds on tree trunks, branches, and fallen timber.

RANGE: Northern Queensland.

Sedentary.

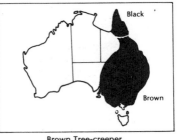

Brown Tree-creeper
Black Tree-creeper

## BLACK-TAILED TREE-CREEPER SEE p. 51
*Climacteris melanura*

15 cm. A dark brown, almost black, tree-creeper with white-streaked throat. **Male:** above, dark brown; wings with pale rufous "window;" below, dark brown; throat and upper breast, streaked black and white. **Female:** similar, but more streaking on breast. Bill, black; eyes, black; legs, black.

The form *melanura* (Kimberleys to north-western Queensland) is much darker on the underparts than the southern, more rufous, form (race *wellsi*), the female of which has a white throat (but its lack of white eyebrows is unlikely to be confused with the White-browed).

VOICE: Loud repetitive piping whistle; a high clear "pink pink pink pink."

HABITAT: Open forest and trees along desert watercourses.

RANGE: Northern and north-western Australia.

Sedentary.

## RUFOUS TREE-CREEPER *Climacteris rufa* SEE p. 51

15 cm. A rufous tree-creeper confined to south-western Australia. Above, rufous-brown; wings with orange-brown "windows;" below, rufous. Bill, black; eyes, black; legs, black.

VOICE: Piercing "peet-peet-peet-peet-peet-peet . . ."

HABITAT: Open forest, where it feeds on tree trunks and branches and among fallen timber on the ground.

RANGE: South-western Australia, north to Geraldton, Western Australia, and east to Eyre Peninsula, South Australia.

Sedentary.

## RED-BROWED TREE-CREEPER *Climacteris erythrops* SEE p. 51

15 cm. A rain-forest tree-creeper with rufous eyebrows and buff patch in wing. **Male:** above, dark reddish-brown; wings with buff

Black-tailed Tree-creeper

Rufous Tree-creeper

"windows;" eyebrows, rufous; throat, white; breast and abdomen, grey, streaked black and white. **Female:** brighter rufous brow and rufous markings on breast. **Immature:** unstreaked below and lacking rufous brow. Bill, black; eyes, dark brown; legs, black.

VOICE: Rapid sibilant chatter.

HABITAT: Rain forest and dense eucalypt forest; feeds on tree trunks.

RANGE: South-eastern Australia.

Sedentary.

## WHITE-BROWED TREE-CREEPER *Climacteris affinis*   SEE p. 51

12·5 cm. A brown tree-creeper with white brow and boldly streaked breast and abdomen. **Male:** above, brown; wing with brownish-orange "window;" prominent white eyebrows and streaking on cheeks; throat, greyish-white; breast and abdomen, boldly streaked black and white. **Female:** buff spot on cheek and buff suffusion above white brow. Bill, black; eyes, brown; legs, black.

Distinguished from Brown Tree-creeper by heavily streaked breast and cheeks; from the White-throated in the east and the Black-tailed (race *wellsi*) in the west by the white eyebrows.

VOICE: Shrill piping, "peet-peet-peet . . ."

HABITAT: Timber, particularly mulga, corkwood, and desert oak.

RANGE: North-western Victoria, western New South Wales, south-western Queensland, northern South Australia, southern Northern Territory, and northern Western Australia, north to Gascoyne River.

Sedentary.

## WHITE-THROATED TREE-CREEPER                     SEE p. 51
*Climacteris leucophaea*

16 cm. A grey-brown tree-creeper with white throat and no pale eyebrows. **Male:** above, dark grey-brown; wing with buff "window;"

Red-browed Tree-creeper

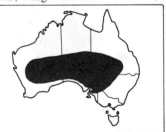
White-browed Tree-creeper

head, dark, with no pale eyebrows; throat, white; breast and abdomen, grey, streaked black and white. **Female:** similar but with pale rufous spot on the cheek. **Immature:** rufous rump. Bill, black; eyes, black; legs, black.

Distinguished from all other tree-creepers in same general range by the lack of pale eyebrows.

VOICE: Loud whistling "peet-peet-peet-peet-peet . . ."

HABITAT: Wet sclerophyll and rain forest.

RANGE: Eastern Australia, from south-eastern Queensland to south-eastern South Australia and New Guinea.

Sedentary.

# FLOWER PECKERS—Dicaeidae

Flower peckers are small, often brilliantly-coloured birds with dumpy bodies, short tails, and rather stout bills. They feed variously on fruit, insects, mistletoe berries, and nectar. Two groups occur in Australia. The sole member of the first, the Mistletoe-bird, is a typical flower pecker, feeding mainly on mistletoe (only the sticky coating of the berries is digested), other berries (very fond of introduced Japanese Pepper), and some insects during nesting season. Flight is rapid and erratic. The pendant nest, of felted plant and animal down, is not unlike a baby's bootie.

Pardalotes are aberrant flower peckers and occur only in Australia. They are dumpy-bodied birds with short tails, thick bills, and strong legs, feeding on insects, particularly scales, among the outer foliage of trees, mainly eucalypts. The flight is direct and undulating and often entices magpies and larger honeyeaters into pursuit. They nest either in a tunnel dug into an earthen bank or sloping ground, or in a hollow in a tree. As some species are quite similar, it is convenient to consider

White-throated Tree-creeper

them in two groups, according to the markings on the crown: striated pardalotes and spotted pardalotes.

**MISTLETOE-BIRD** *Dicaeum hirundinaceum*                SEE p. 53

8·5 cm. A tiny bird with scarlet breast and undertail coverts. **Male:** above, iridescent blue-black; below, breast and undertail coverts, scarlet; abdomen, white, with central longitudinal black stripe and grey flanks. **Female:** above, grey; below, pale grey; undertail coverts, pink. **Immature:** similar to female, but lacking pink undertail coverts, and beak pink instead of dark grey. Bill, black; eyes, red-brown; legs, dark grey.

VOICE: A high-pitched "swee-swit" with the second note higher; often only the second note is given, and in flight a single "wit" is uttered. High-pitched warbling, including mimicry of other species may also be heard (Hutchinson 35).

HABITAT: Closely allied to mistletoe, occurring wherever mistletoe is found, from desert to rain forest.

RANGE: Australia and Aru Islands; absent from Tasmania where mistletoes do not occur.

## SPOTTED PARDALOTES

The four species included here differ from the striated pardalotes in having the crown spotted or freckled instead of streaked. In Tasmania occurs an immature-plumaged form with a freckled crown, the Forty-spotted Pardalote. The Yellow-tailed Pardalote is very similar to the more widely spread Spotted Pardalote, but has a yellow instead of red rump and is confined to mallee. Through the arid interior and tropics occurs the Red-browed Pardalote.

**FORTY-SPOTTED PARDALOTE**                                SEE p. 53
*Pardalotus quadragintus*

10 cm. A greenish pardalote with freckled crown and dully spotted back. Above, greyish-green, freckled lighter; wings, dark, spotted with white; below, grey. Sexes similar. Bill, black; eyes, red-brown; legs, dark grey.

Can be confused with immature Spotted Pardalote, which also occurs in Tasmania, but has a less definitely spotted crown and lacks the brownish-yellow breast. It is more unobtrusive than the Spotted Pardalote.

VOICE: A two-noted call, the first note higher.

HABITAT: Most often observed among outer leaves in eucalypt forest.

RANGE: Tasmania and King Island.

## SPOTTED PARDALOTE *Pardalotus punctatus* SEE p. 53

10 cm. A brilliant spotted pardalote with red rump. **Male:** above, grey and brown, profusely spotted paler; crown, wings, and tail, black, spotted white; eyebrows, white; below, off-white; throat and vent, yellow. **Female:** duller, with buff spots. **Immature:** above, pale brownish spots on back and crown; wings, black, with white spots; eyebrows, white; below, off-white, with brownish-yellow breast. Bill, black; eyes, red-brown; legs, dark grey.

Distinguished from the Yellow-tailed Pardalote by the red instead of yellow rump and the forest, instead of mallee, habitat.

VOICE: A three-noted "sleep baby," the first note higher than the other two.

HABITAT: Eucalypt forest, mostly among outer leaves.

RANGE: Southern Australia, ranging northwards along the forested east coast as far as the Atherton Tableland.

## YELLOW-TAILED PARDALOTE SEE p. 53
*Pardalotus xanthopygus*

10 cm. A brilliant spotted pardalote with a yellow rump. **Male:** similar to the Spotted Pardalote but with a yellow rump; uppertail coverts, red. **Female:** duller, with buff spots. **Immature:** similar to immature Spotted Pardalote. Bill, black; eyes, red-brown; legs, dark grey.

Distinguished from the Spotted Pardalote by the yellow instead of red rump and the mallee habitat.

VOICE: "Sleep baby."

HABITAT: Mallee.

RANGE: Mallee country in New South Wales, Victoria, South Australia, and Western Australia.

Mistletoe-bird                    Forty-spotted Pardalote

**RED-BROWED PARDALOTE**  *Pardalotus rubricatus*        SEE p. 53

10 cm. A pale yellowish pardalote with a spotted crown and red eyebrows. Above, pale yellowish-brown; wings, darker, with each feather edged white or yellow; crown, black, spotted white; brow, red before eyes, pale yellow behind. **Immature:** duller. Bill, black above, pale yellow below; eyes, pale red-brown; legs, grey.

Voice: A five noted "wit-wit-wi-wi-wit."

Habitat: Savannah, particularly along creeks, rivers, and roads, where it nests in the banks.

Range: Arid and northern Australia, south to Wooramel River in Western Australia.

Sedentary.

## STRIATED PARDALOTES

This group of closely related forms is one that has given considerable interest to taxonomists, but should not confuse the field worker if it is remembered that where the various forms come into contact they often interbreed, causing hybrids.

Basically there are five forms: (a) the Yellow-rumped Black-headed Pardalote; (b) the cinnamon-rumped Black-headed Pardalote; (c) the Striated Pardalote; (d) the Yellow-tipped Pardalote; and (e) the Eastern Striated Pardalote, which is a stable hybrid population derived in the past from the Striated and the Yellow-tipped Pardalotes. The Yellow-tipped now breeds only in Tasmania. The Striated Pardalote will hybridise with the Eastern Striated and also with cinnamon-rumped Black-headed Pardalotes in south-eastern Queensland, but apparently not with the yellow-rumped form in north-western Australia. In south-eastern Queensland the Black-headed Pardalote does not interbreed with the Eastern Striated. On Melville Island and the extreme tip of Cape York occurs an orange-rumped form of the Black-headed Pardalote.

Spotted Pardalote

Yellow-tailed Pardalote

In areas where hybridisation is known to occur (see map), observers are best advised to put names only to examples typical of each species.

## YELLOW-TIPPED PARDALOTE *Pardalotus striatus*     SEE p. 53

10 cm. A stripe-crowned pardalote with a yellow spot and a thin white stripe on the wing. Above, back, grey and buff; wing, black, with a yellow spot at the base of a thin white stripe; crown and ear coverts, black, with white streaks; eyebrows, orange-yellow. Below, buff, with yellow throat and darker flanks. Bill, black; eyes, red-brown; legs, grey.

The Yellow-tipped Pardalote breeds in Tasmania and disperses north into south-eastern Australia where it may be confused with the Eastern Striated and Striated Pardalotes. The small yellow spot in the wing, opposed to the red or orange spot of the other two, is the best means of distinguishing it.

VOICE: A three-noted "wit-wi-wit;" a soft trilling warble.

HABITAT: Forest, usually seen among the leaves; nests in hollow trees.

RANGE: Tasmania, south-eastern Australia from south-eastern South Australia to south-eastern Queensland.

Nests in Tasmania, dispersing northwards into south-east Australia.

## EASTERN STRIATED PARDALOTE     SEE p. 53
*Pardalotus ornatus*

10 cm. A stripe-crowned pardalote with a red or orange spot and a thin white stripe in the wing. Above, back, grey and buff; wing, black, with a red or orange spot at the base of a thin white stripe; crown and ear coverts, black, with white streaks; eyebrows, orange-yellow; below, buff, with yellow throat and dark buff flanks. Bill, black; eyes, red-brown; legs, dark grey.

This species is a stabilised hybrid between the Striated and Yellow-tipped Pardalotes. It is distinguished from the Yellow-tipped by the red

Red-browed Pardalote

Yellow-tipped Pardalote

instead of yellow spot in the wing, and from the Striated by the narrow, instead of broad, stripe in the wing. Where the Striated and Eastern Striated overlap in range they may interbreed, and in such areas it is possible to find individuals at all stages of intergradation. It is probably advisable to put names only to typical examples of each species.

VOICE: A three-noted "wit-wi-wit."

HABITAT: Forest, normally among outer leaves; nests in earthen banks or hollow trees.

RANGE: South-eastern Australia.

### STRIATED PARDALOTE *Pardalotus substriatus* SEE p. 53

10 cm. A stripe-crowned pardalote with a red spot and a broad white stripe in the wing. Above, grey and buff; wing, black, with a red spot at the base of a broad white stripe; crown and ear coverts, black, with white streaks; eyebrows, orange-yellow; below, buff, with yellow throat and darker buff flanks. Bill, black; eyes, pale brown; legs, dark grey.

Over much of Australia this is the only stripe-crowned pardalote, but where it overlaps the ranges of the Striated and Eastern Striated Pardalotes in south-eastern Australia, it may be confused with them. From both it may be distinguished by the broad white stripe in the wing, and from the Yellow-tipped by the red, instead of yellow, spot in the wing. In south eastern Queensland it overlaps the range of the Black-headed Pardalote and interbreeds with it. The Black-headed Pardalote lacks the striated crown, but hybrids show varying degrees of striation.

VOICE: A two-noted "wit-witt," often with an echo effect after the first note: "witta-wit."

HABITAT: Basically a bird of drier country, wherever there are trees; usually nests in tree hollows, but it often digs tunnels in eastern Australia.

Eastern Striated Pardalote

Striated Pardalote

RANGE: Australia, except the wetter east and north coasts, where it is replaced by other species.

## BLACK-HEADED PARDALOTE SEE p. 53
*Pardalotus melanocephalus*

10 cm. A black-crowned pardalote. Above, grey and buff; wing, black, with a red spot at the base of a broad white stripe; crown, black; ear coverts, black, streaked white; eyebrows, orange-yellow; below, buff, with yellow throat and darker flanks. Bill, black; eyes, brown; legs, dark grey.

There are three easily recognisable geographic races, distinguishable by rump colour. In Queensland the rump is cinnamon (race *melanocephalus*), in Northern Territory and Western Australia yellow (race *uropygialis*), and on Melville Island and the tip of Cape York orange. Where the races meet (see map), there is intergradation.

The black crown distinguishes the Black-headed Pardalote from the stripe-crowned pardalotes; however, where it overlaps the range of the Striated Pardalote in south-eastern Queensland, interbreeding occurs, and a variable amount of streaking on the crown may be observed.

VOICE: Usually a three-noted call, "wit wi-wit," but also a two-noted call identical to Striated "wit-wit" (Hutchinson 36).

HABITAT: Savannah and forest, usually feeding among outer leaves; nests in earthen banks.

RANGE: Northern and eastern Australia, from south of Brisbane, Queensland, to Broome, Western Australia.

## SUNBIRDS — Nectariniidae

Sunbirds are long-billed birds with iridescent patches of plumage in the male, particularly on the throat. The tongue is tubular, enabling nectar to be drawn from flowers. The sole Australian species is typical

Black-headed Pardalote

of the family. Food consists mainly of spiders and nectar. The nest is a long pendant dome-shaped structure, only rarely attended by the male until the eggs hatch, when he assists the female in feeding the young.

**YELLOW-BREASTED SUNBIRD** *Nectarinia jugularis*    SEE p. 55

12 cm. A long-billed yellow-breasted bird with the throat iridescent black (male) or yellow (female). **Male:** above, olive-yellow; eyebrows, yellow; throat, black, with purple iridescence; breast and abdomen, bright yellow; tail, black, with outer feathers tipped white. **Female:** similar, but with throat yellow. Bill, black; eyes, dark brown; legs, black.

VOICE: Shrill "tsee, tsee, tsee, tss, ss, ss."

HABITAT: Mangroves, rain forest, particularly edges.

RANGE: Tropical coastal Queensland, from Cape York to Gladstone; New Guinea, Andaman Islands through to Bismarck Archipelago. Sedentary.

# SILVEREYES — Zosteropidae

Silvereyes feed on insects, fruit, and nectar and have thin, slightly down-curved, pointed bills with brush-tipped tongues. They take their name from a ring of white feathers round each eye. The nest is cup-shaped and attached by the rim to surrounding twigs. They normally lay two eggs.

**GREY-BREASTED SILVEREYE** *Zosterops lateralis*    SEE p. 55

12 cm. A grey-backed silvereye. Above, olive-green, with back grey; eye-rings, white; throat, yellow, sometimes grey in the centre; breast and abdomen, grey, with buff or brown flanks; undertail coverts, yellow; wings and tail, blackish with greenish-yellow edges. Bill, dark brown, paler at base; eyes, brown; legs, grey brown.

Yellow-breasted Sunbird

Grey-breasted Silvereye

The Tasmanian race (*lateralis*) has brown flanks; it is a non-breeding visitor to eastern Australia from Adelaide, South Australia, to about Caloundra, Queensland. The mainland races have buff flanks.

VOICE: Pleasant warbling song including mimicry; high pitched "chew."

HABITAT: Coastal heath to forest understory.

RANGE: Eastern Australia and Tasmania, Capricorn and Bunker groups (*Z.l. chlorocephala*); islands east to Fiji; recent arrival in New Zealand.

Tasmanian race migrates as far north as Caloundra, Queensland; mainland races probably sedentary or nomadic, depending on locality.

## WESTERN SILVEREYE *Zosterops lateralis gouldi*        SEE p. 55

12 cm. A green-backed silvereye with a grey abdomen. Above, dark olive-green; eye-rings, white; throat and undertail coverts, greenish-yellow; breast and abdomen, grey. Bill, dark brown, paler at base; eyes, light brown; legs, slate-grey.

VOICE: Pleasant warbling song including mimicry; loud "tsee," often tremulous.

HABITAT: Coastal heath to forest undergrowth.

RANGE: South-western Australia and neighbouring islands, from Point Cloates to Kalgoorlie and Eucla.

Sedentary or nomadic.

## YELLOW SILVEREYE *Zosterops lutea*        SEE p. 55

10 cm. A mangrove silvereye with yellow underparts. Above, pale olive-yellow; eye-rings, white; underparts, bright lemon-yellow. Bill, bluish-grey, pale at base; eyes, brown; legs, brownish-grey.

VOICE: Warbling song including mimicry; reedy "tsee."

HABITAT: Mangrove and contiguous vegetation.

Western Silvereye                    Yellow Silvereye

RANGE: Coastal northern Australia, from Shark Bay, Western Australia, to the Edward River, western Cape York Peninsula, with an apparently isolated population on the east coast in the vicinity of Ayr, Queensland.

Sedentary or nomadic.

**PALE SILVEREYE** *Zosterops citrinella chloris*          SEE p. 55

12 cm. A yellowish silvereye with grey breast and abdomen. Above, pale olive-yellow; eye-rings, white; forehead, throat, and undertail coverts, bright lemon-yellow; breast and abdomen, grey, darker on flank and white in the centre. Bill, brown; eyes, brown; legs, greyish-brown.

VOICE: Not recorded.

HABITAT: Island vegetation.

RANGE: Islands off northern Queensland coast; west to Indonesian islands.

Sedentary (?).

## HONEYEATERS — Meliphagidae

Honeyeaters feed on nectar, fruit, and insects, and have down-curved bills and brush-tipped tongues. They are frequently seen feeding on blossoms. They vary considerably in size, from about 10 cm in the Scarlet Honeyeater to nearly 50 cm in the Yellow Wattlebird.

For the purposes of field identification there are a number of well-defined groups: (a) Silvereye-like honeyeaters, superficially similar to silvereyes. (b) Long-billed honeyeaters, the smallest birds of the family. (c) White-gaped honeyeaters, masked honeyeaters, and plumed honey-eaters (genus *Meliphaga*) which may be termed "typical honeyeaters." (d) White-naped honeyeaters, with a distinct black cap and white nape band. (e) Friarbirds, with varying amounts of naked dark skin on the

Pale Silvereye

head. (f) Yellow-winged honeyeaters, with bright flashes of yellow on the edges of the primary and secondary feathers. (g) Fasciated honeyeaters, which build domed nests and which have bars on the breast. (h) Miners, with bare yellow skin about the eyes. (j) Wattlebirds, with pendant wattles of loose skin behind the eyes. As well as these there is one species that fits into none of the above categories, the Striped Honeyeater. *It should be made clear that the groupings included here are for field identification only and do not necessarily indicate taxonomic relationships.*

## SILVEREYE-LIKE HONEYEATERS

In behaviour the Green-backed Honeyeater and the Grey Honeyeater are rather like silvereyes; a further similarity is the ring of pale feathers about each eye. They are largely insect-feeders and seem to depend on nectar less than do other species. The Green-backed Honeyeater inhabits a remarkably small area, at present thought to be less than seventy square miles about the Claudie River in northern Queensland. The Grey Honeyeater, in essence a bird of the mulga, covers an extensive area in the inland, although it is not common. Its nest is like that of a silvereye, but its eggs are quite different.

**GREEN-BACKED HONEYEATER** *Glycichaera fallax*      SEE p. 55

12 cm. A rather silvereye-like honeyeater, with green back and yellowish underparts. Above, light olive-green, darker on head; throat, dull white; breast, greyish-yellow; abdomen, yellow; wings and tail, grey-brown. Bill, pinkish-brown, paler below; eyes, brown; legs, grey.

VOICE: A pleasant twitter uttered in flight or on alighting; chicken-like "peep;" rapid "twit" or twee twee twit twit" (Holland).

HABITAT: Forest canopies.

RANGE: Northern Queensland (Claudie River).

Sedentary.

Green-backed Honeyeater

**GREY HONEYEATER** *Lacustroica whitei* SEE p. 55

12 cm. A rather silvereye-like brownish-grey honeyeater. Above, brownish-grey; wings, brown, with olive-yellow edges; eye-rings, ashy-grey; below, dull white. Bill black; eyes, brown; legs, black.

Behaves rather like a grey silvereye, often accompanying thornbills and warblers in feeding associations. Unlikely to be mistaken for any other honeyeater, but could be confused with White-tailed Warbler, if lack of both white eyebrows and white tail base is overlooked.

VOICE: A silvereye-like giggle; "te-te-dee," or "tsee-you-ee" (second note higher than other two).

HABITAT: Arid scrub, particularly mulga.

RANGE: Central Western Australia to south-western Northern Territory. One record in South Australia.

Sedentary or nomadic.

## LONG-BILLED HONEYEATERS

Grouped here for convenience are the two species of *Lichmera*, three species of *Myzomela*, the similar but unrelated Banded Honeyeater, the Pied Honeyeater, the Black Honeyeater, and the two spinebills. All depend to a considerable degree on nectar for food, although they take insects, and the Pied Honeyeater is partial to berries. There is a nomadic tendency in some species, as they follow flowering eucalypts and melaleucas. In most species the female is less brightly coloured than the male, but the sexes share nesting duties. A characteristic of the spinebills is the loud fluttering made by the wings in flight.

**BROWN HONEYEATER** *Lichmera indistincta* SEE p. 55

Male 15 cm; female 12 cm. A small dull olive-brown honeyeater with a small yellow patch behind the eyes, and, usually, a yellow gape. Above, dull olive-brown; wings and tail, dark grey, edged yellow; head,

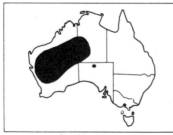
Grey Honeyeater

Brown Honeyeater

greyish-brown, with a black patch below and a yellow patch behind the eyes; gape, yellow at all times in female, and yellow in males except during breeding season (June–October) when it is black; below, yellowish-buff, with darker throat and breast. Bill, black, with yellow or black gape; eyes, reddish-brown; legs, grey.

VOICE: Loud rich "plik;" rich varied song (Hutchinson 37).

HABITAT: Mangrove, forest, woodland, semi-desert, parks, and gardens.

RANGE: Australia, excluding Victoria and south-eastern Western Australia.

Sedentary and nomadic.

## WHITE-STREAKED HONEYEATER SEE p. 55
*Lichmera cockerelli*

14 cm. A small honeyeater with blackish crown, yellow ear-tufts and white-spotted shoulders. Above, mottled dark grey and olive-brown; wings, dark brown, with yellow edges to flight feathers and white spots on the shoulders; head, blackish, with yellow ear-tufts and a yellow line extending the gape; underparts, white, with a grey throat and upper breast, finely streaked white; tail, dark brown, edged yellow. Bill, black; eyes, reddish-brown; legs, dark blue-grey.

VOICE: Similar to Brown Honeyeater.

HABITAT: Melaleuca swamps and riverside vegetation.

RANGE: Cape York, Queensland, south to Shipton's Flat, south of Cooktown on east coast and Archer River on west coast.

Possibly nomadic.

## DUSKY HONEYEATER *Myzomela obscura* SEE p. 57

13–14 cm. A uniform dark grey-brown honeyeater. Above and below, dark grey-brown, rather paler underneath, without any prominent

White-streaked Honeyeater

Dusky Honeyeater

markings. Bill, black; eyes, olive-brown; legs, dark grey, with creamy-yellow soles.

VOICE: Soft "chirp-chirp-chirp;" harsh alarm notes.

HABITAT: Mangrove, swamps, forest, and contiguous vegetation.

RANGE: Northern Australia, from Port Keats, Northern Territory, to Noosa district, Queensland; southern New Guinea, Aru Islands, Moluccas, Misol Island, and Biak Island.

Sedentary and nomadic.

## RED-HEADED HONEYEATER SEE p. 57
*Myzomela erythrocephala*

10–11 cm. A small mangrove honeyeater with red head and rump (male) or crimson-tinged forehead and throat (female). **Male:** above and below, sooty-brown, paler on abdomen; head and rump, crimson. **Female:** above, grey-brown; below, dull white; forehead and throat, tinged crimson. Bill, black; eyes, dark brown; legs, dark grey, with buff-yellow soles.

Female may be confused with female Scarlet Honeyeater which is more olive-brown and lacks crimson-tinged forehead although it often has faint tinge on the chin; however, ranges probably do not overlap.

VOICE: Thin "chirp;" harsh whistle.

HABITAT: Mangrove and contiguous vegetation.

RANGE: Coastal northern Australia, from Derby, Western Australia, to Stewart River, Queensland; Sumba Islands, east to New Guinea.

Sedentary.

## SCARLET HONEYEATER *Myzomela sanguinolenta* SEE p. 57

10–11 cm. A small red-and-black honeyeater (male) or a small olive-brown honeyeater with whitish underparts and no distinctive ear markings (female). **Male:** back, mottled-black and red; wings,

Red-headed Honeyeater

Scarlet Honeyeater

black, with white feather edging; head and breast, crimson; abdomen, pale creamy-grey. **Female:** above, olive-brown; below, whitish, with a tinge of red on the chin. Bill, black; eyes, dark brown; legs, dark grey, with buff-yellow soles.

Female may be confused with other small brown honeyeaters: female Red-headed has crimson-tinged forehead; Brown and Brown-backed have face patterns; female Black has pale eyebrows and is a more dry country bird, although it does enter Scarlet range; immature Rufous-throated Honeyeater has a short bill and yellow edges to wing feathers.

VOICE: High-pitched bell-like "to see-to see."

HABITAT: Mangrove, forest, and woodland.

RANGE: Eastern Australia, from eastern Victoria to northern Queensland; north to Cooktown; Celebes to New Caledonia.

Migratory in south.


## BLACK HONEYEATER *Certhionyx niger* SEE p. 57

12 cm. A small pied honeyeater with a black centre to the white abdomen (male) or a small brown honeyeater with pale eyebrows (female). **Male:** upperparts, tail, throat, breast, and central line on abdomen, black; remainder of underparts, white. Bill, eyes, and legs, black. **Female:** above, buff-brown, with feathers edged pale buff; eyebrows, pale buff; throat and breast, pale grey-brown; abdomen, dull white. Bill, blackish-brown; eyes, dark brown; legs, blackish-brown. Often hovers in front of flowers when feeding.

VOICE: Plaintive "peee."

HABITAT: Arid savannah, occasionally woodland.

RANGE: Drier areas of Australia.

Nomadic, with some north-south migration.

Black Honeyeater

**PIED HONEYEATER** *Certhionyx variegatus*          SEE p. 57

17 cm. A pied honeyeater with white wing and tail patches and a blue spot below eyes (male) or a grey-brown honeyeater with pale edges to wing feathers (female). **Male:** head, throat, and back, black, with small bluish patch below eyes; rump, breast, abdomen, and wing patch, white; tail, white, with black central feather and tip. **Female:** above, grey-brown, with pale edges to wing feathers; throat and breast, pale grey-brown with brown streaks; abdomen, white. Bill, blue-grey; eyes, brown, with blue bare spot below eyes; legs, blue-grey.

Male has a distinctive aerial display, flying straight up, tumbling over and dropping with wings closed and tail fanned.

Female rather similar to female White-winged Triller, but with a longer bill.

VOICE: A plaintive five-noted "tee-titee-tee-tee," usually delivered from top of tree.

HABITAT: Arid savannah.

RANGE: Drier areas of Australia.

Nomadic.


**BANDED HONEYEATER** *Cissomela pectoralis*          SEE p. 57

12 cm. A small long-billed honeyeater with narrow black or dusky breast band. **Adult:** above, black; below, white, with black breast band. **Immature:** above, brown; crown, umber; ear patch, yellow; below, creamy-white, with dusky breast band. Bill, black; eyes, dark brown; legs, black.

In the west, adult male and female are similar in appearance, but in eastern populations the female is said to have a brown back. Possibly specimens obtained were immatures moulting into adult plumage.

VOICE: Tinkling twitter.

HABITAT: Forest and woodland.

Pied Honeyeater

Banded Honeyeater

RANGE: Northern Australia, from Derby, Western Australia, to north Queensland.

Nomadic.

**EASTERN SPINEBILL** *Acanthorhynchus tenuirostris*          SEE p. 57

12–15 cm. A long-billed honeyeater with cinnamon collar and abdomen, black head, and band on side of breast. Above, grey-brown, with cinnamon collar; head, black, continuing as a band to side of breast; throat, white, with reddish-brown patch in centre; abdomen, cinnamon; tail, outer feathers broadly tipped white. **Female:** head, grey. **Immature:** below, brown. Bill, black; eyes, red; legs, blackish-brown.

VOICE: Shrill whistle; soft "chee-chee-chee."

HABITAT: Rain forest to heath.

RANGE: Eastern Australia, from Cairns, Queensland, to Flinders Ranges, South Australia, and Tasmania; Kangaroo Island and Bass Strait islands.

Some regular movement in south-east, elsewhere probably resident.

**WESTERN SPINEBILL** *Acanthorhynchus superciliosus*          SEE p. 57

14 cm. A long-billed honeyeater with cinnamon collar. **Male:** above, dark grey-brown, with broad cinnamon collar extending to throat and breast; head, dark brown, with white eyebrows behind eyes and white moustache; throat and breast, cinnamon, with a white and a black band on lower breast; abdomen, pale buff. **Female:** above, grey-brown, with pale cinnamon collar and faint eyebrows behind eyes; below, pale buff. Bill, black; eyes, red; legs, black.

VOICE: Shrill "kleat-kleat."

HABITAT: Woodland, thickets, and heath, particularly banksias.

RANGE: South-western Australia.

Sedentary.

Eastern Spinebill

Western Spinebill

# TYPICAL HONEYEATERS

The members of the genus *Meliphaga* are often referred to as "typical honeyeaters." In general they are covered in various shades of olive, from pale yellowish-olive to dark olive-brown. The bill length varies from short to medium. Many "typical honeyeaters" are quite similar in appearance and present some difficulties in identification. To aid in field diagnosis, it is perhaps best to consider them in four groups: (a) White-gaped honeyeaters: those with the gape white or pale yellow, usually extending as a line of pale feathers under the eyes, and usually with a patch of pale yellow feathers behind the eyes. In northern Queensland three very similar species occur in the rain forest, the Lewin, Lesser Lewin, and Graceful; they are perhaps best distinguished by their calls, but there are other clues. The Lewin is usually found (in northern Queensland) in upland rain forest only above 500–600 m; the Lesser Lewin has dark eyes, whereas the other two have pale grey-blue eyes; the Graceful is quite slender and has a longer bill. (b) Masked honeyeaters: those with a black mask extending from the beak through the eyes, and usually with a yellow line from the gape joining with a yellow ear patch. Some of them are quite similar in appearance. One species has a yellow mask with black streaks above and below the eyes. (c) Plumed honeyeaters: those without a black mask, and with a yellow or white plume behind the eyes. Some are similar in appearance but range, colour of the face, and the presence or absence of streaks on the breast are aids to identification. (d) Two atypical species occur in northern Queensland, the Tawny-breasted and Macleay's Honeyeater. They have longer bills than other members of the genus.

## WHITE-GAPED HONEYEATER *Meliphaga unicolor* SEE p. 59

18 cm. A dull olive-grey honeyeater with a yellowish-white gape. Above, dull olive-grey with greenish tinge on wings; below, paler. Bill,

White-gaped Honeyeater

black, with yellowish-white gape; eyes, olive-grey; legs, dark grey.

VOICE: Rich, vigorous "ch-ch-ch-choo-wee-a" repeated often (Hutchinson 40).

HABITAT: Mangrove and riverine vegetation.

RANGE: Northern Australia, from Broome, Western Australia, to Townsville, Queensland.

Sedentary. *mt, Spue Qu'land 5/72*

**LEWIN HONEYEATER** *Meliphaga lewinii* SEE p. 59

18 cm. A dark greenish-olive honeyeater with yellowish-white gape, yellow ear patch, and musical staccato call. Above, dark greenish-olive; wings and tail, dark brown, edged lemon-yellow; head, darker with yellowish-white gape extending in a streak below the eyes and a squarish yellow ear-tuft; below, light olive, tinged with yellow. Bill, black, with yellowish-white gape; eyes, pale grey-blue; legs, purplish-grey.

In northern Queensland likely to be confused with Lesser Lewin and Graceful Honeyeaters, best distinguished by calls: Lesser Lewin is paler, has more yellow gape, rounder ear patch, and an "ee-yeu" call; Graceful is smaller, has longer and more slender bill, and the call is a sharp "plik."

VOICE: Loud musical staccato notes.

HABITAT: Rain forest, upland in the north.

RANGE: Eastern Australia, from eastern Victoria to the Atherton Tableland, Queensland.

Sedentary.

**LESSER LEWIN HONEYEATER** *Meliphaga notata* SEE p. 59

16 cm. A greenish-olive honeyeater with yellow gape, yellow ear patch, and "ee-yeu" call. Above, greenish-olive; wings and tail, dark

Lewin Honeyeater

Lesser Lewin Honeyeater

brown, edged lemon-yellow; head, darker, with yellow gape extending in a streak below eyes and a rounded yellow ear-tuft; below, light olive, tinged yellow. Bill, black, with yellow gape; eyes, dark grey-brown; legs, purplish-grey.

In northern Queensland, likely to be confused with Lewin and Graceful Honeyeaters, best distinguished by calls. Lewin is here confined to upland rain forest, above about 600 m, and is darker, has paler gape, more square ear-tuft, and loud staccato call; Graceful is smaller, with more slender and longer bill, and the call is a sharp "plik."

VOICE: Wheezy "ee-yeu, ee-yeu . . . ," descending measured "chew chew chew chew chew."

HABITAT: Rain forest, more particularly lowland.

RANGE: Northern Queensland, from Cape York (Thursday Island) to Cardwell.

Sedentary.

**GRACEFUL HONEYEATER** *Meliphaga gracilis*          SEE p. 59

14 cm. A greenish-olive honeyeater with yellow gape, yellow ear patch and "plik" call. Above, greenish-olive; wings and tail, brown, edged lemon-yellow; head, darker, with yellow gape extending to a streak below the eyes and a rounded yellow ear-tuft; below, light olive, tinged yellow. Bill, black, with yellow gape; eyes, pale blue-grey; legs, purplish-grey.

In northern Queensland likely to be confused with Lewin and Lesser Lewin Honeyeaters. Lewin is much larger, virtually confined in north to upland rain forest, and has a loud staccato call; Lesser Lewin is only slightly bigger, has a shorter stouter bill, and calls "ee-yeu."

VOICE: Sharp "plik;" also a thin reedy whistle.

HABITAT: Rain forest edges and open forest.

Graceful Honeyeater

RANGE: Northern Queensland, from Cape York to Cardwell; Aru Islands; southern and eastern lowlands of New Guinea.
Sedentary.

## WHITE-LINED HONEYEATER *Meliphaga albilineata* SEE p. 59

18 cm. A grey-brown honeyeater with a white streak below the eyes. Above, grey-brown; wings, brown, with feathers edged greenish-yellow; head, darker grey-brown, with white gape extending to a broad streak below eyes; below, dull white, but duskier and mottled on the breast. Bill, brownish-black; eyes, blue-grey; legs, dark grey-brown.

VOICE: Loud, clear "tu-wheer, tu-whit."

HABITAT: Wooded sandstone gorges.

RANGE: Arnhem Land plateau, Northern Territory, from the King River south-west to Oenpelli and possibly the Katherine River Gorge.
Sedentary.

## BRIDLED HONEYEATER *Meliphaga frenata* SEE p. 59

19 cm. A dark plumaged rain forest honeyeater with bi-coloured bill and a yellow "bridle" on the face. Above, blackish-brown, with dull green edges to the wing feathers; crown and face, black, with yellow streak from gape to nape; below, greyish-olive. Bill, black tip and yellow base; eyes, blue-grey; legs, dark blue-grey.

VOICE: "We-are;" "wachita-wachita."

HABITAT: Rain forest on ranges and tableland.

RANGE: North-eastern Queensland, from ranges west of Mackay to Bloomfield River.
Sedentary or locally nomadic. *Portland, Vic 2/72*

## WHITE-EARED HONEYEATER *Meliphaga leucotis* SEE p. 59

20–22 cm. A black-throated honeyeater with white ear patch. Above, dark yellowish-green; crown, dark grey; face, throat, and foreneck,

White-lined Honeyeater

Bridled Honeyeater

black, with white patch behind eyes; breast and abdomen, pale greenish-yellow, with yellow blotches. Bill, black; eyes, grey-brown; legs, dark grey.

There are several other honeyeaters with black throats and white ear patches, but all have yellow edges to wing and tail feathers.

VOICE: Loud "chock;" "cheery-bob."

HABITAT: Open forest, mallee, and heath (sandplain).

RANGE: Southern Australia.

Sedentary or locally nomadic, occasional irruptions.

### YELLOW-THROATED HONEYEATER SEE p. 59
*Meliphaga flavicollis*

20 cm. A yellow-throated Tasmanian honeyeater. Above, dark yellowish-green; crown, dark grey; face and foreneck, black, with white ear-tufts usually tipped yellow; throat, yellow, margined black; breast, grey; abdomen, pale olive, tinged yellow. Bill, black; eyes, brown; legs, dark grey.

VOICE: Loud "tonk tonk," or "chur-ok, chur-ok;" melodious warbling.

HABITAT: Open forest and undergrowth; also suburban gardens.

RANGE: Tasmania and Bass Strait islands.

Sedentary.

### YELLOW-TUFTED HONEYEATER SEE p. 59
*Meliphaga melanops*

18 cm. A masked honeyeater with dark olive-brown back, yellow crown, and underparts. Above, dark yellowish-olive-brown, with greenish-yellow edges to wing and narrowly tipped tail feathers; crown, greenish-yellow; face, broad black mask through the eyes; below, bright yellow, with black chin and streaked on the breast. Bill, black; eyes, brown; legs, dark brown.

White-eared Honeyeater

Yellow-throated Honeyeater

Very similar to larger Helmeted Honeyeater, but is paler, does not have curled feathers on forehead, and has the tail only narrowly tipped white.

VOICE: Harsh "chop-chop;" melodious warble "tooey-t-tooey-t-tooey."

HABITAT: Open forest and woodland with dense undergrowth.

RANGE: South-eastern Australia, from about Caloundra, Queensland, to Naracoorte, South Australia.

Sedentary or locally nomadic.

## HELMETED HONEYEATER *Meliphaga cassidix* SEE p. 59

21 cm. A masked honeyeater with brownish-black back, yellow crown, and underparts. Above, brownish-black, with greenish-yellow edges to wing and broadly tipped tail feathers; crown, greenish-yellow, with feathers curled forward; face, broad black mask through eyes; below, bright yellow with black chin. **Female:** slightly duller in colour. Bill, black; eyes, brown; legs, dark brown.

Very similar to the much more widely-spread Yellow-tufted Honey-eater, but darker on the back, with curled feathers on forehead, and the tail broadly tipped white. Hybrids with the Yellow-tufted Honeyeater have been observed.

VOICE: Harsh "chop-chop;" "tooey-t-tooey."

HABITAT: Creekside vegetation.

RANGE: Restricted, and perhaps dwindling; Woori Yalloch Creek and Cardinia Creek, Dandenong Range, Victoria, and restricted areas in Gippsland, Victoria.

Sedentary.

## YELLOW HONEYEATER *Meliphaga flava* SEE p. 61

17 cm. A plump yellow honeyeater. Above, olive-yellow; wings, brown, with feathers edged yellow; below, bright lemon-yellow. Bill,

Yellow-tufted Honeyeater

Helmeted Honeyeater

brownish-black; eyes, olive-grey; legs, olive-yellow.

VOICE: Loud "cheweer-cheweer-cheweer . . ."

HABITAT: Open forest particularly along rivers; edges of rain forest and mangrove.

RANGE: Coastal northern Queensland, from Norman River district east and south of Yepoon.

Sedentary.

*Langhornes Creek, S A 3/92*

**SINGING HONEYEATER** *Meliphaga virescens*                    SEE p. 61

17–18 cm. A masked honeyeater with faintly streaked buff-white underparts. Above, buff-brown, paler on the rump; wings and tail, brown, with feathers edged sulphur-yellow; face, with broad black streak through eyes, yellow gular stripe, and yellow ear-tuft tipped white; below, buff-white faintly streaked grey-brown. Bill, black; eyes, dark brown; legs, dark grey-brown.

Rather similar to Mangrove Honeyeater, which is restricted to mangroves and has a fasciated yellowish throat; and the Varied Honeyeater, another mangrove species, which has heavily streaked yellow underparts.

VOICE: A loud "prrrp" rather like a postman's whistle; a persistent three-noted drawn call; single whistling "psee."

HABITAT: Wherever there are trees and bushes except rain forest.

RANGE: Australia, except eastern coastal areas, Arnhem Land, and Cape York; Melville Island and Torres Strait islands; New Guinea lowlands.

Sedentary.

**MANGROVE HONEYEATER** *Meliphaga fasciogularis*        SEE p. 61

18 cm. A mangrove-dwelling masked honeyeater with fasciated mustard-yellow throat. Above, dark olive; wings and tail, brown,

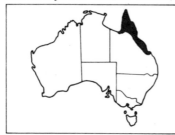

Yellow Honeyeater

Singing Honeyeater

edged sulphur-yellow; face, with broad black streak through eyes, sometimes with a narrow white line above; yellow gular stripe and yellow ear-tuft tipped white; throat and upper breast, mustard-yellow, fasciated with grey-brown; remainder of underparts, buff-white. Bill, black; eyes, dark brown; legs, dark grey-brown.

Rather similar to Singing Honeyeater, which has no throat fasciations, and has an exclusive range; and the Varied Honeyeater, which has yellow, heavily streaked underparts and a more northern range.

VOICE: Rich "wook-a-woow" or "whit-u-we-u."

HABITAT: Mangrove and contiguous vegetation.

RANGE: Coastal eastern Australia, from Rollingstone, Queensland, to Smoky Cape, New South Wales.

Sedentary.

**VARIED HONEYEATER** *Meliphaga versicolor*          SEE p. 61

20 cm. A mangrove-dwelling masked honeyeater with heavily streaked yellow underparts. Above, olive-brown, with rump tinged yellow; wings and tail, brown, with feathers edged yellow; face, with broad black streak through the eyes, yellow gular stripe, and yellow ear-tuft tipped white; below, yellow and heavily streaked with olive-brown. Bill, black; eyes, dark brown; legs, dark grey-brown.

Rather similar to the Mangrove Honeyeater which lacks the heavily streaked yellow underparts and is more southern in range.

VOICE: Loud and varied "ch-ch-weeyo."

HABITAT: Mangrove and contiguous vegetation, including street trees in Cairns, Queensland.

RANGE: Northern Queensland south to about Rollingstone.

Sedentary.

**PURPLE-GAPED HONEYEATER** *Meliphaga cratitia*          SEE p. 61

16 cm. A masked honeyeater with thin purple stripe below the eyes. Above, dark olive-green, with greenish-yellow edges to wing and tail feathers; crown, dark grey, broad black streak through eyes above a purple stripe, below which is a thin yellow stripe; ear coverts, yellow; throat and breast, pale yellowish-olive; abdomen, pale yellow. Bill, black; eyes, dark brown; legs, dark grey-brown.

The purple stripe below the eyes is only visible at close range, and confusion with other species may occur; Singing Honeyeater is much paler; and Grey-headed Honeyeater has a paler grey head and is more yellow in appearance.

VOICE: Harsh, chattering notes.

HABITAT: Mallee and similar eucalypts.

RANGE: Mallee areas of New South Wales, Victoria, South Australia, and Western Australia; Kangaroo Island.

Sedentary or locally nomadic.

## GREY-HEADED HONEYEATER *Meliphaga keartlandi*     SEE p. 61

15 cm. A yellowish-plumaged masked honeyeater with pale grey head. Above, buff-olive, more yellow on rump, and yellow edges to wing and tail feathers; head, grey, with blackish streak through eyes, ending in grey tuft tipped yellow; throat, yellow; breast, buff-yellow, faintly streaked darker; abdomen, whitish. Bill, black; eyes, brown; legs, pale brown.

Rather similar to Purple-gaped Honeyeater, but paler and more yellow in appearance.

VOICE: Loud "kwoyt" or "chee-toyt;" "chip-chip."

HABITAT: Arid savannah, including mulga and mallee, and favouring rocky gullies.

RANGE: Drier areas of Australia.

Sedentary or locally nomadic.      *Portland Vic 8/72*

## YELLOW-FACED HONEYEATER *Meliphaga chrysops*     SEE p. 61

15 cm. An olive-brown honeyeater with a broad yellow facial streak framed above and below with black. Above, dark olive-brown, with greenish-yellow edges to wing and tail feathers; head, olive-brown, with broad yellow streak below and behind the eyes, bordered above and below with black streaks; throat, grey; breast, buff-brown; abdomen, grey, faintly streaked darker. Bill, black; eyes, dark brown; legs, grey-brown.

VOICE: "Chick-up."

HABITAT: Forest and woodland; mangroves.

Mangrove Honeyeater

Varied Honeyeater

RANGE: Eastern Australia.

Migrates from the south leaving April–May, returning August–September.

## FUSCOUS HONEYEATER *Meliphaga fusca*  SEE p. 61

15 cm. A yellow-plumed honeyeater with a small dark smudge around the eyes. Above, dull olive-brown, with wing and tail feathers edged yellow; head, faintly tinged yellow, with a dusky smudge immediately around eyes (which sometimes have a narrow yellow eye-ring), dusky ear-tuft broadly tipped yellow; throat and breast, pale buff-olive; abdomen, whitish. Bill, black (some individuals have a bi-coloured bill, yellow, tipped black, which is apparently retained for life); eyes, dark brown, sometimes with yellow eye-rings; legs, grey-brown.

Northern birds are more yellow and approach the Yellow-tinted Honeyeater in colour.

VOICE: "Arig arig-a-taw-taw."

HABITAT: Open forest.

RANGE: Eastern Australia, from eastern South Australia to Atherton Tableland, Queensland.

Possibly migratory in south, locally nomadic elsewhere.

## YELLOW-TINTED HONEYEATER  SEE p. 61
*Meliphaga flavescens*

15 cm. A yellow-plumed honeyeater with yellowish lores and un-streaked yellowish underparts. Above, buff-olive, with yellow edges to wing and tail feathers; head, yellow, with dusky ear-tuft tipped bright yellow; below, buff-yellow, with obscure ashy streaks on breast. Bill, black (adult), or bi-coloured black with yellow base (immature); eyes, dark brown; legs, grey-brown.

Purple-gaped Honeyeater

Grey-headed Honeyeater

In the north-east (Atherton Tableland), approaches the range of
Fuscous Honeyeater which is much less yellow in general appearance,
but otherwise similar; in the north-west, overlaps the range of Yellow-
fronted Honeyeater which has dusky lores and faintly streaked and
whiter underparts.

VOICE: "Porra-cheu, porra-cheu, chi-porra-cheu, porra-cheu-cheu-
cheu." Contact note a descending "tew tew."

HABITAT: Riverine vegetation and contiguous open forest, particularly *Bauhinea*.

RANGE: Northern Australia, from Broome, Western Australia, to
western slopes of Atherton Tableland, Queensland; Port Moresby area,
New Guinea. Absent from Northern Territory mainland north of the
Roper River. On Melville Island, occurs *M.f. melvillensis*, with underparts deeper yellow with bolder and more extensive streaking.

Sedentary.

## YELLOW-FRONTED HONEYEATER SEE p. 61
*Meliphaga plumula*

15 cm. A yellow-plumed honeyeater with dusky lores and faintly
streaked underparts. Above, olive-brown, with yellow edges to wing
and tail feathers; crown, greenish-yellow; face with dusky lores and a
brownish-black ear-tuft tipped yellow; below, whitish-grey, washed
yellow and faintly streaked grey. Bill, black; eyes, dark brown; legs,
grey-brown.

In northern Australia, may be confused with Yellow-tinted Honeyeater which is more yellow and has yellowish, not dusky, lores, lacks
faint streaking of underparts, except Melville Island race; elsewhere
in its range, may be confused with Yellow-plumed Honeyeater which
has much more heavily streaked underparts and has only a faint black
patch on the ear-tufts.

Yellow-faced Honeyeater                    Fuscous Honeyeater

Voice: "It-wirt, wirt, wirt, wirt."
Habitat: Dry woodland and riverine vegetation.
Range: Drier areas of Australia.
Sedentary.

## WHITE-PLUMED HONEYEATER SEE p. 61
*Meliphaga penicillata*

15 cm. A white-plumed honeyeater. Above, greenish or yellowish-olive, with yellow edges to wing and tail feathers; face, yellow, small dusky ear-tuft broadly tipped white; below, buff-yellow. Bill, black; eyes, brown; legs, grey-brown.

South-eastern birds are tinted green becoming progressively more yellow further west and north. Similar species (Yellow-plumed, Yellow-fronted, and Yellow-tinted) have yellow, instead of white, ear plumes.

Voice: Whistling "chee-uck-oo-wee" (Hutchinson 39).
Habitat: Woodland, particularly along rivers; in central Australia predominantly a bird of river red gums (*E. camaldulensis*).
Range: Eastern and central Australia.
Sedentary.       *Pinaroo, S.A. 10/72*

## YELLOW-PLUMED HONEYEATER *Meliphaga ornata* SEE p. 61

15 cm. A yellow-plumed Honeyeater with streaked underparts. Above, dark olive-brown, with greenish-yellow rump and greenish-yellow edges to wing and tail feathers; face and crown, greenish-yellow, with dusky lores and bright yellow ear-tuft; below, buff-white, streaked dark olive-brown. Bill, black; eyes, dark brown; legs, grey-brown.

The boldly streaked underparts and virtual lack of black in the ear-tuft distinguish it from the similar Yellow-fronted Honeyeater.

Voice: Loud and rather harsh; loud alarm call "see-see-see-see . . ."
Habitat: Woodland, particularly mallee.

Yellow-tinted Honeyeater

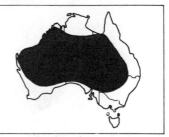

Yellow-fronted Honeyeater

RANGE: Eastern Australia.
Sedentary.

## TAWNY-BREASTED HONEYEATER SEE p. 59
*Meliphaga flaviventer*

20 cm. A brownish honeyeater with speckled nape, white and yellow streaks on face, and a long, rather heavy, bill. Above, olive-brown, speckled pale grey on the nape, and wing feathers edged buff; face pattern, two streaks below the eyes, the upper white separated by black from the lower yellow streak; ear coverts, dark grey; throat, pale grey-brown; breast and abdomen, olive-buff. Bill, black; eyes, dark brown; legs, dark grey.

VOICE: Not recorded.

HABITAT: Mangrove and forest.

RANGE: Cape York south to Archer and Claudie rivers; New Guinea lowlands and neighbouring islands.
Sedentary.

## MACLEAY'S HONEYEATER *Meliphaga macleayana* SEE p. 59

18 cm. A streaked, black-crowned honeyeater with long bill and bare yellow skin below the eyes. Above, blackish-brown, streaked white and buff-yellow; crown, black, with nape speckled white; face, light chestnut, with yellow bare skin below eyes and white gape; ear-tufts, bright yellow; throat, pale olive-grey; breast, darker olive-grey, streaked white and olive-brown; abdomen, blotched olive-brown and black. Bill, black with white gape; eyes, dark brown; legs, dark blue-grey.

VOICE: "Chewit-che-wew" or "tweet your juice."

HABITAT: Rain forest.

RANGE: North-eastern Queensland, from Cardwell to Cooktown.
Sedentary.

White-plumed Honeyeater

Yellow-plumed Honeyeater

## WHITE-NAPED HONEYEATERS

Included in this group are the seven members of the genus *Melithreptus* and the much larger Blue-faced Honeyeater. All have black heads and all except the Black-headed Honeyeater have a white band around the back of the head. Over the eye is a band of bare skin, considerably enlarged and in the Blue-faced Honeyeater covering the whole face. The nest is suspended among outer foliage, usually in eucalypts, and is often attended by a number of birds, as many as seven in the Golden-backed Honeyeater. The Blue-faced Honeyeater often uses the large stick nests of babblers.

*Langhorne's Creek, S.A. 3/72*

## BROWN-HEADED HONEYEATER
*Melithreptus brevirostris* *Kangaroo I. S.A.* SEE p. 63

*10/72*

13 cm. A white-naped honeyeater with brownish head and buff-olive underparts. Above, olive-yellow, more green on rump with yellow edges to tail feathers; crown, grey-brown, with buff-white crescent on nape and greenish-blue or dull yellow skin over eyes; below, buff-olive. Bill, blackish-brown; eyes, brown; legs, pinkish-brown.

Western birds (race *leucogenys*) are darker on the head. The immatures of other white-naped honeyeaters have brown heads and may be confused with the Brown-headed, but all have white underparts and usually yellow gapes.

VOICE: "Chick" in flight; musical warble.

HABITAT: Open forest to arid scrub.

RANGE: Southern Australia, from southern Queensland to Victoria and South Australia; King Island, Kangaroo Island; south-western Australia.

Nomadic.

Tawny-breasted Honeyeater

Macleay's Honeyeater

**WHITE-NAPED HONEYEATER** *Melithreptus lunatus* SEE p. 63

14 cm. A white-naped honeyeater, with the black crown reaching to the chin, and the white crescent not reaching the eyes. Above, olive-green; head, black, extending to lower mandible and chin, with white crescent not reaching eyes, and reddish-orange (eastern) or pale green (western) skin above the eyes; below, white. Bill, black; eyes, brown; legs, dark grey. **Immature:** greyer above, with brown head and white or yellow skin over the eyes; the white crescent is often confined to a spot on the side of the head; gape, yellow.

May be confused with White-throated Honeyeater which has the black head extending only to the gape and not to the chin, and has the white crescent extending to the eyes; the skin above the eyes is bluish-white, and the back is yellower in colour. Immatures are harder to distinguish.

Immature Brown-headed Honeyeaters differ in the buff-olive underparts. Black-chinned Honeyeater has buff-olive underparts and sooty centre of throat, and pale blue skin above the eyes.

VOICE: Harsh "sherp-sherp;" single "tsip."

HABITAT: Open forest and woodland.

RANGE: Eastern Australia, from north Queensland to South Australia, Kangaroo Island, and Bass Strait islands; south-western Australia from Moora to Hopetoun.

Migration in south-east.


**WHITE-THROATED HONEYEATER** SEE p. 63
*Melithreptus albogularis*

14 cm. A white-naped honeyeater with black crown reaching to gape, and the white crescent reaching the eyes. Above, olive-yellow, more yellow on rump; head, black, extending to gape with white crescent

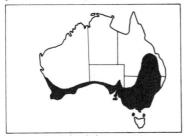

Brown-headed Honeyeater

White-naped Honeyeater

reaching eyes, and bluish-white skin above the eyes; below, white. Bill, black; eyes, reddish-brown; legs, purplish-brown.

May be confused with White-naped Honeyeater, which has the black head extending to the chin and reddish-orange skin above the eyes but its white crescent does not reach to eyes. Immatures are harder to distinguish.

Golden-backed and Black-chinned Honeyeaters have dusky chins.

VOICE: "Tserp-tserp;" loud alarm call "si-si-si-si . . ."

HABITAT: Open forest and woodland.

RANGE: Eastern and northern Australia, from Nambucca Heads, New South Wales, to Broome, Western Australia; southern New Guinea.

Migratory in south.

## BLACK-CHINNED HONEYEATER SEE p. 63
*Melithreptus gularis*

16 cm. A white-naped honeyeater with black chin and black crown extending to gape, the white crescent reaching the eyes, and pale buff-olive underparts. Above, olive-yellow, more yellow on the rump; head, black, extending to gape, with buff-white crescent reaching the eyes, and pale blue skin above the eyes; chin, black, and centre of throat grey; breast and abdomen, pale buff-olive; cheeks, white. Bill, black; eyes, brown; legs, yellowish-brown.

The black chin, dusky throat, and the pale buff-olive underparts distinguish it from all mainland species except the Golden-backed Honeyeater, which has a bright golden-yellow back and is exclusive in range.

VOICE: Rich "ch-ch-ch-cheer."

HABITAT: Open forest and woodland.

RANGE: Extra-tropical eastern Australia and South Australia.

Sedentary.

White-throated Honeyeater

Black-chinned Honeyeater

## GOLDEN-BACKED HONEYEATER SEE p. 63
*Melithreptus laetior*

15 cm. A white-naped honeyeater with bright golden-yellow back. Above, bright golden-yellow; head, black, extending to the gape, with white crescent reaching the eyes and yellowish-green skin above the eyes; chin, black, and centre of throat grey; breast and abdomen, pale greyish-buff; cheeks, white. Bill, black; eyes, dark brown; legs, yellowish-brown. **Immature:** brown head with broad white crescent and dark brown ear coverts; eyes surrounded by purplish skin and beak yellow; back, yellowish-brown.

VOICE: Rich warbling "prrrp, prrrp, prrrp . . ." (Hutchinson 41).

HABITAT: Open woodland and wooded margins of desert waterways.

RANGE: Northern Australia from Exmouth Gulf, Western Australia, to Gulf of Carpentaria, Queensland.

Sedentary and nomadic.

## STRONG-BILLED HONEYEATER SEE p. 63
*Melithreptus validirostris*

15 cm. The only Tasmanian white-naped honeyeater. Above, brownish-olive, rather yellower on the rump; head, black, extending to gape with white crescent reaching the eyes and pale blue skin above the eyes; chin, black; centre of throat, grey; breast and abdomen, pinkish-grey; cheeks, white. Bill, black; eyes, reddish-brown; legs, dull orange.

VOICE: Loud "cheep."

HABITAT: Open forest and woodland; often feeds on tree trunks.

RANGE: Tasmania and Bass Strait islands.

Sedentary.

## BLACK-HEADED HONEYEATER *Melithreptus affinis* SEE p. 63

13 cm. A black-headed Tasmanian honeyeater, rather like a White-naped Honeyeater without the white nape. Above, brownish-olive;

Golden-backed Honeyeater

Strong-billed Honeyeater
Black-headed Honeyeater

head and chin, black; below, off-white, with black patch at side of breast. Bill, black; eyes, brown; legs, pinkish-brown.

VOICE: Sharp whistle.

HABITAT: Open forest, suburban parks, and gardens.

RANGE: Tasmania and Bass Strait islands.

Sedentary.

## BLUE-FACED HONEYEATER *Entomyzon cyanotis* SEE p. 63

25–30 cm. A giant white-naped honeyeater, with blue or yellow bare skin around the eyes and olive-yellow back. Above, olive-yellow; head, black, with white crescent on nape and blue (adult), yellow or green (immature) bare skin around the eyes; centre of throat and breast, grey; remainder of underparts, white. Bill, black; eyes, pale yellow; legs, dark green. Sub-species (*E.c. albipennis*), Wyndham to extreme north-western Queensland, has conspicuous white circle on wing, absent in *E.c. cyanotis* of Norman River eastwards.

VOICE: Harsh "kyowt" (Hutchinson 42).

HABITAT: Open forest.

RANGE: Eastern and northern Australia, from Victoria and Murray Valley to Kimberley, Western Australia; southern New Guinea.

Sedentary, locally nomadic, and some evidence of migration in the south.

## STRIPED HONEYEATERS

The Striped Honeyeater is unlike other honeyeaters in many ways although its call and nest are not unlike those of some of the white-naped honeyeaters. It has a small, uncurved bill and does not often take nectar; much of its food consists of leaf-rolling caterpillars and similar destructive insects.

Blue-faced Honeyeater

**STRIPED HONEYEATER**  *Plectorhyncha lanceolata*      SEE p. 63

20–23 cm. A streaked honeyeater. Above, brownish-grey, streaked black, white, and grey; crown and face, streaked black-grey and white; below, dull white, more buff on abdomen, thinly streaked brown. Bill, bluish-black; eyes, brown; legs, bluish-black.

VOICE: A rich cheerful "cher-cher-cherry-cherry."

HABITAT: Woodland, forest, and occasionally mangrove.

RANGE: Eastern Australia and South Australia, more common inland.

Sedentary and nomadic.

## FRIAR-BIRDS

Six species of friar-bird inhabit eastern and northern Australia. They are easily distinguished from other large honeyeaters by the bare dark grey or black skin on the head and, in all but one, the knob at the base of the bill. In the northern areas of the Northern Territory occur three knob-billed species which may cause confusion. The Silver-crowned Friar-bird is very like the Noisy Friar-bird of the east coast, but with a strip of silver feathers covering the crown; the knob on the bill is abrupt. The other two species have less obvious knobs on the bill, and may be distinguished by the colour of the facial skin and the habitat.

**LITTLE FRIAR-BIRD**  *Philemon citreogularis*      SEE p. 67

25–28 cm. The only friar-bird lacking a knob on the forehead in the adult. Above, dull grey-brown, with whitish fringe on nape and sides of neck; facial skin blue-black; underparts, pale grey-brown, paler on the abdomen. Bill, black; eyes, brown; legs, bluish-black. **Immature:** yellow on side of neck and spots on breast.

VOICE: Raucous "ar-coo;" "rackety crookshank."

HABITAT: Open forest and woodland.

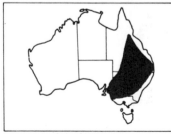

Striped Honeyeater

Little Friar-bird

RANGE: Northern and eastern Australia and Murray Valley in South Australia; southern New Guinea.

Some seasonal migration in the south; resident or nomadic farther north.

## MELVILLE ISLAND FRIAR-BIRD *Philemon gordoni*     SEE p. 67

30–32·5 cm. A large friar-bird found mainly in mangroves in coastal Northern Territory. Above, dull grey-brown, with frilled whitish nape; facial skin, plumbeous-slate; knob on culmen, gently sloping; below, pale grey-brown, paler on abdomen; throat, off-white. Bill, black; eyes, crimson; legs, slate.

Often recorded in small flocks, mainly in mangroves, but also in monsoon forest and adjacent suburban gardens. Distinguished from Sandstone Friar-bird mainly by habitat, slightly smaller size, and plumbeous-slate, not black, facial skin. Distinguished from adult Silver-crowned by large size and less pronounced knob on culmen.

VOICE: "Watch out, watch out" (first syllable stressed).

RANGE: Melville Island and coastal Northern Territory.

Occasionally wanders from normal mangrove and monsoon forest habitats into adjacent open forest.

## SANDSTONE FRIAR-BIRD *Philemon buceroides*     SEE p. 67

34–35·5 cm. A very large friar-bird, found in the sandstone country of Arnhem Land. Above, dull grey-brown, with frilled whitish nape; facial skin, black above gape, dark grey below; knob on culmen, gently sloping and not conspicuous in field; below, pale grey-brown, paler on abdomen; throat, silvery-white. Bill, black; eyes, crimson; legs, dark grey-brown.

As far as is known, inhabits the sandstone gorges of Arnhem Land; recorded in ones, twos, and threes, and may differ in this respect from

Melville Island Friar-bird

Sandstone Friar-bird

the Melville Island Friar-bird, which is usually gregarious. The Melville Island Friar-bird may be distinguished further by its plumbeous-slate facial skin, its preference for mangroves, and its slightly smaller size.

The Sandstone and Melville Island Friar-birds differ from the adult Silver-crowned in their much larger size and less pronounced knob on the culmen.

VOICE: A metallic "Chilanc chilanc" (first syllable stressed and slightly higher than second); a monotonous "chank chank chank;" "wack-a-where" with upward inflection on first syllable and downward on third.

HABITAT: Open forest to dense thickets, sandstone country.

RANGE: Arnhem Land, Lesser Sundas.

## HELMETED (NEW GUINEA) FRIAR-BIRD                SEE p. 67
*Philemon novaeguineae*

35 cm. A large silver-crowned friar-bird with a large knob on forehead and a frilled whitish nape. Above, dull grey-brown, with a frilled whitish nape; crown, silver; facial skin, leaden-grey, and large gently-sloping knob on forehead; below, pale grey-brown, paler on abdomen. Bill, black; eyes, reddish-brown; legs, bluish-black.

Distinguished from Silver-crowned Friar-bird by much larger size, larger but less conspicuous knob on forehead, and frilled whitish nape.

VOICE: Harsh "poor devil, poor devil" and "sergeant-major."

HABITAT: Forest and woodland.

RANGE: North-eastern Queensland south to Mackay; New Guinea and adjacent islands; Aru Islands.

Sedentary or locally nomadic.

## SILVER-CROWNED FRIAR-BIRD *Philemon argenticeps*    SEE p. 67

28–29·5 cm. A medium-sized friar-bird with pronounced knob on culmen in adult and smooth, not frilled, nape. Above, dull grey-brown,

Helmeted Friar-bird

Silver-crowned Friar-bird

smooth whitish nape; crown, silver; facial skin, leaden-grey; knob on culmen terminating abruptly and thus very conspicuous; below, pale grey-brown, paler on abdomen. Bill, black; eyes, crimson; legs, bluish-black or dark grey.

The smooth nape, smaller size, and more conspicuous knob on culmen distinguish this species from the Sandstone, Melville Island, and Helmeted Friar-birds.

VOICE: Raucous and parrot-like; at least twelve distinct phrases.

HABITAT: Open forest, monsoon forest, riverine woodland, mangroves.

RANGE: Across northern Australia from the Kimberleys to Townsville.

Nomadic.

## NOISY FRIAR-BIRD *Philemon corniculatus*      SEE p. 67

31–36 cm. A large bare-headed friar-bird. Above, dull grey-brown; head, bare, and brownish-black, with large knob on forehead; below, pale grey-brown, with lanceolate dark-centred hackles on the throat and breast. Bill, black; eyes, red; legs, bluish-black.

VOICE: Loud raucous "four o'clock;" "chok-chok."

HABITAT: Open forest and woodland.

RANGE: Eastern Australia, from Lakes Entrance, Victoria, and Murray Valley, to Cape York; southern New Guinea.

Regular movements in southern range; elsewhere nomadic.

# YELLOW-WINGED HONEYEATERS

While many honeyeaters have yellowish edges to the wing feathers, there are some in which the yellow is so obvious that it becomes a feature of the bird. Those grouped here as "yellow-winged honeyeaters"

Noisy Friar-bird

are not necessarily closely allied, but have this one characteristic in common. An exception is the Tawny-crowned Honeyeater, which has no yellow on the wing, but must be included here because of its close relationship with other yellow-winged species.

## CRESCENT HONEYEATER *Phylidonyris pyrrhoptera*     SEE p. 65

15 cm. A yellow-winged honeyeater with a broad black band on side of breast (indistinct in female). **Male:** above, sooty-black, with bright yellow edges to wing and tail feathers; head, sooty-black, with white eyebrows; throat, white, streaked brown; remainder of underparts, white, with broad black band on side of breast; tail, tipped white on outer feathers. **Female:** above, dusky-brown; indistinct breast band; yellow in wings, and tail rather duller. Bill, black; eyes, red; legs, dark grey.

VOICE: Loud "egypt."

HABITAT: Forest with bushy undergrowth.

RANGE: South-eastern Australia, from Newcastle, New South Wales, to South Australia, Bass Strait islands, and Tasmania.

Some evidence of migration.

## NEW HOLLAND HONEYEATER     SEE p. 65
*Phylidonyris novaehollandiae*

18 cm. A yellow-winged, boldly streaked honeyeater with white eyes and small white ear patch. Above, brownish-black, streaked white and brown with wing and tail feathers edged bright yellow; head, and throat, black, with white eyebrows, moustache, and ear patch, and scattered white hairs on throat; breast and abdomen, streaked black and white; tail, tipped white on outer feathers. Bill, black; eyes, white; legs, black.

Rather similar to the White-cheeked Honeyeater, but with white eyes, small ear patch, white moustache, and white tip on tail.

VOICE: Weak whistle; shrill chatter; loud "tchlik."

Crescent Honeyeater

New Holland Honeyeater

HABITAT: Woodland, heath, banksia and dryandra scrub, and swampy vegetation.

RANGE: South-eastern Australia, from south-eastern Queensland to South Australia; Kangaroo Island; Bass Strait islands, and Tasmania; and south-western Australia.

Sedentary and nomadic.

## WHITE-CHEEKED HONEYEATER *Phylidonyris niger* SEE p. 65

18 cm. A yellow-winged honeyeater with dark eyes and large white ear patch. Above, brownish-black, streaked white and brown with wing and tail feathers edged bright yellow; head and throat, black, with white eyebrows and large ear patch; breast and abdomen, streaked black and white; tail, not tipped white. Bill, black; eyes, dark brown; legs, black.

Rather similar to the New Holland Honeyeater but with dark eyes, large white ear patch, and no white tipping to the tail.

VOICE: "Chip-choo-chippy-choo;" "twee-ee-twee-ee;" rapid "tee-tee-tee . . . ;" harsh "chak a chak."

HABITAT: Woodland, heath, banksia and dryandra thickets, but rather more open and more swampy country than that for the New Holland, although both often occur together.

RANGE: Eastern Queensland and New South Wales; south-western Australia.

Sedentary and nomadic. *Kangaroo, S.A., 10/72*

## WHITE-FRONTED HONEYEATER SEE p. 65
*Phylidonyris albifrons*

18 cm. A yellow-winged honeyeater with white forehead and face; the dry country representative of the yellow-winged honeyeaters. Above, brownish-black, streaked grey and brown, with wing and tail

White-cheeked Honeyeater

White-fronted Honeyeater

feathers edged dull yellow; head and throat, black, with white forehead (except in the centre), face, moustache, and ear patch; crown, scalloped white; breast, black; abdomen, white, streaked black. Bill, black; eyes, brown, with small red wattle behind; legs, black.

In western birds, the dark breast is more sharply demarcated from the white abdomen than in eastern birds.

VOICE: Musical "tsooee;" metallic nasal "tneep;" harsh "truk;" mimics other species.

HABITAT: Arid woodland, heath, and scrub, favouring Eremophila bushes.

RANGE: Drier areas of Australia; once Kangaroo Island.

Nomadic.

## TAWNY-CROWNED HONEYEATER    SEE p. 65
*Gliciphila melanops*

15–16 cm: A tawny-crowned honeyeater with black stripe through eyes to side of breast. Above, grey-brown, streaked blackish-brown; forehead, reddish-cinnamon; eyebrows, white; blackish band through eyes to side of breast; below, dull white, with reddish-cinnamon underwing. Bill, black; eyes, brown; legs, grey.

VOICE: Musical flute-like ventriloquial; nasal, sneezing "kneep."

HABITAT: Heaths and mallee.

RANGE: Southern Australia, Tasmania, Bass Strait islands, and Kangaroo Island.

Sedentary or locally nomadic; some evidence of migration.

## RUFOUS-BANDED HONEYEATER                              SEE p. 65
*Conopophila albogularis*

12 cm. A small yellow-winged honeyeater with white throat and reddish-brown breast band. Above, dark fawn, with wing and tail feathers edged bright yellow; head, grey; below, white, with upper

Tawny-crowned Honeyeater

Rufous-banded Honeyeater

breast reddish-brown. Bill, dark grey; eyes, reddish-brown; legs, bluish-grey.

VOICE: "Swee-whit-chi-ti;" hard "zivee."

HABITAT: Mangrove and swamp vegetation.

RANGE: Northern Australia, as far east as Townsville, Queensland; New Guinea and neighbouring islands.

Nomadic.

## RUFOUS-THROATED HONEYEATER SEE p. 65
*Conopophila rufogularis*

12 cm. A small yellow-winged honeyeater with reddish-brown throat. Above, fawn, with wing and tail feathers edged bright yellow; head, grey, with reddish-brown throat; below, white. Bill, dark grey; eyes, olive-grey; legs, dark grey.

VOICE: Rasping chatter.

HABITAT: Forest and woodland, especially riverine vegetation.

RANGE: Northern Australia, from Broome, Western Australia, to Bundaberg, Queensland.

Sedentary in coastal areas and along rivers, but migratory in open woodlands, moving out after wet season.

## PAINTED HONEYEATER *Conopophila picta* SEE p. 65

15 cm. A yellow-winged honeyeater, black above and white below, with pink bill. Above, black, with wing and tail feathers edged bright yellow; head, black, with white ear patch; below, white, with fine streaks on breast and flanks. Bill, pink, tipped brown; eyes, light brown; legs, black. **Female:** rather more grey above and lacking streaks on underparts.

VOICE: "George-ee;" "kow-kow-kow."

HABITAT: Open forest and woodland, favouring mistletoe.

Rufous-throated Honeyeater

Painted Honeyeater

RANGE: Eastern Australia, from Leichhardt River, Queensland, to northern Victoria; an early record from McArthur River Station, Northern Territory.

Nomadic, perhaps migratory (summer visitor) in south.

### REGENT HONEYEATER *Zanthomiza phrygia*          SEE p. 65

22 cm. A striking honeyeater, scalloped black and yellow. Above and below, scalloped black and yellow; head, black, with bare warty skin around eyes, yellow. Bill, black; eyes, reddish-brown; legs, dark grey-brown.

VOICE: Bell-like "tink, tink-tink."

HABITAT: Open forest and woodland.

RANGE: South-eastern Australia, from southern Queensland to South Australia; Kangaroo Island.

Nomadic.

## FASCIATED HONEYEATERS

Two species are characterised by bars on the breast; faint in one, the Brown-backed; and bold in the other, the Bar-breasted. Both are often associated with flowering melaleucas. They differ from all other Australian honeyeaters in the construction of the nest, which is built with a dome. All other species build cup-shaped nests.

### BAR-BREASTED HONEYEATER          SEE p. 55
*Ramsayornis fasciatus*

12 cm. A small honeyeater with a boldly barred breast. Above, mottled dark grey-brown, scalloped white on the crown; below, white, with barred breast and streaked flank; underwing, pale cinnamon. Bill, dark brown; eyes, reddish-brown; legs, dull red. **Immature:** similar, but with tear drop markings on the breast.

Regent Honeyeater

Bar-breasted Honeyeater

VOICE: Sharp high-pitched call.

HABITAT: Melaleuca swamps and river margins.

RANGE: Northern Australia, from Derby, Western Australia, to Mackay, Queensland.

Nomadic, following melaleuca flowering.

## BROWN-BACKED HONEYEATER SEE p. 55
*Ramsayornis modestus*

11 cm. A small dull-brown honeyeater with a faintly barred breast. Above, dull mottled-brown; head, darker, with white streak below eyes; below, dull white, with faintly barred breast and faintly streaked flank; underwing, pale cinnamon. Bill, brown; eyes, reddish-brown; legs, pinkish-brown.

VOICE: Rapid "mick;" chattering "shee-shee-shee."

HABITAT: Mangrove and melaleuca swamps and contiguous vegetation.

RANGE: North-eastern Queensland south to Ayr; New Guinea and satellite islands.

Apparently migratory in southern range.

## MINERS

Four species of miners occur in Australia. The origin of the name is obscure, but probably refers to the bare yellow or orange skin on the face, a feature of the unrelated mynas of India and South-east Asia. The Bell Miner is well known because of its tinkling, bell-like call, and the Noisy Miner because it often visits suburban gardens, where it makes its presence known by loud calls and aggressive behaviour towards cats, dogs, and other honeyeaters. Like the other miners it associates in small groups and exhibits interesting social behaviour. The two other species are similar but may be distinguished either by

Brown-backed Honeyeater

facial pattern and distribution in the Black-eared (or Dusky) Miner, or by rump colour in the White-rumped Miner.

**BELL MINER** *Manorina melanophrys*                          SEE p. 67

18 cm. A yellow-green miner with a bell-like call. Above, dark yellow-green; head, darker, particularly on forehead, with yellow lores and orange-red bare skin below and behind eyes; below, light greenish-yellow. Bill, yellow; eyes, dark brown; legs, yellow.

VOICE: Bell-like "tink-tink."

HABITAT: Dry sclerophyll forest.

RANGE: South-eastern Australia, from Brisbane, Queensland, to Melbourne, Victoria; an old record from Casterton, Victoria.

Sedentary. *Langhornes Creek S.A. - 3/72*

**NOISY MINER** *Manorina melanocephala*                       SEE p. 67

26–28 cm. A black-crowned miner with white forehead and grey-brown rump. Above, grey-brown, with rump same colour as back, and with wing and tail feathers edged greenish-yellow; crown, black; forehead and lores, white; ear patch, black, with bare yellow skin behind eyes; below, pale grey, lightly barred brown on breast and paler on abdomen. Bill, yellow; eyes, brown; legs, yellow.

Distinguished from the White-rumped Miner by the uniform rump; and from the Black-eared Miner by the black crown and white forehead.

VOICE: Variable with as many as twenty different meaningful sounds.

HABITAT: Woodland, suburban gardens.

RANGE: Eastern Australia, South Australia, and Tasmania. Sedentary.

**YELLOW-THROATED MINER** *Manorina flavigula*                 SEE p. 67

26–28 cm. A grey-crowned miner with yellow forehead and white rump (grey-white in south-west). Above, grey-brown; rump, white,

Bell Miner

Noisy Miner

with wing and tail feathers edged yellow; crown, grey; forehead, olive-yellow; lores and ear patch, black, with bare yellow skin behind eyes; throat and breast, grey, with darker bars and a yellow patch on side of neck; abdomen, white. Bill, yellow; eyes, brown; legs, yellow.

Distinguished from other miners by the pale rump. Hybridisation with Noisy Miner has been observed.

VOICE: Variable.

HABITAT: Dry woodland.

RANGE: Australia, west of the Dividing Range.

### BLACK-EARED (DUSKY) MINER *Manorina melanotis* SEE p. 67

26–28 cm. A grey-crowned miner with faintly yellow forehead and grey-brown rump. Above, dark grey-brown, with rump same colour as back and wings and tail feathers edged yellow; crown, grey; forehead, tinged yellow; lores and ear patch, black, with bare yellow skin behind eyes; throat and breast, grey; abdomen, white. Bill, yellow; eyes, brown; legs, yellow.

VOICE: Variable.

HABITAT: Mallee.

RANGE: Mallee areas surrounding the junction of the borders of South Australia, Victoria, and New South Wales.

Nomadic within a small area.

## WATTLE-BIRDS

Wattle-birds are large honeyeaters. They feed mostly on insects and nectar, and are partial to large flowers such as banksia, introduced coral tree, and dryandra. Obvious both because of their large size and their loud calls, they also attract attention when they chase small birds such as pardalotes high into the air. Of the four species of wattle-birds grouped here only two, the Yellow and the Red Wattle-birds, have

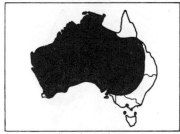

Yellow-throated Miner

Black-eared Miner

visible wattles, flaps of coloured skin that dangle like earrings. Of the others, the Little Wattle-bird occurs in open forest and heaths where there are banksias and similar plants with large, nectar-rich flowers. The Spiny-cheeked Honeyeater lives generally in more arid country; it is easily distinguished by the unique pink and black bill. Apart from insects and nectar it eats berries and fruit, particularly from the introduced pepper-tree (*Schinus molle*), nestlings of other birds, and small lizards.

## SPINY-CHEEKED HONEYEATER SEE p. 67
*Anthochaera rufogularis*   *Pinaroo, SA - 10/72*

24–26 cm. A streaked honeyeater with a bi-coloured bill. Above, streaked greyish-olive and brownish-black with a pale rump; head, greyer, with black band through eyes and another from base of bill enclosing a silvery ear patch; bare skin below eyes, pink; throat and upper breast, pale cinnamon; lower breast and abdomen, pale yellowish-buff streaked with black. Bill, pink, with a black tip; eyes, pale blue; legs, dark grey.

VOICE: "Wee-you-weer, wh wh wh wh . . .;" "quok;" a querulous bubbling.

HABITAT: Woodland to arid scrub.

RANGE: Australia, avoiding forested areas; one record from Kangaroo Island.

Some evidence of regular seasonal movement in south-east, nomadic or sedentary elsewhere.

## LITTLE WATTLE-BIRD *Anthochaera chrysoptera*   SEE p. 67

27–30 cm. A streaked wattle-less wattle-bird with whitish ear patch. Above and below, dark olive-brown streaked and speckled white; head, paler, with dark streaks through eyes and from base of bill enclosing whitish ear patch; wing patch (visible in flight), cinnamon;

Spiny-cheeked Honeyeater

Little Wattle-bird

tail, tipped white on outer feathers. Bill, black; eyes, reddish-brown; legs, dark grey.

VOICE: Chuckling cackle; "kraa-cook."

HABITAT: Open forest and coastal heath, especially banksia and dryandra.

RANGE: South-eastern Australia, from south-eastern Queensland to South Australia; Kangaroo Island, and Tasmania.

Sedentary.

## RED WATTLE-BIRD *Anthochaera carunculata* SEE p. 67

32–35 cm. A wattle-bird with red ear wattle. Above, dark olive-grey, streaked white; head, blackish-brown, and with triangular silver ear patch and red pendulous ear wattle; below, dusky-brown, streaked white with yellow patch on abdomen; wing and tail feathers, tipped white, obvious in flight. Bill, black; eyes, red; legs, pinkish-brown.

VOICE: "Chock a lock;" barking "cheock."

HABITAT: Open forest, suburban gardens.

RANGE: Southern Australia, from southern Queensland to south-west Australia; straggler to New Zealand.

North-south migration in west, altitudinal migration in east.

## YELLOW WATTLE-BIRD *Anthochaera paradoxa* SEE p. 67

40–45 cm. A wattle-bird with a yellow ear wattle. Above, dark olive-brown streaked white; head, streaked dark brown and white, with long pendulous yellow wattles; throat, white; breast and abdomen, dusky-brown, streaked white with yellow patch on abdomen. Bill, black; eyes, red; legs, pinkish-brown.

VOICE: Raucous sounds.

HABITAT: Open forest and suburban gardens.

RANGE: Tasmania and Bass Strait islands.

Sedentary or nomadic.

Red Wattle-bird

Yellow Wattle-bird

## GRASS FINCHES—Spermestidae

Grass finches are generally birds of savannah grassland and open grassland, usually near water. Some species are found in forests. They feed on seeds, taken either on the ground or on seedheads. Although all grass finches have stout, conical bills, some prefer unripe soft seed. Insects, particularly flying ants, may be taken in the breeding season. Grass finches usually move in flocks, ranging in size from a few individuals to enormous congregations in some tropical forms. These flocks tend to disperse during the breeding season. The nest is a dome-shaped structure built from grass, usually with a spout leading to the entrance. Some species build roosting nests which are distinct from the breeding nest. Interbreeding between Chestnut-breasted and Yellow-rumped Finches has been observed in the field, and hybrids between them occur frequently. All species are easily identifiable; a number have distinctive forms, but as they change gradually from one to the other, they are not treated separately here. One or two cases have not as yet been studied in sufficient detail to enable a confident final classification to be made.

**RED-BROWED FINCH** *Aegintha temporalis*                              SEE p. 69

12 cm. A red-rumped finch with red brow. Above, yellowish-olive, with a yellowish patch on side of neck, and crimson rump; head, grey, with crimson eyebrows; below, grey; tail, dusky-brown. Bill, red, with black above and below; eyes, reddish-brown; legs, pinkish-brown.

VOICE: High-pitched "see."

HABITAT: Mangrove, forest, and near-by open country.

RANGE: Eastern Australia, from Cape York to Victoria, south-eastern South Australia and Kangaroo Island; introduced to Tahiti. Sedentary, with some nomadism.

Red-browed Finch

**PAINTED FINCH** *Emblema picta* SEE p. 69

10 cm. A spinifex red-rumped finch with crimson face and abdomen and black sides spotted white. Above, brown, with scarlet rump; forehead, face, and chin, scarlet; below, black, spotted white, with scarlet centre to abdomen; tail, brownish-black. Bill, red, with black above and blue at base of lower mandible; eyes, white; legs, pinkish-brown.

VOICE: Loud harsh "trut;" song "che che che-che-che-che-che werreee-oooeeee."

HABITAT: Spinifex, particularly in rocky areas.

RANGE: Arid areas of Australia.

Sedentary.

**RED-EARED FIRETAIL** *Emblema oculata* SEE p. 69

12 cm. A south-western red-rumped finch with red ear patch and black abdomen spotted white. Above, olive-brown, finely barred black with crimson rump; face, black; ear patch, crimson; throat and upper breast, pale buff barred black; abdomen, black, with large white spot. Bill, red; eyes, red with ring of naked blue skin; legs, dark brown.

VOICE: Mournful "oowee."

HABITAT: Moist grassy areas in forests.

RANGE: South-western Australia; only Finch in lower south-west.

Sedentary.

**BEAUTIFUL FIRETAIL** *Emblema bella* SEE p. 69

12 cm. A south-eastern red-rumped finch with barred underparts. Above, olive-brown, finely barred black, with crimson rump; face, black; below, grey, barred black, with undertail and centre of abdomen black. Bill, red; eyes, reddish-brown, with ring of naked blue skin; legs, pinkish-brown.

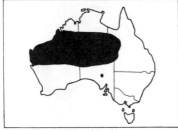

Painted Finch

Red-eared Firetail

VOICE: Low "weee."

HABITAT: Heath and woodland.

RANGE: South-eastern Australia, from Newcastle, New South Wales, to south-eastern South Australia and Kangaroo Island; only Finch in Tasmania.

Sedentary.

## DIAMOND FIRETAIL *Emblema guttata*                SEE p. 69

11 cm. A red-rumped finch with a grey head and black breast band. Above, pale buff-brown, with crimson rump; head, grey, with black lores; throat, white; breast, black; flanks, black, spotted white; centre of abdomen, white; tail, black. Bill, red, with blue base; eyes, red; legs, dark bluish-grey. **Immature:** more olive in colour, with olive-barred flanks.

VOICE: Long "twooo-heee."

HABITAT: Woodland including mallee, usually but not always near water.

RANGE: South-eastern Australia, from Dawson River, Queensland, to Eyre Peninsula, South Australia, and Kangaroo Island.

Sedentary.

## CRIMSON FINCH *Neochmia phaeton*                  SEE p. 69

14 cm. A largely crimson finch. **Male:** above, greyish-olive, tinged dull crimson; crown and nape, dark grey; face, throat, breast, and flanks, dull crimson, with white spots on sides; abdomen, black (over most of range) or white (tip of Cape York, race *albiventer*). Bill, red, with white (race *phaeton*) or blue (race *albiventer*) at base of lower mandible; eyes, brownish-yellow; legs, brownish-yellow. **Female:** similar, but breast greyish-olive, flanks greyish-brown, and abdomen dull white. Bill, orange. **Immature:** rather more grey-brown, and bill, black.

Beautiful Firetail

Diamond Firetail

VOICE: Loud "chee chee chee."

HABITAT: River and swampy vegetation, particularly pandanus.

RANGE: Northern Australia, from Derby, Western Australia, to Rockhampton, Queensland; southern New Guinea.

Sedentary.

## STAR FINCH *Bathilda ruficauda* SEE p. 69

12 cm. A red-rumped finch with red face and yellowish-spotted underparts. Above, yellowish-olive, with lower rump dull-scarlet spotted white; face and chin, crimson, spotted white; below, yellowish-olive, spotted white with central abdomen yellow; tail, dull-scarlet central feathers, and black outer feathers. Bill, scarlet; eyes, orange; legs, yellow.

VOICE: High-pitched "seet;" quicker "pslit."

HABITAT: Grassy river and swamp margins; grassy areas interspersed with bushes, near water.

RANGE: Northern Australia, from about Rockhampton, Queensland, to the Ashburton River, Western Australia. Once occurred in central New South Wales and southern Queensland.

Sedentary.

## ZEBRA FINCH *Taeniopygia guttata* SEE p. 69

10 cm. A greyish-brown finch with barred rump and tail coverts. **Male:** above, grey-brown, with rump and extended upper tail coverts barred black and white; head, grey, with chestnut ear patch and white face bordered with black streaks; throat and breast, grey, finely barred black; flanks, chestnut, spotted white. **Female:** lacking the chestnut ear patch and plain dull buffy-white below. Bill, red; eyes, red; legs, orange.

VOICE: Nasal "tang" (not unlike White-fronted Chat); trilling song; aggressive "woot."

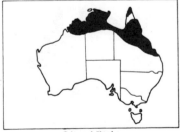

Crimson Finch

Star Finch

HABITAT: Woodland to open arid country, interspersed with bushes, abundant about windmills and agricultural bores in dry country.

RANGE: Australia, except in eastern and south-western forests; Lesser Sunda Islands.

Sedentary in good conditions; nomadic in dry seasons.

### DOUBLE-BAR FINCH *Stizoptera bichenovii* SEE p. 69

11 cm. A brownish-grey finch with two narrow breast bars. Above, brownish-grey, finely barred black and rump white (east of Burketown) or black (west of Burketown, race *annulosa*); wings, black, spotted white; face and throat, white, bordered with a narrow black band extending across upper breast; below, buffy-white, with another black band across the breast. Bill, blue-grey; eyes, dark brown; legs, blue-grey.

VOICE: Loud nasal "tiaaat-tiaaat;" and low "tat-tat."

HABITAT: Open grassy woodland.

RANGE: Northern Australia, from central-western New South Wales to Broome, Western Australia.

Sedentary.

### MASKED FINCH *Poephila personata* SEE p. 71

12 cm. A pinkish-brown finch with black face and long tail. Above, pinkish-brown, with white rump; face and chin, black; below, pinkish-buff, with black patch on lower flank and white undertail coverts. On Cape York occurs a white-cheeked form, race *leucotis*. Bill, yellow; eyes, reddish-brown; legs, red.

VOICE: Loud "tsit;" quiet "tat-tat."

HABITAT: Open woodland and grassland.

RANGE: Northern Australia, from Derby, Western Australia, to Cape York, Queensland.

Sedentary.

Zebra Finch

Double-bar Finch

**BLACK-THROATED FINCH** *Poephila cincta* SEE p. 71

10 cm. A pinkish-brown finch with black bill, black throat, and short tail. Above, pinkish-brown, with rump white (south of about Townsville, race *cincta*) or black (north of about Cairns, race *atropygialis*, with hybrid zone between Townsville and Cairns); head, grey, with white ear patch, black lores and throat; breast and abdomen, pinkish-buff; lower flank, black; undertail coverts, white. Bill, black; eyes, brown; legs, reddish-orange.

VOICE: Plaintive "weet."

HABITAT: Forest and woodland with ground cover.

RANGE: North-eastern Australia, from about Tenterfield, New South Wales, to Cape York, Queensland.

Sedentary.

**LONG-TAILED FINCH** *Poephila acuticauda* SEE p. 71

15 cm. A pinkish-brown finch with yellow or orange bill, black throat, and long tail. Above, pinkish-brown, with white rump; head, grey, with white ear patch, black lores, and black throat; breast and abdomen, pinkish-buff, with black patch on lower flanks; undertail coverts, white. Bill, orange (east of Wyndham) or yellow (west of Wyndham, race *hecki*); eyes, brown; legs, reddish-orange.

VOICE: A loud "teeweet;" a very soft "tet;" a warbler-like song (Hutchinson 43).

HABITAT: Open forest and well-grassed woodland.

RANGE: Northern Australia, from Derby, Western Australia, to Leichhardt River, Queensland.

Sedentary.

**BLUE-FACED FINCH** *Erythrura trichroa* SEE p. 69

12 cm. A seldom-seen red-rumped finch with a blue face. Above dark grass-green, with dull-scarlet rump and tail; forehead and face,

Masked Finch

Black-throated Finch

blue; below, pale grass-green. Bill, black; eyes, dark brown; legs, pale brown.

VOICE: Not recorded.

HABITAT: Edges of mangrove and rain forest.

RANGE: Coastal north-eastern Queensland, south to Cairns and Atherton Tableland; New Guinea; Celebes, Solomon Islands, and Micronesia.

Probably sedentary.

**PLUM-HEADED FINCH** *Aidemosyne modesta*          SEE p. 69

11 cm. An olive-brown finch with barred rump, purple crown, and barred underparts. Above, olive-brown, with white tips to wing feathers and rump barred black and white; crown and chin, purple; below, white, barred pale olive-brown; tail, black. Bill, black, with blue at base; eyes, dark brown; legs, pinkish-brown.

VOICE: Soft "tlip;" loud "pyiit;" almost inaudible song.

HABITAT: Tangled vegetation along rivers and creeks; savannah with undergrowth.

RANGE: Restricted to savannah woodland in south-eastern Australia from Mogoa River and Port Denison, Queensland, to southern and central-western New South Wales. Recorded once in Victoria.

Sedentary near water; elsewhere nomadic.

**GOULDIAN FINCH** *Chloebia gouldiae*          SEE p. 71

14 cm. A colourful finch with a purple breast. Above, green, with blue rump; head, black, red, or yellow; breast, purple; abdomen, yellow; long tail, black. Bill, whitish, with red tip; eyes, dark brown; legs, yellow.

Black-headed Gouldian Finches outnumber red-headed three to one; yellow-headed birds occur only once in every few thousand.

VOICE: Soft "ssit-ssit."

HABITAT: Savannah.

Long-tailed Finch

Blue-faced Finch

RANGE: Northern Australia, from Derby, Western Australia, to about Charters Towers, Queensland.

Sedentary and nomadic, with regular southwards movement in wet season.

## CHESTNUT-BREASTED FINCH SEE p. 71
*Lonchura castaneothorax*

10 cm. An orange-yellow rumped finch with black face and chestnut breast. Above, cinnamon-brown, with orange-yellow rump; crown and nape, mottled grey-brown; face and throat, black, with pale streaks on cheeks; breast, chestnut; abdomen, white, with barred flanks. Bill, blue-grey; eyes, dark brown; legs, purplish-grey. **Immature:** plain greyish-brown with yellowish rump; indistinguishable from immature yellow-rumped Finch.

The Chestnut-breasted and Yellow-rumped Finches often interbreed in the Kimberleys, and many individuals display characteristics of both species.

VOICE: Bell-like "treet."

HABITAT: Grasslands and reedy swamp margins.

RANGE: Northern and eastern Australia, from Derby, Western Australia, to Sydney, New South Wales; New Guinea.

Sedentary and nomadic.

## YELLOW-RUMPED FINCH *Lonchura flaviprymna* SEE p. 71

10 cm. A yellow-rumped finch with grey head and creamy-buff underparts. Above, cinnamon-brown, with yellow rump; crown and nape, grey; face and underparts, creamy-buff, rather richer on breast. Bill, blue-grey; eyes, dark brown; legs, purplish-grey. **Immature:** plain greyish-brown, with yellowish rump; indistinguishable from immature Chestnut-breasted Finch.

Plum-headed Finch

Gouldian Finch

The Yellow-rumped and Chestnut-breasted Finches often interbreed in the Kimberleys, and many individuals display characteristics of both species.

VOICE: Bell-like "treet."

HABITAT: Grassland and reedy swamp margins.

RANGE: Northern Australia, from Derby, Western Australia, to north-western Queensland.

Sedentary and nomadic.

### PICTORELLA FINCH *Heteromunia pectoralis*        SEE p. 71

11 cm. A grey-brown finch with black face and white barred breast. Above, grey-brown, darker on head and rump; face and throat, black, edged pale cinnamon-buff; breast, black, profusely barred white; abdomen, purplish-buff, with white markings on flanks. Bill, blue-grey; eyes, dark brown; legs, pinkish-buff. **Immature:** dark brownish-grey above, paler below; bill, brownish-black.

VOICE: Double-noted "k-rt, k-rt."

HABITAT: Dry savannah, grasslands, and spinifex.

RANGE: Northern Australia, from Derby, Western Australia, to Charters Towers, Queensland.

Sedentary and nomadic.

### SPICE FINCH *Lonchura punctulata*        SEE p. 71

10 cm. A yellow-rumped finch with chestnut face and marbled breast and flanks. Above, cinnamon-brown, with golden-yellow rump; head and throat, chestnut-brown; breast and flanks, marbled-black and white; centre of abdomen, white. Bill, black; eyes, reddish-brown; legs, blue-grey. **Immature:** above, pale brown, with brownish rump; below, brownish-yellow.

Chestnut-breasted Finch

Yellow-rumped Finch

VOICE: High-pitched "kit-teee;" sharp "tret-tret;" juvenile call like alarm note of Black-fronted Dotterel.

HABITAT: Bushy savannah.

RANGE: (Introduced.) Near Sydney; coastal Queensland, from Brisbane to Cooktown.

Sedentary and nomadic.

### BLACK-HEADED MANNIKIN *Lonchura atricapilla*  SEE p. 71

10 cm. An introduced brown and black finch with a reddish-brown rump. Above, brown; rump, reddish-brown; head, neck, and breast, black; below, brown with a black patch in the centre of the abdomen. Bill, silver-grey; eyes, brown; legs, black.

VOICE: Almost inaudible.

HABITAT: Grassland with scattered trees.

RANGE: Small flocks around Sydney.

Sedentary.

## SPARROWS AND WEAVERS—Ploceidae

The four species found in Australia were all introduced. They are similar in shape to the grass finches, but differ in the manner of building the nest. Sparrows build untidy domed structures from grass, bark, paper, string, etc., and usually place them in a crevice. Weavers build intricately-woven suspended nests, and often congregate in huge colonies.

### HOUSE SPARROW *Passer domesticus*  SEE p. 71

15 cm. A streaked sparrow with grey forehead, chestnut nape, and clear white cheeks (male) or with dull white underparts (female). **Male:** above, streaked brown and black, with white bar on shoulder and grey rump; forehead, grey, and nape, chestnut; below, grey, with black bib.

Pictorella Finch

Spice Finch

**Female:** above, streaked brown and black, with buff bar on shoulder; below, dull white. Bill, black (male), yellowish-brown (female); eyes, brown; legs, light brown.

Male distinguished from the similar Tree Sparrow by the grey forehead and clear white cheeks.

VOICE: Constant chirruping.

HABITAT: Cities, towns, and cultivations.

RANGE: Eastern Australia, from north Queensland to central South Australia and Tasmania; range is extending; widely spread throughout the world.

Sedentary.

### TREE SPARROW *Passer montanus* SEE p. 71

15 cm. A streaked sparrow, with chestnut forehead and nape and black spot in white cheeks. Above, streaked brown and black; forehead to nape, chestnut; cheek, white, with black spot; below, grey, with the black bib smaller than in House Sparrow. Bill, black; eyes, reddish-brown; legs, light brown.

Distinguished from male House Sparrow by chestnut crown and black spot on cheek; rather more retiring than the House Sparrow.

VOICE: More twittering than House Sparrow; "tek" in flight.

HABITAT: Less attached to human habitations than House Sparrow.

RANGE: South-eastern Australia, north to Sydney.

Sedentary.

### GRENADIER WEAVER (RED BISHOP BIRD) SEE p. 71
*Euplectes orix*

13–14 cm male; 12–13 cm female. A scarlet and black finch (male breeding) or streaked brownish-buff and black (female and non-breeding male). **Male breeding:** scarlet, with black crown and abdomen; bill, black.

Black-headed Mannikin

House Sparrow

**Male non-breeding and female:** above, streaked brownish-buff and black, with pale stripe over eyes; below, buff, paler on the abdomen and streaked on breast and flanks. Bill, horn.

The male in breeding plumage is unmistakable, but female and male in non-breeding dress are rather similar to female House Sparrow in colour.

VOICE: Noisy chattering.

HABITAT: Savannah grassland.

RANGE: Bend of the Murray River, South Australia. Introduced from Africa.

Sedentary.

**WHITE-WINGED WHYDAH** *Coliuspasser albonotatus* SEE p. 71

Male 17 cm; female 15 cm. A black introduced sparrow with a gold and white patch on the wing (male) or a brown sparrow with pale patch in the wing (female). **Breeding male:** above and below, black, with a gold and white patch on the shoulder and white bases to the flight feathers; underwing coverts, white. **Non-breeding male:** above, brown, streaked darker; wing, similar to breeding male; below, buffy-white. **Female:** above, brown, streaked darker; wing, brown, with light bases to the flight feathers and pale buff underwing coverts; below, pale buff, darker on the breast.

VOICE: Cheerful twittering but usually silent.

HABITAT: Long grass in open country with scattered trees.

RANGE: Aviary escapees in vicinity of Sydney.

## FINCHES — Fringillidae

The two species found in Australia were introduced. They are similar to grass finches, but build cup-shaped nests and feed the young on insects as well as seeds.

Tree Sparrow

Grenadier Weaver

**GOLDFINCH** *Carduelis carduelis* SEE p. 71

12 cm. A red-faced finch with gold band in wing. Above, brown, with whitish rump; wing, black, with broad gold band; tail, black, tipped white; face and throat, red; crown, black, extending behind white cheeks; below, buffy-white, with buff breast. Bill, pale yellow; eyes, brown; legs, pinkish.

VOICE: Tinkling "swit-wit."

HABITAT: Parks, gardens, and overgrown cultivations, particularly among thistles and cosmos.

RANGE: South-eastern Australia; in Western Australia in the vicinity of Perth and Albany.

Sedentary.

**GREENFINCH** *Chloris chloris* SEE p. 71

15 cm. A green finch with yellow in wings and tail. Above, olive-green, yellower on rump; wings and tail, with yellow patches; below, yellowish-olive-green. Bill, white; eyes, brown; legs, pale pink.

VOICE: Sharp "swee-e-e-e;" trilling notes.

HABITAT: Woodland, gardens.

RANGE: Victoria; south-eastern New South Wales; southern South Australia; and Tasmania.

Sedentary.

## STARLINGS — Sturnidae

Starlings are omnivorous birds, typically black with iridescent plumage. They generally move in large flocks, particularly towards evening. Although these birds usually nest in hollows and crevices, the sole native Australian species breeds colonially, weaving hanging dome-shaped nests from vine tendrils. Two species, the English Starling and the Indian Myna, have been introduced; the former has spread

White-winged Whydah

Goldfinch

alarmingly in the south-east, as it has in many parts of the world. The Indian Myna is brown and black, with white "windows" in the wings. Its spread has been confined more or less to urban areas and cultivated farmland.

### SHINING STARLING  *Aplonis metallica*                    SEE p. 73

25 cm. An iridescent black starling with red eyes and long graduated tail. Above and below, black, glossed green and purple. **Immature:** underparts, white, streaked black. Bill, black; eyes, red; legs, black.

VOICE: Harsh rather lorikeet-like screeching.

HABITAT: Rain forest.

RANGE: North-eastern Queensland south to Hinchinbrook and Dunk Island; Moluccas, New Guinea, and Solomon Islands; Timor; Laut and Damar islands; Bismarck Archipelago.

Regular migrant to New Guinea, leaving May and arriving August, but some birds remain.

### ENGLISH STARLING  *Sturnus vulgaris*                    SEE p. 73

20 cm. An often-spotted iridescent black starling with yellow or dull brown bill and short tail. Above and below, black, glossed green and purple, speckled pale buff in fresh plumage; wings and tail, brownish (breeding) or dull brown (non-breeding); eyes, dark brown; legs, reddish-brown. **Immature:** plain grey-brown above and below.

VOICE: Very variable with harsh or shrill whistles, and mimicry of other species.

HABITAT: Cities, towns, and cultivations, but spreading into more natural bush.

RANGE: South-eastern Australia, from south-east Queensland to Eyre Peninsula, South Australia, and Tasmania; spreading; found in many parts of the world.

Sedentary.

Greenfinch

Shining Starling

**INDIAN MYNA** *Acridotheres tristis* SEE p. 73

24 cm. A chocolate-brown bird with yellow bill and face patch, and white "bull's-eye" in the wing. Above, chocolate, with large white spot in wing; head and neck, black, glossed green, with yellow naked skin behind eyes; below, paler brown. Bill, yellow; eyes, yellow; legs, yellow.

VOICE: Loud raucous notes.

HABITAT: Cities, towns, and cultivations.

RANGE: Mainly coastal eastern Australia and northern Tasmania; in vicinity of cities and towns; spreading; introduced from South-east Asia.

Sedentary.

# OLD WORLD ORIOLES—Oriolidae

Orioles are birds of forest and woodland, where they feed on insects and fruit, particularly native figs. They also enjoy fruit and berries of introduced plants, such as mulberries and Japanese pepper. They fly with undulating flight, rather like bower-birds, and often move in small flocks in which orioles and figbirds may mingle. The two species of orioles are typical of the family, being yellowish-green in colour and having reddish bills. The two figbirds are aberrant orioles, with stouter bills and naked skin, bright scarlet in males, around the eyes. Male figbirds are more brightly-coloured than females.

**OLIVE-BACKED ORIOLE** *Oriolus sagittatus* SEE p. 73

25–28 cm. A slender oriole with olive back and heavily streaked underparts. Above, olive-green (male) or olive-grey (female), faintly streaked black; tail, tipped on inner webs; below, white, boldly streaked black and yellowish on flanks. Bill, reddish-brown; eyes, red; legs, dark blue-grey.

English Starling                    Indian Myna

May be confused with Yellow Oriole (which is more green than yellow), but distinguished by duller colour, white streaked underparts, and lack of yellow edges to wing feathers; more similar to female and immature figbirds, which are more heavily built, have shorter, stouter bills, bare purplish skin around the eyes, and have more white (female) or no white (immature) in tail.

VOICE: Sneezing "chee-et;" musical whistles, based on "or-ee-ee."

HABITAT: Forest and woodland.

RANGE: Northern and eastern Australia, from Derby, Western Australia, to Adelaide, South Australia; southern New Guinea.

Migratory in south, sedentary in north.

### YELLOW ORIOLE *Oriolus flavocinctus* SEE p. 73

25–28 cm. A slender yellowish-green oriole with yellow edging to wing feathers. Above, yellowish-green, with black centres to feathers; wings, blackish, with feathers edged yellow; throat and breast, yellowish-green, narrowly streaked black; abdomen, yellow. Bill, reddish-brown; eyes, red; legs, dark blue-grey. **Female:** duller and more streaked.

May be confused with Olive-backed Oriole, which generally inhabits drier forest and has white heavily streaked underparts and lacks the yellow edges to the wing feathers.

VOICE: Melodious liquid song "cholonk cholonk;" harsh sneezing note.

HABITAT: Wet forest and mangrove.

RANGE: Northern Australia, Aru Islands, and southern New Guinea. Nomadic.

### SOUTHERN FIGBIRD *Sphecotheres vieilloti* SEE p. 73

28 cm. A stout oriole with dark head, red eye patch, and green underparts (male) or with olive-brown upperparts, purplish eye patch, and

Olive-backed Oriole    Yellow Oriole

heavily streaked white underparts. **Male:** above, yellowish-green, with head black and hindneck grey; naked skin around eyes, red (but loses and gains colour rapidly); throat and breast, grey; abdomen, yellowish-green, becoming white under the tail, which is black, broadly tipped white. **Female:** above, olive-brown, streaked darker; naked skin around eyes, purplish-grey; below, white, boldly streaked dark brown; tail, broadly tipped white. **Immature:** tail, without white tip. Bill, black; eyes, reddish-brown; legs, pale buff.

Female may be confused with Olive-backed Oriole, but is stouter, has a shorter bill and a purplish-grey eye patch; almost identical to female Yellow Figbird, which is more northern in range and has browner upperparts. Male distinguished from male Yellow Figbird by green underparts and grey collar.

VOICE: Loud "sluck;" high-pitched whistling, clucking, and lorikeet-like warbling.

HABITAT: Forest, woodland, particularly native figs.

RANGE: South-eastern Australia, from about Townsville, Queensland, to about Sydney, New South Wales; southern New Guinea.
Migratory in south, sedentary farther north.

*Cairns, Qu'land 5/72*

**YELLOW FIGBIRD** *Sphecotheres flaviventris*          SEE p. 73

28 cm. A stout oriole with dark head, red eye patch, and yellow underparts (male) or with brown upperparts, purplish eye patch, and heavily streaked white underparts. **Male:** above, yellowish-green, with black head; naked skin around eyes, red (but loses and gains colour rapidly); below, yellow, with white undertail coverts; tail, black, broadly tipped white. **Female:** above, brown, streaked darker, tinged olive on rump; naked skin around eyes, purplish-grey; below, white boldly

Southern Figbird

Yellow Figbird

streaked dark brown; tail, broadly tipped white. **Immature:** tail, without white tip. Bill, black; eyes, brown; legs, pale buff.

Female may be confused with Olive-backed Oriole, but is stouter, has shorter beak, is browner on the back, and has purplish-grey skin around the eyes; almost identical to female Southern Figbird, but more northern in range and browner above. Male differs from the male Southern Figbird in the yellow underparts and lack of grey collar.

VOICE: Similar to Southern Figbird.

HABITAT: Forest and woodland.

RANGE: Northern Australia, from Port Keats, Northern Territory, to about Townsville, Queensland; Kei Island near Timor.

Sedentary.

# DRONGOS—Dicruridae

Drongos are easily-recognisable iridescent black birds with stout bills, surrounded by bristles, and long fishtail-shaped tails. Most of their food consists of flying insects, taken in flight. The sole Australian species is migratory, arriving in October and leaving in March. It builds a cup-shaped nest suspended by the rim among outer branches, and lays three to five eggs. The nesting territory is strongly defended.

## SPANGLED DRONGO *Dicrurus bracteatus*  SEE p. 73

28–30 cm. An iridescent black bird, with fishtail fork in tail. Above, black, with green iridescence; below, black, with blue spangles on head, neck, and breast. Bill, black; eyes, red; legs, black.

VOICE: Harsh cackle; creaking whistle.

HABITAT: Forest, mangrove.

RANGE: Eastern Australia, from Cape York, Queensland, to eastern Victoria; winter visitor to southern New Guinea.

Migratory in southern range, sedentary in north.

Spangled Drongo

# WOOD-SWALLOWS — Artamidae

Wood-swallows are unusual birds in several respects. They are the only small passerines that soar persistently, and they are the only passerines with powderdown feathers. They are easily identifiable by their robust build, black-tipped blue bill, and long wings. They feed on insects and in some species on nectar; in such cases the forehead is often yellow or orange with pollen. Some also scavenge in rubbish dumps. Another peculiarity of wood-swallows is their habit of clustering, particularly in cold weather. Some species roost in densely-packed clusters. The nest is a scanty cup-shaped structure placed in a clump of leaves or twigs; in a shallow hollow in a tree trunk, branch, or rock face; or behind a loose sheet of bark.

## WHITE-BREASTED WOOD-SWALLOW                              SEE p. 75
*Artamus leucorhynchus*

17 cm. A white-breasted wood-swallow with white rump. Above, dark grey, browner on the back, with rump white; head and throat, dark grey; breast and abdomen, white. Bill, blue-grey, with black tip; eyes, dark brown; legs, blue-grey.

VOICE: Harsh "cyeck" (Hutchinson 45).

HABITAT: Forest, woodland, and mangrove; telephone wires.

RANGE: Northern and eastern Australia, from Shark Bay, Western Australia, to the Murray Valley, Victoria and South Australia.

Sedentary in northern coastal areas; nomadic or migratory inland and farther south.

## MASKED WOOD-SWALLOW *Artamus personatus*          SEE p. 75

18–20 cm. A grey wood-swallow with face black (male) or dusky (female) and with rump and tail grey. **Male:** above, grey; forehead, face,

White-breasted Wood-swallow

and throat, black, bordered with white except on forehead; below, pale grey; tail, tipped white. **Female:** similar, but with face and throat dusky shading to dark grey on upper breast. **Immature:** above, grey spotted white on wings; below, rather brownish-grey. Bill, whitish-blue with black tip; eyes, dark brown; legs, black.

Immature may be confused with immature White-browed Wood-swallow, but is paler in colour. In flying flocks of Masked only, such as occur in Western Australia, the browner immatures may give the impression that the White-browed is present.

VOICE: Loud penetrating "chyet;" often heard when passing birds are flying overhead almost out of sight.

HABITAT: Inland savannah and shrub savannah.

RANGE: Drier areas of Australia, irrupting on occasions.

Nomadic.

## WHITE-BROWED WOOD-SWALLOW SEE p. 75
*Artamus superciliosus*

18–20 cm. A white-browed wood-swallow with breast chestnut (male) or greyish-chestnut (female). **Male:** above, dark grey, bluer on the rump, tail, and wings; head, sooty-black, with white eyebrows; throat and upper breast, sooty-black; lower breast and abdomen, chestnut. **Female:** head and upper breast, blue-grey, with black lores; eyebrows, less distinct than male; breast, greyish-chestnut. **Immature:** similar to female, but spotted white on wings. Bill, whitish-blue, with black tip; eyes, dark brown; legs, black.

VOICE: Loud querulous "chirp," often heard when passing birds are flying overhead almost out of sight.

HABITAT: Savannah and open woodland.

RANGE: Drier areas of Australia, irrupting on occasions, and much more common in eastern than western Australia.

Nomadic, with regular migrations into southern Victoria.

White-browed Wood-swallow
and Masked Wood-swallow

**BLACK-FACED WOOD-SWALLOW** *Artamus cinereus*     SEE p. 75

18 cm. A dark smoky-grey wood-swallow with black face, rump, and tail. Above, smoky-brownish-grey with blue-grey wings, black rump and tail, which has a white tip; face, black; underparts, variable: race *hypoleucos* (northern and eastern Queensland), vinous grey to buff-grey with undertail coverts white; race *cinereus* (rest of Australia), undertail coverts black. **Immature:** streaked buffy-brown, and grey on head and back. Bill, whitish-blue, with black tip; eyes, dark brown; legs, dark blue-grey.

The black rump and tail, more dumpy shape, and smaller black face distinguish the Black-faced from the Masked Wood-swallow.

VOICE: Twittering "quet-quet" (Hutchinson 46).

HABITAT: Savannah woodland.

RANGE: Most of Australia except Tasmania and extreme south-west; most common in areas of less than 500 mm rainfall; Timor.

Sedentary, with some local nomadism. *Portland Vic 2/72*

**DUSKY WOOD-SWALLOW** *Artamus cyanopterus*     SEE p. 75

18 cm. A dark grey-brown wood-swallow with white edge to wing. Above and below, dark grey-brown; wing, blackish, with the second, third, and, in the east, fourth wing feathers white; tail, blackish, with white tip. **Immature:** streaked buff and dark grey on head and back. Bill, whitish-blue, with black tip; eyes, dark brown; legs, dark blue-grey.

Distinguished from the Black-faced and Little Wood-swallows by the white in the wing.

VOICE: "Check."

HABITAT: Forest and woodland.

RANGE: Southern Australia, Tasmania, and Bass Strait islands; generally in areas of more than 500 mm rainfall.

Generally migratory in south, but some sedentary.

Black-faced Wood-swallow

Dusky Wood-swallow

**LITTLE WOOD-SWALLOW** *Artamus minor*          SEE p. 75

12 cm. A small chocolate-brown wood-swallow. Above and below, chocolate-brown, with dark blue-grey wings; rump and tail, black, with white tip. Bill, whitish-blue, with dark tip; eyes, dark brown; legs, black.

VOICE: "Choo-choo-swit-swit," mimicry of other species.

HABITAT: Forest to savannah, breeding mainly in rocky country (breakaways).

RANGE: Northern Australia, more or less exclusive of the range of the Dusky Wood-swallow.

Nomadic over much of its range.

## BUTCHER-BIRDS, MAGPIES, AND CURRAWONGS (BELL-MAGPIES)—Cracticidae

The butcher-birds are so named from their habit of wedging their prey in a suitable branch fork to assist them in feeding. They do not store surplus food in the manner of the Old World shrikes, which are often also called "butcher-birds." Magpies are strongly territorial birds that live in small groups, often in towns and cities. They are aggressive towards other groups of magpies, birds of prey, cats, and dogs, particularly during their breeding season. Currawongs, alternatively known as Bell-magpies, are largely black-and-white birds with long stout beaks and loud voices, often pure and pleasing to human ears. They build cup-shaped nests from twigs and grass, and these are vigorously defended by some species to the extent of causing injury to humans. Currawongs are pied or grey-and-white birds, frequently observed in loose flocks; they often visit towns in winter. Basically two forms occur, pied and grey, but they have distinctive races in Tasmania. As they are easily identifiable in the field, they are treated here separately.

Little Wood-swallow

## PIED BUTCHER-BIRD *Cracticus nigrogularis* SEE p. 77

32–35 cm. A pied butcher-bird with a black throat. **Adult:** above, black, with white rump, collar, tail tip, and edges to wing feathers; head, throat, and upper breast, black; lower breast and abdomen, white. **Immature:** dark brown areas, with throat and upper breast buff. Bill, bluish-grey, with black tip; eyes, blackish-brown; legs, grey.

VOICE: Beautiful flute-like calls, one of the most common recalling the opening bars of Beethoven's Fifth Symphony (Hutchinson 47).

HABITAT: Woodland.

RANGE: Australia, except extreme south, and tip of Cape York, Queensland.

Sedentary.

## GREY BUTCHER-BIRD *Cracticus torquatus* SEE p. 77

28–32 cm. A grey-backed butcher-bird with white throat. **Adult:** above, grey with white collar, rump, and tail tip; wings, black, with white edges to feathers; head, black, with white lores; below, white, with speckled necklace in south-western birds (race *leucopterus*). **Immature:** above, blackish-brown, below, buff-white. Bill, blue-grey, with black tip; eyes, dark brown; legs, bluish-grey.

In northern Queensland may be confused with Black-backed Butcher-bird which is darker on the back and lacks the white lores.

VOICE: A rich rollicking "crr-crr-crr-crroa-crrk;" mimics other species.

HABITAT: Forest and woodland.

RANGE: Southern and eastern Australia north to Palmer River, Queensland, Alice Springs and Ashburton River, Western Australia; isolated population in the Kimberleys and north-western Northern Territory (known as Silver-backed Butcher-bird).

Sedentary.

Pied Butcher-bird

Grey Butcher-bird

## BLACK-BACKED BUTCHER-BIRD *Cracticus mentalis*    SEE p. 77

25 cm. A pied butcher-bird with white throat. **Adult:** above, black, with white collar, upper back, and tail tip; rump, grey, shading to white at base of tail; wings, black, with extensive white edges to wing feathers; head, black, with black lores; below, white. **Immature:** a brownish version of adult. Bill, blue-grey, with black tip; eyes, dark brown; legs, blue-grey.

In northern Queensland may be confused with the Grey Butcher-Bird which has grey back and white lores and the Black-throated Butcher-bird which has black throat.

VOICE: Rich, mellow piping.

HABITAT: Woodland.

RANGE: Cape York, Queensland, north of Palmer River; southern New Guinea.

Sedentary.

## BLACK BUTCHER-BIRD *Cracticus quoyi*    SEE p. 77

32–36 cm. A black (adult) or cinnamon-brown (immature) butcher-bird. **Adult:** black. **Immature:** either black or cinnamon-brown, streaked darker on head. Bill, blue-grey, with black tip; eyes, dark reddish-brown; legs, black.

VOICE: "Ah-oo-ah;" musical calls.

HABITAT: Rain forest, mangrove.

RANGE: Northern Australia; New Guinea and satellite islands, Misol, Salawati, Waigeu, and Japen; Aru Islands.

Sedentary.

## BLACK-BACKED MAGPIE *Gymnorhina tibicen*    SEE p. 77

36–40 cm. A northern and eastern magpie with black back. **Male:** above, black, with white nape, shoulder, rump and tail, which is tipped

Black-backed Butcher-bird

Black Butcher-bird

black; below, black, with white undertail coverts. **Female:** similar, but nape dusky-white. **Immature:** dark areas, mottled brownish-black. Bill, bluish-white, with black tip; eyes, rich reddish-brown; legs, black.

Sometimes interbreeds with the White-backed Magpie and Western Magpie where their ranges meet; in southern Northern Territory the two appear to occur together without interbreeding.

VOICE: Loud flute-like warble.

HABITAT: Open timbered areas, cultivated paddocks, urban parks, and gardens.

RANGE: Northern and eastern Australia.

Sedentary. *Parkland Vic - 2/72*

## WHITE-BACKED MAGPIE *Gymnorhina hypoleuca*                SEE p. 77

36–40 cm. A south-eastern magpie with back white (male) or grey (female). **Male:** black, with white back, rump, shoulder, undertail coverts, and tail which is tipped black. **Female:** similar, but back pale grey. **Immature:** probably indistinguishable in the field from other species. Bill, bluish-white; eyes, rich reddish-brown; legs, black.

Sometimes interbreeds with Black-backed Magpie where ranges meet; in southern Northern Territory the two appear to occur together without interbreeding.

VOICE: Loud flute-like warble.

HABITAT: Open timbered country, cultivated paddocks, urban parks, and gardens.

RANGE: South-eastern Australia from south-eastern New South Wales to South Australia; Tasmania.

Sedentary.

## WESTERN MAGPIE *Gymnorhina dorsalis*                SEE p. 77

36–40 cm. A south-western magpie, with back white (male) or black with feathers edged white (female). **Male:** black with white back, rump,

Black-backed Magpie

White-backed Magpie

shoulder, undertail coverts, and tail, which is tipped black. **Female:** similar, but with back black with white edges to feathers. **Immature:** probably indistinguishable from other species. Bill, bluish-white, with black tip; eyes, rich reddish-brown; legs, black.

Interbreeds with Black-backed Magpie where their ranges meet.

VOICE: Loud flute-like warble.

HABITAT: Open timbered country, cultivated paddocks, urban parks, and gardens.

RANGE: South-western Australia.

Sedentary.

*Kangaroo Is., S.A. 4/72*

**PIED CURRAWONG** *Strepera graculina* SEE p. 81

45 cm. A black currawong with tail tip, "bull's-eye" in wing and, except in some Victorian birds, base of tail and undertail coverts white. Bill, black; eyes, yellow; legs, black.

On the mainland, may be confused with Grey Currawong which is paler and lacks the white base to the tail.

VOICE: Loud "kadow-kadang" or "curra-wong;" loud whistle; "quok."

HABITAT: Forest and well-vegetated urban areas.

RANGE: Eastern Australia from Cape York, Queensland, to south-western Victoria; the amount of white increases northwards.

Sedentary in many areas, but regular altitudinal movements in some areas.

**BLACK CURRAWONG** *Strepera graculina fuliginosa* SEE p. 81

45 cm. A Tasmanian currawong with black undertail coverts. Above and below, black, with tail tip and small patch in wing, white. Bill, black; eyes, yellow; legs, black.

The Tasmanian representative of the Pied Currawong; may be

Western Magpie

Pied Currawong

confused with the Clinking Currawong, but it lacks the white undertail coverts and has a smaller white patch in the wing.

VOICE: Loud "kadow-kadang;" loud whistle.

HABITAT: Forest and vegetation, urban areas.

RANGE: Tasmania and Bass Strait islands.

Nomadic.

## CLINKING CURRAWONG *Strepera versicolor arguta*   SEE p. 81

50 cm. A Tasmanian currawong with white undertail coverts. Above and below, sooty black with tail tip; undertail coverts and large patch in wing, white. Bill, black; eyes, yellow; legs, black.

This bird is the Tasmanian representative of the Grey Currawong. It may be confused with the Black Currawong, but can be identified by its white undertail coverts and a larger white patch in the wing.

VOICE: Loud "clink;" squeaking meow.

HABITAT: Forest and woodland.

RANGE: Tasmania and Bass Strait islands.

Nomadic.  *Pinaroo S.A. 10/72*

## GREY CURRAWONG *Strepera versicolor*   SEE p. 81

50 cm. A dark grey or sooty currawong with tail tip, "bull's-eye" in wing, and undertail coverts white. Bill, black; eyes, yellow; legs, black.

On the mainland may be confused with Pied Currawong, but lacks the white base to the tail and is paler in colour, except the race *melanoptera*, known as Black-winged Currawong in south-eastern South Australia and north-western Victoria, which lacks white in the wing.

VOICE: Loud metallic "clink" or "tew;" squeaking meow.

HABITAT: Forest and woodland; the Black-winged inhabits mallee.

RANGE: Southern Australia from south-eastern New South Wales to south-western Australia.

Sedentary.

Black Currawong and Clinking Currawong

## BOWER-BIRDS — Ptilonorhynchidae

Bower-birds are among the most remarkable of birds. They are closely related to birds of paradise, but their specialisation in courtship is directed towards display grounds called "bowers." Other birds, such as whydahs, lyrebirds, grouse, and ruffs clear courtship arenas, but none is so elaborate as those of the bower-birds. Not all species build bowers, but those that do may be classified according to the nature of the display area: (a) Stage-makers, which clear an area on the rain forest floor and strew it with selected leaves. (b) Avenue-builders, which construct a bower consisting of two parallel walls. The cleared surrounding area is decorated with bones, berries, and flowers, and the twigs in the bower walls are often "painted" with a mixture of saliva and charcoal or vegetable matter. (c) Maypole-builders, which heap piles of twigs around two adjacent small trees, usually joined by a fallen branch. These piles sometimes reach 2 m in height, and some species join them to form an overhanging roof. Decorations include lichen, shells, and flowers.

Bowers are attended by the male bower-birds for considerable periods, and in many cases for much of the year. In those species that have been studied males are promiscuous. Females visit the bowers often, but the mating period covers only the latter part of the year. The female builds and tends the nest alone; it is a cup-shaped structure, made of twigs, and placed among the branches of a tree.

### GREEN CATBIRD *Ailuroedus crassirostris* SEE p. 79

33 cm. A green bower-bird with head and underparts spotted yellowish-green. Above, dark green, with wing and tail feathers tipped white; head, yellowish-green, spotted and mottled with black and white;

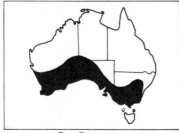

Grey Currawong

Green Catbird

below, yellowish-green, with larger pale yellow spots. Bill, pinkish-white; eyes, red; legs, blue-grey.

Very similar to the Spotted Catbird, but ranges are exclusive.

VOICE: Cat-like meow; gutteral clicking sounds.

HABITAT: Rain forest.

RANGE: South-east Queensland and eastern New South Wales. Sedentary. *mt S plc Qui'lund 5/72*

### SPOTTED CATBIRD *Ailuroedus melanotis*          SEE p. 79

23 cm. A small green bower-bird with head spotted brownish-grey and underparts spotted green. Above, dark green, only faintly spotted on wings; head, dark brownish-grey, spotted and mottled black and white; below, green, with white spots. Bill, pinkish-white; eyes, red; legs, blue-grey.

VOICE: Nasal meow.

HABITAT: Rain forest.

RANGE: North-eastern Queensland; southern New Guinea; Aru Islands, and Misol Island.

Sedentary.

### STAGE-MAKER (TOOTH-BILLED BOWER-BIRD)          SEE p. 79
*Scenopoeetes dentirostris*

23 cm. A brown heavy-billed bower-bird with streaked underparts. Above, dark olive-brown; underparts, buffy-white, streaked dark grey-brown. Bill, black; eyes, dark brown; legs, dark grey-brown.

Bower: a cleared "stage" up to 3 m in diameter, usually among dense saplings in rain forest, and decorated with green leaves turned underside up; one or more singing perches over or near the stage are used for lengthy periods from September to December when stage can easily be found by walking towards the song. In favoured areas, stages may be less than 50 m apart.

Spotted Catbird                                    Stage-maker

VOICE: A very loud, variable song, including mimicry, almost incessant during display season (September to December); at other times loud "chuck."

HABITAT: Mountain rain forest more or less above 600 m, lower in winter.

RANGE: North-eastern Queensland.

Sedentary with some altitudinal movement.

**GOLDEN BOWER-BIRD** *Prionodura newtoniana*                SEE p. 79

23–26 cm. A gold-and-yellow bower-bird (male) or olive-brown above and ash-grey below (female). **Male:** above, dull golden-brown; centre of crown, nape, underparts, and outer tail feathers, bright orange-yellow, with opalescent sheen. Bill, dark brown, paler on the lower mandible; eyes, yellowish-white; legs, brownish-grey. **Female:** above, dark olive-brown; below, ash-grey.

Bower: a maypole bower consisting of two pyramids of sticks stacked around two adjacent saplings a few metres apart and joined by a horizontal branch; the pyramids may be as high as 2 m, but more usually 0·5–1·2 m, one higher than the other, and decorated with seed pods of *Melicope broadbentiana*, white flowers, yellow-green lichen, and occasional berries. Also builds small "gunyahs" on the ground usually near bower.

VOICE: Croaking and rattling sounds; mimicry of other species.

HABITAT: Mountain rain forest, more or less above 900 m, lower in winter.

RANGE: North-eastern Queensland.

Sedentary with some altitudinal movement.

**REGENT BOWER-BIRD** *Sericulus chrysocephalus*           SEE p. 79

23–28 cm. A black-and-yellow bower-bird (male) or scalloped brown with black crown and throat (female). **Male:** black, with orange-yellow

Golden Bower-bird

Regent Bower-bird

crown, nape, centre of wing and bill. Bill, yellow; eyes, yellow; legs, black. **Female:** above, blackish-brown, spotted dull white; wings and tail, brown; forehead, face, and hindneck, rusty-brown; crown, mantle, and centre of throat, black; upper breast, blackish-brown, spotted white; lower breast and abdomen, dull white, scalloped blackish-brown. Bill, blackish-brown; eyes, yellow flecked brown; legs, blackish-brown.

Bower: apparently two forms of bower. (1) An ephemeral avenue bower of two scanty walls consisting of a dozen or so twigs, used only for a few days; (2) a permanent avenue bower of more substance with two walls flanking a low platform usually placed under a dense bush, often introduced lantana in rain forest; the bower is 15–30 cm long with walls about 15 cm high; green berries and leaves are placed in the bower, rarely on the cleared areas at each end of the avenue; attended for much of the year in at least some cases.

VOICE: Harsh "te-ar;" mimics other species.

HABITAT: Rain forest.

RANGE: Central eastern Australia.

Sedentary, with some local nomadism.

## SATIN BOWER-BIRD *Ptilinorhynchus violaceus* SEE p. 79

27–33 cm. A violet-black bower-bird (male) or olive-green with reddish-brown wings. **Male:** above and below, violet-black. **Female:** above, olive-green, with reddish-brown feathers in wings; below, paler, tinged yellow on abdomen, scalloped blackish-brown. Bill, bluish, tip greenish-yellow with nostrils covered with feathers; eyes, bright violet-blue with red circumference; legs, greenish-yellow.

Bower: an avenue bower with two walls about 20–30 cm high flanking a platform about 5–8 cm thick; an area of up to 90 cm around the bower is cleared and strewn with leaves and grass; decorations of primarily blue flowers, berries, and other objects placed in and around the bower;

Satin Bower-bird

twigs in the wall are "painted" with a mixture of saliva and masticated berries or charcoal by both races, the southern, large *violaceus* and the northern, small *minor*. Bowers are attended over much of the year (April to December), and are placed under overhanging vegetation in rain forest.

VOICE: Creaking and hissing sounds; loud "wee-you;" mimics other birds; in display at the bower has a staccato, hissing, machine-gun-like call.

HABITAT: Rain forest and contiguous vegetation.

RANGE: Eastern Australia.

Localised during breeding season, nomadic at other times; the northern race may be more sedentary.

## SPOTTED BOWER-BIRD *Chlamydera maculata* SEE p. 79

27–31 cm. A brown bower-bird with pale buff spots on the back. Above, dark brown, with pale buff spots; neck, grey; head, mottled-brown, with darker streaks and concealed lilac patch on nape, spread in display; below, pale buff faintly barred darker on flanks. Bill, black; eyes, dark brown; legs, brown.

Similar to the more brightly spotted Western Bower-bird, but apparently their ranges do not meet.

Bower: an avenue bower with two walls 15–20 cm apart, made from sticks and grass stems 30–40 cm long, flanking a platform 8–10 cm thick; an area of up to 180 cm is cleared and strewn with white bones, stones, green berries, and other objects, mostly around one end of the bower; a hoard of favourite articles is kept in the bower; twigs in the wall are painted with saliva mixed with masticated grass. Bowers are attended over most of the year (April to December), and are usually placed under a wilga or lime bush.

VOICE: Loud hiss; mimics other species.

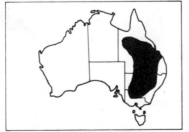

Spotted Bower-bird

HABITAT: Woodland to arid savannah, particularly wilga trees.
RANGE: Dry interior of eastern Australia.
Sedentary with some nomadism.

## WESTERN BOWER-BIRD *Chlamydera guttata*        SEE p. 79

26–28 cm. A brown bower-bird with rich buff spots on the back. Above, black, with rich buff spots; neck, black, with small spots; head, dark brown, spotted and mottled paler, and with concealed lilac patch on nape, spread in display; below, buff, faintly barred on flanks. Bill, black; eyes, brown; legs, brown.

Similar to less brightly coloured Spotted Bower-bird, but apparently their ranges do not meet.

Bower: an avenue bower with two walls 15–20 cm apart, made from twigs 30–40 cm long, flanking a platform 15–20 cm thick; grass stems are only rarely used; an area of up to 180 cm is cleared and strewn with white bones, stones, green berries, and other objects, mostly around one end of the bower; a hoard of favourite articles is kept in the bower. Bowers are attended over much of the year, at least from May to December.

VOICE: Loud hiss; mimics other species (Hutchinson 48).

HABITAT: Rocky hills in association with native figs (*Ficus platypoda*).

RANGE: Dry interior of Western and central Australia, coastal in region of North West Cape.

Sedentary.

## GREAT BOWER-BIRD *Chlamydera nuchalis*        SEE p. 79

30–33 cm. A greyish northern bower-bird. Above, brownish-grey, with feathers edged paler; concealed tuft on nape, lilac, spread in display, often lacking in female; below, buffy-grey. Bill, black; eyes, brown; legs, dark brown.

Western Bower-bird                    Great Bower-bird

Found north of the ranges of Spotted and Western Bower-birds, looks much larger and greyer, lacks prominent spotting on the back and markings on the underparts.

Bower: a large avenue bower with two walls 20 cm apart made from twigs about 38 cm long, flanking a platform 15–20 cm deep; an area of up to 180 cm is cleared and strewn with white bones, snail shells, stones, green berries, and other objects, mostly around one end of the bower, with a hoard of favourite articles in the bower. Bowers are attended from May or June to December.

VOICE: Loud hiss; mimics other species (Hutchinson 49).

HABITAT: Woodland and open forest with rainfall of more than 500 mm.

RANGE: Northern Australia, from about Broome, Western Australia, to Mackay, Queensland.

Sedentary.

## FAWN-BREASTED BOWER-BIRD SEE p. 79
*Chlamydera cerviniventris*

23 cm. A small brown bower-bird with cinnamon-buff underparts, and lacking the lilac nape feathers. Above, dark brown with each feather tipped grey; head, greyish-brown, streaked greyish-white; throat and upper breast, buff streaked brown; breast and abdomen, cinnamon-buff. Bill, black; eyes, dark brown; legs, greyish-brown.

Bower: a large avenue bower with two walls 20 cm apart made from twigs about 30–38 cm long, flanking a base up to 30 cm thick; at each end of the bower spreads a platform about 60 cm across and 10–36 cm thick, although one end is usually larger; green berries, leaves, and seed pods are laid on the platforms, principally on the larger.

VOICE: Harsh churring; mimics other birds.

HABITAT: Low-lying woodland and melaleuca thickets, near mangrove swamps.

Fawn-breasted Bower-bird

RANGE: Cape York Peninsula, Queensland, south to Cape Flattery; Torres Strait islands; eastern New Guinea.

Sedentary.

# BIRDS OF PARADISE—Paradisaeidae

Birds of paradise are closely related to bower-birds, but their specialisation in courtship is directed towards plumage elaboration in males. The few species occurring in Australia are among the least gaudy of the family, but their iridescent plumage is nevertheless very attractive. The rifle-birds are closely similar to each other, with slight variations on a basic theme of black plumage with iridescent feathers on crown, throat, and tail. The females are reddish-brown above with barred or speckled pale underparts. The nest is cup-shaped and often decorated with cast snake-skins.

### MANUCODE *Phonygammus keraudreni* SEE p. 81

30 cm. An iridescent black bird with long neck feathers. Above and below, black, glossed green, purple, and blue. Bill, black; eyes, red; legs, black.

May be confused with Shining Starling and Spangled Drongo, but long round broad tail and loud trumpet-like call are diagnostic; the Shining Starling also has lanceolate neck feathers, but has a long pointed tail.

VOICE: Loud, low, trumpet-like call.

HABITAT: Rain forest.

RANGE: Cape York, Queensland, south to Iron Range; New Guinea; Aru and D'Entrecasteaux archipelagos.

Possibly migratory.

Manucode

**PARADISE RIFLE-BIRD** *Ptiloris paradiseus*  SEE p. 81

28 cm. A rifle-bird with olive-green edges to belly feathers (male) or with buff underparts profusely marked with dark chevrons (female). **Male:** above, black, with iridescent green and purple crown and central tail feathers; throat, iridescent green and purple; breast, black; abdomen, black, with olive-green edges to the feathers. **Female:** above, brown, with broad whitish eyebrows and rufous edges to feathers; throat, buff-white; breast and abdomen, cinnamon-buff, with brownish-black chevrons. Bill, black; eyes, dark brown; legs, black.

May be confused with Victoria Rifle-bird where ranges approach near Mackay, Queensland, but distinguished by the green edges to belly feathers of the male and the paler and more profusely-marked underparts of the female.

VOICE: "Ya-a-ass."

HABITAT: Rain forest.

RANGE: Eastern Australia, from about Mackay, Queensland, to Hunter River, New South Wales.

Sedentary.

**VICTORIA RIFLE-BIRD** *Ptiloris victoriae*  SEE p. 81

24 cm. A rifle-bird with greyish belly feathers (male) or with cinnamon-buff underparts sparsely marked with dark chevrons (female). **Male:** above, black, with iridescent green, and purple crown and central tail feathers; throat, iridescent green and purple; breast, black; abdomen, grey, with black centres to the feathers. **Female:** above, grey-brown, with broad white eyebrows; below, cinnamon-buff, with sparse blackish-brown chevrons. Bill, black; eyes, dark brown; legs, black.

May be confused with Paradise Rifle-bird where ranges approach near Mackay, Queensland, but distinguished by greyish abdomen of male and richer and less profusely-marked underparts of the female;

Paradise Rifle-bird

Victoria Rifle-bird

there is a big gap between the ranges of the Victoria and Magnificent Rifle-birds.

VOICE: "Ya-a-ar."

HABITAT: Rain forest.

RANGE: North-eastern Queensland, from about Mackay to Cooktown.

Sedentary.

## MAGNIFICENT RIFLE-BIRD *Ptiloris magnificus*    SEE p. 81

30 cm. A rifle-bird with purplish-black belly feathers and plume-like flank feathers (male) or with white underparts profusely barred blackish-brown. **Male:** above, black, with iridescent green and purple crown and central tail feathers; throat and breast, iridescent green and purple, separated by an iridescent golden-green band from the purplish-black abdomen; flank feathers elongated into plumes. **Female:** above, cinnamon-brown with broad white eye stripe; throat, white with black streak on edge; below, white speckled and barred blackish-brown.

VOICE: Loud "whee-you, whee-you, whee-you, wheee."

HABITAT: Rain forest.

RANGE: Cape York, Queensland, south to Rocky River; New Guinea.

Sedentary.

# CROWS AND RAVENS—Corvidae

Unless one has had extensive experience with them, the five Australian species of corvids are probably the most difficult of all passerines to identify in the field. This is borne out by the fact that two hitherto unsuspected species have been described in the past ten years. They are all similar in shape and colour, and all have white eyes in the adult stage. Only in Tasmania and on Flinders Island does only one species occur;

Magnificent Rifle-bird

elsewhere at least two species are likely to be encountered. Of the characteristics which might aid identification, the best are the call, range, habitat, and the length of the throat hackles. Size as a means of identification is only relative, and is useful only when two species whose size may be relevant are seen together (e.g. Little Crow and Australian Raven). Even so, there are small individuals of large species to cloud the issue. The three ravens have dusky bases to the feathers and the two crows have white bases; these may be seen if the wind ruffles the neck feathers, or if the bird is preening.

## AUSTRALIAN RAVEN *Corvus coronoides* SEE p. 82

50–56 cm. A glossy-black corvid with grey bases to feathers, long throat hackles. Above and below, glossy black with grey bases to feathers. Bill, black; eyes, white, with blue inner ring (adult), brown or hazel (immature), or blue (juvenile); legs, black.

When calling, often fans the throat hackles and occasionally lowers the tail with each note. Distinguished in the field from other corvids by the throat hackles and call. In the hand, the grey bases to the feathers distinguish it from the Australian Crow and Little Crow; the area at the base of the lower bill is, if stretched, largely bare in the Australian Raven and feathered in the other ravens.

VOICE: Powerful "aah aah aah aaaaaahh" dying away like a death rattle.

HABITAT: Woodland; virtually extends over the sheep country of the east, but confined to the eucalypt forests and associated farmland in Western Australia.

RANGE: Eastern Australia except Cape York; South Australia, Kangaroo Island; south coast of Western Australia and south-western Australia.

Adults resident, immatures nomadic.

Australian Raven

## LITTLE RAVEN *Corvus mellori* SEE p. 82

40–45 cm. A glossy-black corvid with grey bases to feathers; throat hackles short relative to Australian Raven. Above and below, glossy-black, with grey bases to feathers. Bill, black; eyes, white with blue inner ring (adult), brown or hazel (immature), or blue-grey (juvenile); legs, black.

When calling, the Little Raven flips its wings upwards as it utters each note. In the hand, the grey bases to the feathers distinguish it from the Australian Crow and Little Crow; the feathered skin at the base of the lower bill distinguishes it from the Australian Raven, as do the smaller hackles on the throat which, if removed, tend to be bifurcated at the tip rather than long and lanceolate. The Forest Raven tends to inhabit denser forest and is confined to only a few areas within the range of the Little Raven (see maps below).

VOICE: Guttural "kar-kar-kar-kar," lacking the nasal quality of the Little Crow, which is probably closest to it in call.

HABITAT: Woodland and associated farmland; during breeding tends to nest in lower trees than the Australian Raven.

RANGE: South-eastern Australia; King Island.

Nomadic, and perhaps migratory to King Island.

## FOREST RAVEN *Corvus tasmanicus* SEE p. 82

50–56 cm. A glossy-black short-tailed corvid with grey bases to feathers, throat hackles short relative to Australian Raven. The only corvid in Tasmania and Flinders Island. Above and below, glossy-black. Bill, black; eyes, white, with blue inner ring (adult), brown or hazel (immature), or blue-grey (juvenile); legs, black.

Normally inhabits more timbered country on the mainland, and in its southern population has a noticeably shorter tail than the other corvids. Consult the map for likely occurrences on the mainland.

Little Raven                                     Forest Raven

VOICE: Slow, deep "caw-caw-caw-caaaw."

HABITAT: Wet sclerophyll to savannah woodland in Tasmania, wet sclerophyll on the mainland.

RANGE: Tasmania, Flinders Island; Wilsons Promontory and Otway Ranges, Victoria; New England Tableland, New South Wales.

Sedentary.

## AUSTRALIAN CROW *Corvus orru* SEE p. 83

50–56 cm. A glossy-black corvid with white bases to feathers, no throat hackles. Above and below, glossy-black. Bill, black; eyes, white, with blue inner ring (adult), brown or hazel (immature), or blue-grey (juvenile); legs, black.

Shuffles its wings exaggeratedly on alighting (other corvids normally shuffle them only once). Distinguished from the Ravens by the white bases to the feathers. Call distinguishes it from Little Crow; in the hand the two are very similar, with the Little Crow rather smaller.

VOICE: Nasal, high-pitched staccato "oh-oh-oh-oh-oh" (Hutchinson 50).

HABITAT: Woodland and associated farmland in the east and north; vegetation, particularly eucalypts, along watercourses and ranges in arid country.

RANGE: Northern Australia south to north-eastern New South Wales; Alice Springs, Northern Territory; and about Kalgoorlie, Western Australia. New Guinea, Moluccas, Bismarck Archipelago, Tanimbar Island, and Babar Island.

Sedentary.

## LITTLE CROW *Corvus bennetti* SEE pp. 81, 83

40–44 cm. A glossy-black corvid with white bases to feathers, no throat hackles. Above and below, glossy-black. Bill, black; eyes, white,

Australian Crow

Little Crow

with blue inner ring (adult), brown or hazel (immature), or blue-grey (juvenile); legs, black.

Often performs elaborate acrobatics when travelling in flocks. Distinguished from the Ravens by white bases to feathers. Call distinguishes it from Australian Crow; in the hand the two are very similar with the Australian Crow rather bigger.

VOICE: Nasal "nark-nark-nark-nark," lacking the guttural quality of the Little Raven which is probably closest to it in call.

HABITAT: Woodland, including mulga; in arid areas localised to some extent near windmills and other sources of water.

RANGE: Arid areas of Australia, from south-western Queensland and western New South Wales through South Australia and southern Northern Territory to the mulga belt of Western Australia. In adverse seasons probably moves into outer areas.

Nomadic.

## INDIAN CROW *Corvus splendens*                                  SEE p. 81

40 cm. A dull black corvid with dark eyes, ashy-brown nape, upper back, and breast. Above and below, black, with ashy-brown nape, upper back, and breast. Bill, black; eyes, dark brown; legs, black.

Occasionally arrives at Fremantle, Western Australia, on ships from India and Ceylon. Distinguished from local Corvids by the ashy-brown patches in the plumage and the dark eyes. May be confused with Grey Currawong which has white in the wing and under the tail and has yellow eyes.

VOICE: Noisy cawing.

HABITAT: Human habitations.

RANGE: India, Ceylon, Singapore; occasionally arrives on ships at Fremantle, Western Australia, and rarely at other ports.

# SELECTED BIBLIOGRAPHY

The following books have been selected as reliable and accurate references for students of Australian ornithology:

Bourke, P. A., (1955),    *A Handbook of Elementary Bird Study*. Perth, Paterson Brokensha Pty Ltd.

Cayley, N. W., (1974),    *What Bird is That?* 5th ed. Sydney, Angus and Robertson Ltd.

Condon, H. T., (1967),    *Field Guide to the Hawks of Australia*. 4th ed. Melbourne, Bird Observers' Club.

Condon, H. T. and McGill, A. R., (1966),    *Field Guide to the Waders*. 4th ed. Melbourne, Bird Observers' Club.

CSIRO, (1969),    *An Index of Australian Bird Names*. Canberra.

Forshaw, J. M., (1969),    *Australian Parrots*. Melbourne, Lansdowne Press.

Frith, H. J., (1962),    *The Mallee Fowl*. Sydney, Angus and Robertson Ltd.

Frith, H. J., (1967),    *Waterfowl in Australia*. Sydney, Angus and Robertson Ltd.

Frith, H. J. (Ed.), (1969),    *Birds in the Australian High Country*. Sydney, A. H. and A. W. Reed.

Immelmann, K., (1965),    *Australian Finches in Bush and Aviary*. Sydney, Angus and Robertson Ltd.

Macdonald, J. D., (1973),    *Birds of Australia*. Sydney, A. H. and A. W. Reed.

Marshall, A. J., (1954),    *Bower Birds*. Oxford, Clarendon Press.

Officer, H. R., (1964),    *Australian Honeyeaters*. Melbourne, Bird Observers' Club.

Officer, H. R., (1969),    *Australian Flycatchers and their Allies*. Melbourne, Bird Observers' Club.

Serventy, D. L. and Whittell, H. M., (1967),    *Birds of Western Australia*. Perth, Lamb Publications Pty Ltd.

Sharland, M. R., (1958), *Tasmanian Birds*. Sydney, Angus and Robertson Ltd.

Slater, P., *et al.*, (1970), *A Field Guide to Australian Birds—Non-Passerines*. Adelaide, Rigby Ltd.

Whittell, H. M., (1954), *The Literature of Australian Birds*. Perth, Paterson Brokensha Pty Ltd.

The Official Checklist of the Birds of Australia published by the Royal Australian Ornithologists' Union in 1926 is out of print, but a facsimile edition is available from the State Library of South Australia. The first part of a new, up-to-date edition will be published this year (1974).

Details of birds occurring in several States can be found in:

Condon, H. T., (1968), *A Handlist of the Birds of South Australia*. Adelaide, South Australian Ornithological Association.

Lavery, H. J., (1969), *List of Birds in Queensland*. Canberra, Winston Churchill Memorial Trust.

McGill, A. R., (1960), *A Handlist of the Birds of New South Wales*. Sydney, Fauna Protection Panel.

Storr, G. M., (1967), *List of the Birds of the Northern Territory*. Perth, Spec. Publ. W.A. Museum No. 4.

Wheeler, W. R., (1967), *A Handlist of the Birds of Victoria*. Victorian Ornithological Research Group.

Small handlists are available for recording field observations in given localities:

Anon., (1966), *A Field List of the Birds of Canberra and District*. Canberra, R.A.O.U.

Elks, R., (n.d.), *Field List of Birds of Queensland's South-East Corner*. Caloundra, Qld, Published by the author.

For a general survey of birds of the world:

Austin, O. L. and Singer, A., (1961), *Birds of the World*. London, Paul Hamlyn.

Fisher, J. and Peterson, R. T., (1964), *The World of Birds*. London, MacDonald & Co.

# INDEX OF COMMON NAMES

*Figures in italics refer to plates*

# INDEX OF SCIENTIFIC NAMES

*Figures in italics refer to plates*

307